CW01671769

Fighting Corruption

International Corporate Integrity Handbook

Edited by
Fritz Heimann and
François Vincke

ICC
International Chamber of Commerce
The world business organization

First edition, *Fighting Bribery*, published April 1999.
Second edition, *Fighting Corruption*, published April 2003.

ICC Publication No. 678
ISBN: 978-92-842-0013-9

ICC Services
International Chamber of Commerce
The world business organization

Publications
38, Cours Albert 1er
75008 Paris – France
www.iccbooks.com

Table of Contents

Appendices

Foreword

Corruption – whether in the form of bribes, extortion, money laundering or other illegal acts – is the scourge of international commerce, costing untold billions of dollars in losses and distorting trade. For more than two decades, the International Chamber of Commerce (ICC), has taken the lead among business organizations in denouncing corruption and developing rules of conduct to combat it. As early as 1977, ICC issued its *Rules of Conduct and Recommendations for Combating Extortion and Bribery*, which broke new ground in setting forth practical ways in which companies should conduct themselves when dealing with bribery, both public and private, and when confronted with demands for illegal payments (extortion). The Rules, which have been revised twice since they were first issued, were followed by ICC guidelines on whistleblowing; publication, along with other organizations, of the "Business Case Against Corruption"; and active cooperation with OECD, the UN and other international organizations that have developed anti-corruption conventions.

In 1999, to reinforce its anti-corruption drive, ICC published a corporate practices handbook, in which ICC experts from the Anti-Corruption Commission examined diverse forms of corruption and made precise recommendations to combat them. The present handbook is the third edition of that publication, expanded to cover new issues and updated to take account of the latest developments in the field.

In these pages, readers will find expert commentary and recommendations concerning bribery and its many forms, as well as other fields in which corruption often distorts trade and governance – corporate gifts, political contributions, accounting and the insidious "facilitation payments" that have long plagued international commerce.

Compliance officers, managers, lawyers, accountants, bankers, customs officials and everyone concerned with stamping out corruption in all its forms would do well to follow the recommendations in this classic text.

Victor Fung
ICC Chairman

Introduction

By François Vincke and Fritz Heimann

This is the third edition of ICC's handbook on anti-corruption. Most of the authors are members of the Anti-Corruption Commission of the International Chamber of Commerce. This handbook is written by experts from the business community for members of the business community. Our aim is to give concrete, practical help to those on the frontline combating extortion and bribery. Our goal is to help achieve – at last – a corruption-free, level playing field so that executives will no longer offer a bribe because of their suspicion that their competitors will do so or because corrupt officials will be demanding it. Our hope is that, by following our recommendations, companies will be able to compete on the quality of their products and services.

The pace of change in anti-corruption has continued to accelerate. Thus, every chapter of this handbook has been substantially revised and updated, and a new chapter on the UN Convention Against Corruption has been added. The handbook has been divided into three parts. Part I describes the international legal framework within which corporate self-regulation must operate, including the development of the OECD and UN Conventions and of ICC Rules of Conduct, and the evolving prohibitions of direct and indirect corruption. Part II covers management initiatives, including the responsibilities of top officers; accounting, auditing and financial controls; dealing with whistleblowing; and compliance by SMEs.
Part III deals with specialized problem areas, including money laundering, political contributions, private-to-private bribery, extortion, and compliance with Customs regulations. The concluding chapter, "Moving Anti-corruption to the Next Level", looks ahead at the priorities for the next five or more years.

Combating corruption requires strong top-management commitment, high-quality human resources and systematic organization to ensure that anti-corruption becomes part of the corporate culture at all levels. This handbook proposes straightforward answers to the question of how to best organize the prevention of extortion and bribery. We have addressed difficult matters, including how to deal with whistleblowing, facilitation payments and gifts and entertainment in different cultural environments.

While self-regulation is key to corporate ethics, it is also clear that combating corruption requires strong government and international action. The OECD Convention on Combating Bribery of Foreign Public Officials, adopted in 1997, signaled a turning point in anti-corruption. All signatory states have passed laws prohibiting foreign bribery. The OECD actively monitors national enforcement, and the authors stress the need for continuing rigorous follow-up. ICC has developed a long-term advocacy relationship with the OECD and has urged that the scope of its anti-corruption instruments be broadened.

The United Nations Convention Against Corruption (UNCAC) of 2003 is an equally important milestone because of its worldwide participation and comprehensive scope. The principle of monitoring the national implementation of UNCAC's provisions has been agreed, but the necessary monitoring mechanism has not yet been established. This obviously troubles the business community, as the executives of ICC's member companies regularly report that companies from non-OECD countries still have not aligned their practices to the new anti-corruption norms. ICC will, therefore, continue to press for a strong, efficient and sustainable monitoring system for UNCAC, coordinated with the monitoring programs of other existing anti-corruption treaties, including those of the Organization of American States, the Council of Europe, the European Union and the African Union, all of which contribute to the fight against corruption.

This edition of the handbook is appearing in the midst of a massive financial crisis. It will take years to analyze its causes. However, it is already clear that there will be strong pressure for reforms, including greater transparency and accountability, as well as greater international cooperation. These are issues that the ICC has long supported. We are convinced that combating corruption is crucial to corporate integrity. Companies cannot engage in corruptive practices without disabling their management control systems, thereby undermining their integrity.

It should be recognized that the authors are writing as individual experts. Their views do not necessarily represent the position of ICC or of the other organizations with which they are affiliated.

We wish to express our appreciation for the numerous contributions to the preparation of this handbook made by Ron Katz, Rachelle Bijou and Viviane Schiavi of the ICC Secretariat in Paris.

Part I

Historical and Legal Perspectives

Chapter 1

ICC Rules of Conduct and the OECD Convention

By Fritz Heimann

ICC Rules of Conduct on Extortion and Bribery in International Business Transactions and the OECD Convention on Combating Bribery of Foreign Public Officials are key reference points for corporate compliance programs. This chapter describes their evolution and principal requirements.

ICC COMMISSION ON ANTI-CORRUPTION

ICC effort to fight extortion and bribery in international business transactions began in 1975 when it established a committee chaired by Lord Shawcross, a former Attorney General of Great Britain and Nuremberg prosecutor. The committee was established in response to widely publicized corruption scandals, including bribe payments by US companies to government leaders in Japan, Italy and the Netherlands. The Shawcross Committee issued a ground-breaking report in 1977, which called for complementary and mutually supportive action by the business community, national governments, and international organizations. In doing so, ICC became the first international organization to take a stand against international corruption.

The Shawcross Report identified self-regulation by international business as a particularly critical step. To provide a basis for corporate action, the Shawcross Committee drafted "Rules of Conduct to Combat Extortion and Bribery". These have become widely known as ICC Rules. The Committee also recommended an ambitious agenda for action by governments and international organizations, including a United Nations convention outlawing bribery and extortion and a panel of experts to which complaints about bribery and extortion could be submitted.

The Shawcross Report was ahead of its time. Although a UN convention was considered by the UN General Assembly in the early 1980s, it became stalemated in an acrimonious North-South debate. Representatives of industrialized countries claimed that corruption was primarily a problem in the developing world. Leaders of developing countries argued that multinational corporations were the real culprits. International financial institutions were unwilling to confront corruption. The US made bribery of foreign officials a crime in 1977, and ICC Rules served as a model for compliance programs of many US companies. No other country prohibited foreign bribery. During the 1980s, corruption faded from view as an international issue.

In the 1990s, a new wave of corruption scandals struck virtually all parts of the world, including Italy, France, Belgium, Japan, South Korea, Indonesia, India, Pakistan, Brazil, Venezuela, Mexico, Nigeria and Zaire. In 1994, ICC established an ad hoc committee chaired by François Vincke, then Secretary General of Petrofina of Belgium, to review and revise the 1977 Report. The Vincke Committee worked for more than a year and produced a report which was adopted by ICC's Executive Board in March 1996.

The 1996 Report reconfirmed the dual premises of the 1977 Reports: the need for corporate self-regulation based on ICC Rules of Conduct, as well as a comprehensive programme of action by national governments and international organizations. The Vincke Committee revised the Rules of Conduct, making them stricter and more explicit. The recommendations to governments and international organizations were revised to reflect changed conditions and shifted the principal focus for multilateral action from the UN to OECD. When the ICC Executive Board approved the 1996 Report, it reconstituted the Vincke Committee as a standing Committee on Extortion and Bribery to promote widespread use of ICC Rules of Conduct and adoption of the Report's recommendations to international organizations and governments.

The Committee became the ICC Commission on Anti-Corruption in 2002. It continues to be chaired by François Vincke. The Commission's members are designated by ICC national committees; it currently has members from over 30 countries and meets two or three times a year. As part of its work to promote corporate self-regulation, the Commission revised ICC Rules for a third time in 2005. The Commission also publishes this handbook, written mainly by Commission members, to assist companies to develop and manage integrity programs, of which this is the third edition.

The Commission's international advocacy work has included active participation in the adoption, ratification and monitoring of the OECD Convention and in similar work on the UN Convention Against Corruption (UNCAC). The ICC Commission closely follows the work of the OECD Working Group on Bribery and has made practical proposals for strengthening OECD's anti-corruption instruments. The Commission welcomed the adoption of UNCAC, because such a comprehensive and universal instrument provides the best prospect for achieving the level global playing field that international business wants. The Commission will continue to deploy its efforts to promote effective monitoring of UNCAC's provisions by the States Parties. In addition, the Commission follows regional anti-corruption initiatives, including those of the Council of Europe, the European Union, the Organization of American States and the African Union.

Part II of this Chapter discusses ICC Rules of Conduct; Part III covers the OECD Convention; and Part IV describes the ICC Commission's advocacy work with international organizations and governments.

ICC Rules of Conduct

When the Shawcross Committee developed the 1977 ICC Rules, it wrote on a clean slate. There was no established body of laws and practices. The concept was to set forth basic principles on which companies could build their own codes of conduct. The principal focus was on bribery and extortion "for obtaining and retaining business". The 1977 Rules got the fundamentals right, covering both active and passive bribery (extortion), bribery of public officials as well as bribery within the private sector. The evolution of ICC Rules since 1977 reflects the progress made by the adoption of international treaties and national laws, and even more importantly the development of corporate experience in combating corruption.

When the 1996 ICC Rules were adopted, the OECD Working Group on Bribery had already published recommendations that foreshadowed the Convention. There was also experience from the US Foreign Corrupt Practices Act (FCPA), particularly by American companies. The most important change made by the 1996 Rules was to prohibit extortion and bribery for any purpose and not only for obtaining or retaining business, thereby covering judicial proceedings, tax matters, environmental and other regulatory cases, as well as legislative proceedings. Other changes made by the 1996 Rules were to:

- Broaden the prohibition of bribery to bar not only kickbacks, but also other techniques such as subcontracts and consulting agreements that channel payments to government officials, their relatives or their business associates.
- Sharpen the provision dealing with the use of agents, to provide that payments to agents be limited to "appropriate remuneration for legitimate services" and require companies to take steps to ensure that agents do not pay bribes.
- Make more explicit the financial provisions of the Rules to prohibit the use of "off-the-books" or secret accounts and call for the establishment of independent auditing systems to bring to light any transactions which contravene the Rules.

- Urge boards of directors to establish and maintain proper systems of control, to conduct periodic compliance reviews and to take approprivate action against any director or employee who contravenes the Rules.
- Provide that political contributions may be made only in accordance with applicable law, that all requirements for public disclosure shall be full complied with, and that all such contributions must be reported to senior corporate management.

By the time the 2005 ICC Rules were adopted, the relevant body of anti-corruption law and practice had expanded greatly. The OECD Convention had been adopted by 36 parties, and these countries had also passed laws implementing the Convention's prohibitions. Many more companies had adopted anti-corruption policies, including large numbers of non-US companies. Other organizations, including Transparency International, the World Economic Forum and the UN Global Compact were promoting and obtaining experience with corporate compliance programs.

The 2005 Rules reflect the growing sophistication in anti-corruption practice:

- There has been a substantial policy change regarding facilitation payments, from toleration as a "lesser problem" to elimination wherever possible,and strict controls where they cannot be eliminated. This reflects the evolution of thinking in the international business community during the last decade. (Article 6).
- The basic prohibition of bribery and extortion in Section 1 has been expanded to explicitly cover:
  - Public officials at national, local or international levels;
  - Political parties, party officials or candidates;
  - Directors, officers, employees or agents of a private enterprise.
  - The provision dealing with agents has been expanded to cover other intermediaries, such as subcontractors, lawyers and consultants, and to require that agents explicitly agree not to pay bribes (Article 2).
- Anti-bribery provisions are made applicable to joint ventures and outsourcing agreements (Article 3).
- Provisions dealing with political contributions have been made more explicit and made applicable to charitable contributions and sponsorships (Article 4).
- A new provision has been added dealing with gifts, hospitality and expenses (Article 5).
- Procedural rules covering corporate policies have been expanded, including those providing confidential channels for whistleblowers (Article 7).

- A new provision has been added dealing with the responsibility of boards of directors for anti-corruption compliance, including making resources available, sanctioning violations, taking corrective action and public disclosure.

The evolution of anti-corruption policies and programs is continuing to advance rapidly, and ICC is committed to spearheading corporate efforts to fight all forms of corruption. The Commission will ensure that ICC Rules are correctly aligned with the major international instruments. ICC Rules will also be coordinated, wherever possible, with other programs to promote corporate self-regulation. Therefore, a new edition of ICC Rules and of this handbook is likely to be needed within the next five years.

The OECD convention

Origins

The OECD established a Working Group on Bribery in 1989. In the spring of 1994, the OECD Ministerial adopted a Recommendation calling on member states to take "effective measures to deter, prevent and combat the bribery of foreign public officials". The Recommendation proposed a half-dozen measures for consideration by member states, including making it a crime to bribe foreign officials and ending tax deductibility of bribes. OECD members were asked to report back on the steps they were prepared to take. It was a modest beginning after five years of deliberations by the OECD's Working Group, but it got the ball rolling.

The Working Group continued to meet, trying to develop a consensus on how the proposed steps could be turned into specific legislative or regulatory proposals for adoption by member states. Initially, criminalization of bribes seemed too controversial, so attention shifted to the tax deductibility issue. At the spring 1996 Ministerial, a new, somewhat convoluted Recommendation was approved. It urged "those Member countries which do not disallow the deductibility of bribes to foreign public officials to re-examine such treatment with the intention of denying this deductibility". This was firmer than the 1994 Recommendation, but not an unambiguous call for action.

By early 1997, the Working Group had reached a consensus on "Agreed Common Elements of Criminal Legislation and Related Action". This defined in considerable detail eight key subjects to be covered by national laws criminalizing foreign bribery. Instead of adopting a new Recommendation calling for national legislation embodying the "Agreed Common Elements", however, the spring 1997 OECD Ministerial decided on a different approach.

At the urging of France, Germany and Japan, it was decided that criminalization should be dealt with by means of an international convention. This was an unusual move, because the OECD normally uses recommendations and has only rarely used conventions. The US reluctantly concurred, in return for commitments that the convention would be based on the "Agreed Common Elements" and on a firm schedule. This called for completing the drafting of the convention by the end of 1997 and obtaining ratification by national legislatures by the end of 1998. Amazingly, the compromise worked. The Convention was signed in Paris on 17 December 1997, and sufficient ratifications were secured by 15 December 1998 to meet the Convention's entry-into-force requirement. As a result, the Convention entered into effect on 15 February 1999.

Moving from the soft recommendation of 1994 to bringing the Convention into effect less than five years later is an outstanding accomplishment. It is a tribute to the remarkable leadership of Professor Dr.Mark Pieth, the Chairman of the OECD Working Group. It also reflects a sea change in public perceptions and political positions on the need to combat international bribery.

As of 2008, the Convention has been signed and ratified, not only by all 30 OECD members, but also by seven countries that are not OECD members, including Argentina, Chile and Brazil. Accession discussions with additional countries are underway.

Importance of the Convention

The Convention is of great strategic importance in the fight against international corruption, because the OECD member states are the home states of most major international corporations. This makes the OECD the ideal forum for curbing the supply side of international corruption. Action by OECD members to prohibit foreign bribery affects a preponderant share of international trade and investment. The Convention was a major breakthrough, because it overcame a previously insurmountable obstacle. After the US passed its Foreign Corrupt Practices Act in 1977, the first law making foreign bribery a crime, it became clear that other countries were unwilling to prohibit foreign bribery without assurance that their major competitors would do so at the same time. Agreement at the OECD cut the Gordian Knot.

The Convention provides a solid framework for an effective system to prohibit bribery of foreign officials:

- Both "bribery" and "foreign officials" are broadly defined, as discussed in Chapter Three in this handbook.
- Penalties must be "effective, proportionate and dissuasive". They must be comparable to those for the bribery of domestic officials, including provisions for prison terms.

- Bribes and "the proceeds of the bribery" are subject to seizure and confiscation. Proceeds are defined as "the profits or other benefits derived by the briber".
- Accounting and auditing standards are required to prohibit the establishment of off-the-books accounts and other techniques for hiding bribery, as discussed in Chapter Five in this handbook.
- Mutual legal assistance must be provided in connection with criminal investigations and other proceedings. Bank secrecy may not be asserted, and extradition is provided for.

Monitoring programme

Article 12 of the Convention requires the parties to cooperate in carrying out "a programme of systematic follow-up to monitor and promote the full implementation of this Convention". This is of critical importance to assure that all parties will be held to high standards in carrying out the Convention's requirements. The monitoring programme is conducted by the Working Group on Bribery, which drafted the Convention.

Phase 1, evaluating the adequacy of national laws implementing the requirements of the Convention, began in 1999 and was largely completed by the end of 2001, except for new parties. The laws passed by more than 35 countries have been reviewed. The Working Group did an excellent job and did not shrink from criticizing deficiencies in the laws passed by some of the most powerful OECD members. Most of the deficiencies identified by the Working Group have been corrected.

Phase 2, reviewing the adequacy of national enforcement programmes, began in 2001. This is the most critical test of the effectiveness of the Convention. Reviews of enforcement programs are, by their nature, much more complex than reviews of laws, requiring field visits to each of the countries under review. Because of budget constraints, Phase 2 reviews had a slow start, and only four countries were reviewed in the first two years. After agreement in 2003 on an increased budget, with sufficient funding for country visits, the pace of Phase 2 monitoring stepped up to about six per year. As of 2008 almost all parties have been reviewed.

Phase 2 reviews are conducted by a team consisting of representatives from two "lead review" governments, plus staff from the OECD Secretariat, usually about ten people. The lead review governments include one with a similar legal system as the country being reviewed and one with a different legal system. Participation by members of the OECD Secretariat helps ensure consistency. Country visits generally last one week and include meetings with government officials, as well as with representatives of the private sector and civil society. The review team prepares a detailed report, often more that 50 pages long, which is first submitted in draft form to the government under review and then presented for discussion and approval at a meeting of the full Working Group. Governments are expected to report back to the

Working Group on the actions taken to correct deficiencies, orally after one year and in writing after two years. When the Working Group is dissatisfied with the adequacy of corrective action, it can order a second country visit, a so-called 2bis review. This has been done several times, including for the UK and Japan.

OECD's monitoring program has received excellent marks. The reports are extremely thorough and of high professional quality. They are published and are available on the OECD website. The Working Group consults regularly, not only with ICC, but also with its business and trade union advisory groups (BIAC and TUAC) and with Transparency International.

The progress of foreign bribery enforcement by parties to the Convention is still uneven, but is continuing to improve. According to an annual progress report prepared by Transparency International, there was significant enforcement in 16 countries in 2008, compared with 14 in 2007, 12 in 2006, and eight in 2005.

Controversy over national security exceptions

The termination by the UK government in December 2006 of the investigation of bribery involving a major arms order in Saudi Arabia, based on the assertion of overriding national security interests, was a serious setback for the Convention. The Working Group on Bribery reviewed the UK's action and expressed its dissatisfaction with the justification provided by the UK Government. In July 2008, the House of Lords decided that the termination was valid under UK law; it refused to rule on the availability of a national security exception under the OECD Convention. This is a matter of continuing controversy. (No explicit national security exception is provided, and the terms of Article 5 arguably preclude such an exception. However, the UK maintained that is has an implicit right to assert that national security interests override the Convention.) This raises important issues for the future of the Convention. Should the UK action serve as a precedent for an unlimited, unilateral right for governments to exercise national security exceptions? Should OECD develop restrictions on the exercise of such restrictions, similar to those contained in other treaties?

Future scope of working Group in bribery

With the OECD's Phase 2 country reviews nearing completion, the Working Group has launched a wide-ranging consultation on its future activities. The ICC Commission has participated in this consultation. Decisions are likely to be taken in 2009. The key issues that the ICC Commission has urged the Working Groups to address include the following:

- Continuation of rigorous monitoring by the Working Group, including country visits, is essential because the goal of the Convention to establish a corruption-free level playing field for international trade and investment has not yet been achieved. The continued monitoring program should have two key objectives:

- To assure that governments which have taken little or no enforcement action against foreign bribery undertake significant enforcement without further delays;
- To assure that governments correct deficiencies identified in Phase 2 reviews.

❖ Because self-regulation by companies is essential for the success of the Convention, the Working Group should promote corporate integrity programs at the international, national and industry sectorlevel, governments should encourage the adoption of effective integrity programs by taking them into account in sentencing guidelines.

❖ While the prime focus of the Convention is on the supply side of corruption, international business continues to be exposed to widespread extortion by foreign officials. The Working Group should address this issue by promoting cooperative action by member governments to assist their companies in overcoming extortion threats, including joint intervention with governments where such threats are common.

❖ Two long-recognized inadequacies in the coverage of the Convention need to be addressed:

- Bribe payments to foreign political parties, party officials and candidates for office;
- Bribe payments by foreign subsidiaries of companies based in OECD countries.

❖ On bribery in the private sector, ICC proposes that OECD introduce provisions in its anti-corruption instruments prohibiting private-to-private corruption.

❖ Facilitation payments were not covered when the Convention was adopted. ICC notes that the thinking of the business community on these payments has changed substantially in recent years, reflecting greater recognition of the damage caused by such payments. Multinational companies, confronted with divergent practices in different countries, increasingly opt for zero tolerance policies. ICC believes that OECD should re-examine its position on facilitation payments, by governments and other means.

❖ Whistleblower protection: corporations recognize that readily accessible complaint procedures can contribute substantially to uncovering corruption and other economic fraud and make it possible to solve problems at an early stage. Effective protection of whistleblowers against retaliation is essential. ICC published guidelines on whistleblowing in July 2008 and recommends that OECD urge member governments to provide whistleblower protection.

- Uncertainties about the issue of national security exceptions need to be resolved. Allowing unlimited, unilateral exceptions risks serious erosion of the Convention. The Working Group should agree to reasonable restrictions on their use, consistent with restrictions on the use of national security exceptions under many other treaties.
- Cooperation between OECD and the monitoring programs of other anti-corruption conventions - including the UN Convention Against Corruption, the GRECO program of the Council of Europe, the Inter-American Convention and the African Union Convention – is important to avoid duplicative monitoring and to build on the experience of different programmes.
- Accession to OECD instruments by major trading countries, including China, India and Russia is important for the achievement of a corruption free level playing field.

Chapters of this handbook cover the substance of most of the foregoing issues. Chapter Three discusses foreign subsidiaries and facilitation payments; Chapter Seven, whistleblower protection; Chapter Nine, money laundering; Chapter Ten, political party bribery; Chapter Eleven, private sector bribery; Chapter Twelve, preventing extortion.

ICC advocacy programme

From the beginning, the ICC Commission has promoted anti-corruption programs by international organizations and national governments. This reflects the conviction that there is a complementary relationship between corporate self-regulation and the efforts of governments and international organizations. The success of ICC Rules of Conduct requires supportive action by governments and international organizations, just as the success of anti-corruption programs of international organizations and national governments requires support from the business community.

ICC's most intensive involvement has been with the OECD Convention. It began with efforts to encourage the adoption and ratification of the Convention, participation in monitoring reviews in many countries, and in the consultations to define the ongoing role of the Working Group on Bribery. The scope of this work has been covered in Part III, above.

The second most active priority for the ICC Commission has been the UN Convention Against Corruption (UNCAC). This reflects the recognition that global corruption must be addressed on a global scale. The ICC Commission participated in the Vienna negotiations in 20022003 that led to the adoption of UNCAC and encouraged efforts by ICC national committees to secure its ratification. The Commission also participated in the First and Second Conference of States Parties in Jordan in 2006 and in Bali in 2008. There, ICC pressed for action to establish an

UNCAC monitoring mechanism, which has not yet been done. This effort is continuing in anticipation of the Third Conference of States Parties to be held in Qatar in late 2009. The adoption of an effective monitoring program is widely regarded as the key step to transform UNCAC from words to deeds. The scope of ICC work to encourage national implementation of UNCAC provisions important to the business community can be expected to expand substantially.

The ICC Commission has also worked with the World Bank, urging the Bank to use its lending programs to promote more transparent government procurement, including requiring bidders on Bank-financed programs to adopt ICC Rules and to disclose payments to agents.

The Commission is also cooperating closely with other organizations engaged in anti-corruption work, for example working with Transparency International, the World Economic Forum and the UN Global Compact to promote corporate integrity programs. An important objective has been to promote consistent standards and to learn from each others' experience.

Fritz Heimann is Vice-Chair of the ICC Commission on Anti-Corruption.
He is also the author of Chapters 2, 3 and 14 in this handbook.

Chapter 2

UNCAC: Anti-Corruption's Expanding Frontier

By Fritz Heimann

The UN Convention Against Corruption (UNCAC) is of compelling interest for international business because it provides a global framework for combating corruption. UNCAC has 140 parties, including key players in international trade, such as China, Russia, India and Indonesia, in addition to the major OECD countries. UNCAC also has a much broader scope than the OECD Convention. Thus, UNCAC is capable of tackling many issues that cannot be effectively dealt with by OECD or by regional anti-corruption conventions.

UNCAC's broad scope and worldwide participation are its greatest strengths. However, they also present difficult challenges in moving from words to deeds. There is as yet no agreement to establish a follow-up monitoring programme to ensure effective implementation by the parties. ICC strongly supported the Convention during the negotiations leading to its adoption, but has also pleaded for effective monitoring. Without monitoring, the goal of creating a corruption-free level playing field for international business will not be achieved.

This chapter is divided into four parts. Section 1 will provide an overview of UNCAC's scope and its potential effect on anti-corruption laws and programmes. Section 2 will deal with UNCAC provisions directly affecting international business. Section 3 will consider the preventive measures designed to strengthen national integrity systems. Section 4 will describe the need for an effective monitoring programme.

Overview of UNCAC

UNCAC was adopted in 2003 and became effective in December 2005. It has been signed by 140 countries and has been ratified by more than 120 (as of mid-2008). UNCAC's parties include industrialized, emerging, developing and failing economies. By comparison, OECD includes only 37 industrialized countries, while the regional conventions only cover countries in their regions. (The regional conventions and their websites are listed in the Appendix.)

UNCAC's scope is extremely ambitious. There are 28 articles covering criminalization and law enforcement, covering foreign and domestic corruption, extortion as well as bribery, corruption in the public sector and the private sector, (embezzlement, illicit enrichment of public officials, abuse of functions and trading in influence). In addition, UNCAC contains important preventive measures designed to strengthen the capability of states to fight corruption; provisions on international cooperation, including mutual legal assistance, extradition and joint investigations; ground-breaking provisions on asset recovery; as well as provisions on technical assistance and information exchanges.

Several examples can be used to illustrate UNCAC provisions of particular relevance to multinational enterprises:

- The provisions for international cooperation should substantially improve cooperation among national enforcement officials. There are detailed articles dealing with mutual legal assistance and extradition. These should expedite prosecutors ability to obtain evidence and witnesses located in other countries, thereby overcoming one of the biggest obstacles obstructing foreign bribery cases.
- The criminalization provisions break important new ground. Particularly noteworthy is the article on "compensation for damages" which provides for private rights of action to enable those damaged by acts of corruption to obtain compensation from those responsible for the damage. Also of interest is the article requiring governments to "address consequences of corruption", including annulling contracts and withdrawing concessions.
- UNCAC includes innovative provisions on asset recovery designed to enable governments, most commonly in the South, to recover funds deposited abroad by corrupt officials, often in the North but increasingly elsewhere. In the past, asset recovery has been very difficult to pursue. The UNCAC provisions are likely to increase and accelerate this process. Companies dealing with corrupt officials must exercise high levels of diligence to ensure that any assets that they may obtain as a result of dealings with corrupt officials, or other politically exposed persons (PEPs), cannot be frozen and confiscated in asset recovery proceedings.

UNCAC's broad scope and worldwide participation provide unique potential for global progress against corruption. However, these same factors present difficulties and complexities in their implementation that will take time to overcome. The parties are at different levels of political, legal and economic development. Most UNCAC provisions are not self-executing and require governments to pass new legislation, to build and strengthen organizations and provide them with adequate funding and staffing. Some UNCAC provisions are mandatory ("governments shall adopt laws"), others are discretionary ("governments shall consider adopting laws"). Some are spelled out in great detail: the article on mutual legal assistance includes thirty sections, others are expressed only in broad generalities.

The rate at which UNCAC implementation will progress is difficult to predict. That over 80 per cent of the parties have ratified UNCAC is a positive sign that governments recognize the need for comprehensive international action. There is widespread recognition of two fundamental points: (a) globalization of economic life will continue to expand, and (b) corruption operates on a global scale and is continuing to grow. Therefore, there is a compelling need for UNCAC to evolve from a promising legal framework into effective action programs.

UNCAC provisions directly affecting international business

The provisions of most direct impact on international business are primarily in the Chapter on Criminalization and Law Enforcement.

Article 15 "Bribery of national public officials", is a mandatory requirement that governments criminalize domestic bribery (active corruption) and solicitation (passive corruption). The OECD Convention only deals with bribery of foreign public officials. Bribery of national officials is prohibited by the criminal laws of most countries.

Article 16 "Bribery of foreign public officials and officials of public international organizations", is a mandatory requirement that governments criminalize foreign bribery. However, the criminalization of solicitation by foreign public officials is left discretionary. The prohibition of solicitation under Article 15 would apply whether the company solicited is domestic or foreign. The OECD Convention covers bribery of foreign public officials, but does not deal with solicitation.

UNCAC Convention Article 16

Article 16

Bribery of foreign public officials and officials of public international organizations

1. Each State Party shall adopt such legislative and other measures as may be necessary to establish as a criminal offence, when committed intentionally, the promise, offering or giving to a foreign public official or an official of a public international organization, directly or indirectly, of an undue advantage, for the official himself or herself or another person or entity, in order that the official act or refrain from acting in the exercise of his or her official duties, in order to obtai n or retain business or other undue advantage in relation to the conduct of international business.

2. Each State Party shall consider adopting such legislative and other measures as may be necessary to establish as a criminal offence, when committed intentionally, the solicitation or accept ance by a foreign public official or an official of a public international organization, directly or indirectly, of an undue advantage, for the official himself or herself or another person or entity, in order that the official act or refrain from acting in the exercise of his or her official duties."

Article 18 "Trading in influence", **Article 19**, "Abuse of functions" and **Article 20**, "Illicit Enrichment", are discretionary provisions which have considerable potential for broadening the reach of criminal law beyond the traditional prohibitions of bribery and extortion. Article 20 is particularly important because it shifts the burden of proof on to public officials who get rich in office. These provisions go beyond the OECD Convention. Companies need to consider whether to cover Article 18 under their anti-bribery policies; this raises the difficult issue of distinguishing between legitimate lobbying activities and improper trading in influence.

UNCAC Convention, Articles 20 and 21

Article 20

Illicit enrichissment

Subject to its constitution and the fundamental principles of its legal system, each State Party shall consider adopting such legislative and other measures as may be necessary to establish as a criminal offence, when committed intentionally, illicit enrichment, that is, a significant increase in the assets of a public official that he or she cannot reasonably explain in relation to his or her lawful income."

Article 21

Bribery in the private sector

Each State Party shall consider adopting such legislative and other measures as may be necessary to establish as criminal offences, when committed intentionally in the course of economic, financial or commercial activities:

a) The promise, offering or giving, directly or indirectly, of an undue advantage to any person who directs or works, in any capacity, for a private sector entity, for the person himself or herself or for another person, in order that he or she, in breach of his or her duties, act or refrain from acting;

b) The solicitation or acceptance, directly or indirectly, of an undue advantage by any person who directs or works, in any capacity, for a private sector entity, for the person himself or for another person in order that he or she, in breach of his or her duties, act or refrain from acting."

Article 21 "Bribery in the private sector", and Article 23, "Embezzlement of property in the private sector", are both discretionary provisions. Their implementation is important because the line of division between the private sector and the public sector has become blurred with the private sector taking on traditional public functions. These provisions go beyond the OECD Convention.

Article 23 "Laundering of proceeds of crime", is a mandatory provision. It provides that the corruption offences covered by UNCAC shall be predicate offences triggering the anti-money laundering prohibitions. This provision goes beyond the OECD Convention, which makes foreign bribery a predicate offence only in countries where bribery of domestic officials is a predicate offence.

Article 26 "Liability of legal persons", is a mandatory provision calling for corporate liability for the offences covered by UNCAC. This is an important step, because it should accelerate the abandonment of the antiquated concept that only individuals and not corporations shall be criminally liable for offences. Article 26 provides that the liability of corporations may be criminal, civil or administrative; thus, it does not require that corporations shall be criminally liable. Governments must provide that corporations are "subject to effective, proportionate and dissuasive criminal or non-criminal sanctions, including monetary sanctions". UNCAC's treatment of corporate liability is similar to that of the OECD Convention.

UNCAC Convention article 26

Article 26

Liability of legal persons

1. Each State Party shall adopt such measures as may be necessary, consistent with its legal principles, to establish the liability of legal persons for participation in the offences established in accordance with this Convention.
2. Subject to the legal principles of the State Party, the liability of legal persons may be criminal, civil or administrative.
3. Such liability shall be without prejudice to the criminal liability of the natural persons who have committed the offences.
4. Each State Party shall, in particular, ensure that legal persons held liable in accordance with this article are subject to effective, proportionate and dissuasive criminal or non-criminal sanctions, including monetary sanctions."

Article 29 "Statute of limitations", is a mandatory provision calling for long statutes of limitations for corruption offences. It also provides for a longer limitations period or a suspension of the statute where there is evasion by the offender. Article 29 is stronger than the OECD Convention.

Article 31 "Freezing, seizure and confiscation", is a mandatory provision calling for the confiscation of the proceeds of corruption and of property used in or destined for use in corruption. Bank and other financial records shall be made available and bank secrecy may not be asserted. The OECD Convention provides that bribes and the proceeds of bribery are subject to seizure and confiscation.

Article 33 "Protection of reporting persons", is a discretionary provision for protection of persons who report offences under the Convention to the competent authorities (whistleblowers). This is not covered in the OECD Convention.

Article 34 "Consequences of acts of corruption", provides for annulling or rescinding contracts or withdrawing concessions in case of corruption. This is not covered in the OECD Convention.

Article 35 "Compensation for damages", is a mandatory provision calling for measures to enable persons damaged by acts of corruption to obtain compensation from those responsible for such damages. This provision for private rights of action has far-reaching implications. Private suits could make up for the reluctance of public prosecutors to take action. The OECD Convention does not provide for private rights of action.

Article 35 is broadly worded. Its scope and effect will depend on implementing legislation and court decisions. Presumably suits could be brought by unsuccessful competitors and by various other damaged parties. It will be interesting to see how broadly courts will construe the category of potential plaintiffs: "entities and persons who have suffered damage as a result of an act of corruption". Similar questions are raised regarding the category of potential defendants: "those responsible for that damage". Presumably suits could be brought against corrupt companies and against corrupt officials. Can suits also be brought against governments that maintain corrupt procurement systems?

Article 37 "Cooperation with law enforcement authorities", provides that governments may mitigate punishment or grant immunity to persons cooperating in investigations and prosecutions of corruption. This is not covered by OECD Convention.

Chapter IV "International Cooperation", includes provisions on mutual legal assistance, law enforcement cooperation, joint investigations and special investigative techniques. These are important to international business, because they should speed up the traditionally cumbersome and time-consuming procedures for dealing with international corruption.

Chapter V "Asset Recovery", is of principal benefit to countries whose corrupt officials have deposited stolen assets in foreign countries. Companies making foreign acquisitions need to assess, as part of their due diligence reviews, whether properties to be acquired could be subject to seizure and confiscation because of corruption by prior owners.

The successful implementation of UNCAC's asset recovery chapter would be of far-reaching importance, because the attractiveness of corruption would be sharply reduced if corrupt leaders could no longer count on safely depositing the proceeds of corruption in foreign banks. In addition, recovery of stolen assets would contribute greatly to international development, because a large share of the estimated tens of billions dollars of such assets came from the poorest countries in the world.

Strengthening national integrity systems

Many of the provisions in UNCAC's Section on "Preventive Measures" are important to companies because they will strengthen integrity and accountability, thereby curtailing corruption, as well as improving conditions for doing business more broadly. The OECD Convention does not include preventive measures.

Article 5 "Preventive anti-corruption policies and practices", requires governments to develop anti-corruption policies that reflect the rule of law, integrity, transparency and accountability. Periodic evaluations are called for to determine the adequacy of anti-corruption measures. This article should provide a useful advocacy tool for private sector and civil society groups.

Article 6 "Preventive anti-corruption bodies", requires governments to establish organizations to implement the policies referred to in Article 5. Such bodies shall be granted the necessary independence to enable them to carry out their functions, as well as the necessary material resources and specialized staff.

Article 8 "Codes of conduct for public officials", requires governments to promote integrity, honesty and responsibility among its public officials by means of codes of conduct. Such codes should encourage reporting of violations. Also called for are declarations by public officials of outside activities, investments, assets and substantial gifts from which conflict of interest may result.

Article 9 "Public procurement and management of public finances", addresses two areas of government activity long subject to widespread corruption. Governments are required to establish public procurement systems based on transparency, competition and objective criteria in decision-making, including effective systems of appeal. They shall also promote transparency and accountability in the management of public finances, encompassing procedures for the adoption of the national budget, timely reporting on revenue and expenditure, accounting and auditing standards and risk management and internal control. Improvements in these areas would be of great benefit to business.

UNCAC Convention Articles 9 (excerpted) and 10

Article 9

Public procurement and management of public finances

Each State Party shall, in accordance with the fundamental principles of its legal system, take the necessary steps to establish appropriate systems of procurement, based on transparency, competition and objective criteria in decision-making, that are effective, inter alia, in preventing corruption ...

Article 10

Public reporting

Taking into account the need to combat corruption, each State Party shall, in accordance with the fundamental principles of its domestic law, take such measures as may be necessary to enhance transparency in its public administration, including with regard to its organization, functioning and decision-making processes, where appropriate. Such measures may include, inter alia:

a) Adopting procedures or regulations allowing members of the general public to obtain, where appropriate, information on the organization functioning and decision-making processes of its public administration and, with due regard for the protection of privacy and personal data, on decisions and legal acts that concern members of the public;

b) Simplifying administrative procedures, where appropriate, in order to facilitate public access to the competent decision-making authorities.

c) Publishing information, which may include periodic reports on the risks of corruption in its public administration."

Article 10 "Public reporting", provides for public access to decision-making authorities and periodic reports on the risks of corruption in public administration.

Article 12 "Private sector", calls for governments to take measures to prevent corruption in the private sector, including enhanced accounting and auditing standards, codes of conduct, prevention of conflicts of interest, restrictions on employment of former public officials, internal controls, prohibitions of off-the-books transactions and disallowance of tax deductibility of bribes. These measures would apply directly to business conduct.

UNCAC Convention Article 12 (excerpted)

Article 12

Private sector

Each State Party shall take measures, in accordance with the fundamental principles of its domestic law, to prevent corruption involving the private sector, enhance accounting and auditing standards in the private sector and, where appropriate, provide effective, proportionate and dissuasive civil, administrative or criminal penalties for failure to comply with such measures.

3. In order to prevent corruption, each State Party shall take such measures as may be necessary, in accordance with its domestic laws and regulations regarding the maintenance of books and records, financial statement disclosures and accounting and auditing standards, to prohibit the following acts carried out for the purpose of committing any of the offences established in accordance with this Convention:

a) The establishment of off-the-books accounts;

b) The making of off-the-books or inadequately identified transactions;

c) The recording of non-existent expenditure;

d) The entry of liabilities with incorrect identification of their objects;

e) The use of false documents; and

f) The intentional destruction of bookkeeping documents earlier than foreseen by the law.

4. Each State Party shall disallow the tax deductibility of expenses that constitute bribes, the latter being one of the constituent elements of the offences established in accordance with articles 15 and 16 of this Convention and, where appropriate, other expenses incurred in furtherance of corrupt conduct."

Article 13 "Participation of society", requires governments to promote active participation of individuals and groups outside the public sector in the fight against corruption. This includes business as well as NGOs. Article 13 calls for ensuring that the public has effective access to information and protects the freedom to publish and disseminate information concerning corruption. Anti-corruption bodies are required to provide access for reporting, including anonymously, of corruption offences.

Article 14 "Measures to prevent money laundering", calls for a comprehensive regulatory and supervisory regime for banks and other financial institutions to deter and detect all forms of money laundering.

The foregoing preventive measures provide an invaluable foundation for strengthening government capability to combat corruption, strengthening private participation and enhancing corporate integrity programs.

The need for an effective monitoring programme

The most serious cloud hanging over the future of UNCAC is the unresolved controversy over monitoring of government implementation. Experience has shown that follow-up monitoring is essential to make anti-corruption conventions work. It is particularly important for a convention as complex as UNCAC.

The need for monitoring was debated during the 2002 Vienna negotiations that led to the adoption of the Convention. There were strong proponents of monitoring. However, many developing countries objected because they feared that UNCAC monitoring would become another process for criticizing them. A number of industrialized countries expressed reservations about the cost and effectiveness of UNCAC monitoring and about duplication with monitoring programmes of OECD and regional conventions. When it proved impossible to reach agreement, a decision on monitoring was deferred until the First Conference of States Parties (CoSP), to be held one year after UNCAC became effective.

The First CoSP, held in Jordan in December 2006, agreed that "effective and efficient review of implementation of the Convention … is of paramount importance and urgent". A working group was established to develop proposals for a review mechanism. The working group failed to develop proposals for action at the Second CoSP, held in Indonesia in early 2008. Leaders of the G77 continued to express reservations. The working group is expected to present proposals at the Third CoSP, to be held in Qatar in late 2009.

Business objectives for UNCAC

Declaration by the business community to the Conference of States Parties to the United Nations Convention against Corruption (excerpted).

"No tangible progress will be achieved without a systematic and continuous review mechanism to ensure the effective implementation of the Convention by all signatory countries. The Conference of States Parties is urged to promptly establish a full monitoring program, based on self-evaluation and peer reviews, before the momentum created by the adoption of UNCAC is allowed to fade out. Such a program, which will require a strong secretariat and dependable funding from the UN budget, should be effective as from 2007 and begin with a survey of implementation and technical assistance needs ...

An open and transparent review mechanism should help focus attention on corruption issues which are pervasive in all segments of society. Participation by business in the monitoring of UNCAC will be essential to provide a complete picture of country progress in implementing and enforcing the Convention. It also gives an opportunity for non-governmental stakeholders who are directly affected by corruption, such as the business community, to press for action when governments are lagging and to raise concerns about potential abuse of UNCAC provisions."

Surveys of implementation conducted by UNODC, based on self-assessment by governments, have shown that implementation has been uneven, varying between regions and for different UNCAC provisions. Without monitoring, UNCAC will be an erratic patchwork quilt, with governments picking and choosing provisions that are easy to implement and ignoring the rest. Unless there is consistent global implementation, important UNCAC programmes cannot achieve their objectives. For example, asset recovery can be circumvented as long as some banking centres fail to implement UNCAC's asset recovery provisions. Stolen funds will flow to countries with little or no implementation, particularly those that retain banking secrecy laws.

The key elements necessary for a sound monitoring program include the following:

Management responsibility: The Conference of States Parties should be responsible for establishing policies and providing oversight. However, responsibility for the day-to-day management of the monitoring program should be assigned to UNODC, the UNCAC Secretariat. Because the CoSP meets only every two years, and decisions require consensus by more than 120 parties, CoSP management of the monitoring process would be completely unwieldy.

Flexible administration: The monitoring program should be flexible recognizing that some countries and some UNCAC articles will need more time for implementation than others. A range of review methods should be used, including self-assessment surveys, expert and peer reviews and country visits. The review process should be allowed to evolve over time.

Adequate and dependable funding: The Secretariat will require strong leadership and a small technical staff. Because monitoring must be a long-term programme, adequate and dependable funding will be required. The funding should come from the regular UN budget.

Board of experts: A board of distinguished experts in the major fields covered by UNCAC should be established to provide technical advice and assistance to the CoSP and the Secretariat. This would strengthen the quality of monitoring reviews, enhance its objectivity and promote public credibility.

Transparency and non-governmental participation: Monitoring reviews should be transparent with opportunities for participation by the private sector and civil society. Such participation will provide essential inputs on the status of government anti-corruption programmes. A transparent process will have much greater credibility than reviews conducted behind closed doors.

Cooperation with other monitoring programmes: Arrangements for cooperation should be established between the UNODC and the monitoring organizations of the other anti-corruption conventions. This is necessary to avoid duplicative reviews, because most UNCAC parties are also parties to other conventions.

Technical assistance: Many developing countries will require technical assistance to implement UNCAC provisions. Such assistance will be essential for the success of the Convention. While many donors already fund governance programmes in developing countries, greater assistance and increased coordination will be needed. Assurance of adequate technical assistance is also necessary in overcoming G77 concerns that monitoring will result in unfair criticism.

Until a monitoring program with the foregoing elements is established, UNCAC will not achieve the momentum necessary to reverse the growth of global corruption, and the objective of establishing an effective global framework for combating corruption will recede into the indefinite future.

Conclusion

It should be clear, even from this brief overview, that UNCAC is crucially important. Making UNCAC work will take time and effort. Establishing an effective follow-up monitoring programme is the most critical step. UNCAC is unique in providing a comprehensive global framework for combating corruption. That in itself provides enough incentive to justify the efforts required.

Fritz Heimann is also the author of Chapters 1, 3 and 14 in this handbook.

Chapter 3

Prohibiting Bribery and Extortion: Narrowing the Problem Areas

By Fritz Heimann

This chapter outlines the basic prohibitions of ICC Rules and the OECD Convention concerning bribery and extortion. It then deals with four important problem areas: facilitation payments; gifts, entertainment and travel expenses; parent company responsibility for foreign subsidiaries; and offset arrangements.

RELEVANT PROVISIONS OF ICC RULES AND THE OECD CONVENTION

Basic definitions and prohibitions

ICC Rules

Article 1 Prohibition of Bribery and Extortion

Enterprises should prohibit bribery and extortion at all times and in any form, whether direct or indirect, including through agents and other intermediaries:

a) Bribery is the offering, promising, or giving of any undue pecuniary or other advantage to:

- A public official, at national, local or international level;
- A political party, party official, or candidate; and
- A director, officer, employee or agent of a private enterprise;

b) Extortion or solicitation is the demanding of a bribe, whether or not coupled with a threat if the demand is refused. "Bribery" as used in the Rules shall include extortion.

c) Enterprises should not (i) kick back any portion of a contract payment to government officials or to employees of the contract ing party, or (ii) utilize intermediaries such as agents, sub contrac tors, consultants or other third parties, to channel payements to government officials, or to employees of the contracting party, or their relatives, friends or business associates".

This Article is substantially broader than the corresponding provision of the OECD Convention, which deals only with bribery of foreign public officials. Article 1 of ICC Rules covers extortion as well as bribery; corruption in the private sector and the public sector; domestic as well as foreign corruption; bribery of political parties, party officials and candidates, as well as public officials.

The opening sentence of Article 1 makes clear that the prohibition of "direct and indirect" corruption includes agents and other intermediaries. The last sentence amplifies the prohibition of bribery for "other improper advantage" by adding as examples "in connection with regulatory permits, taxation, customs, judicial and legislative proceedings".

Paragraph b) of Article 1 defines extortion broadly to cover solicitation of a bribe "whether or not coupled with a threat if the demand is refused".

Paragraph c) further amplifies the broad scope of Article 1 by prohibiting kick backs of contract payments and the use of intermediaries such as agents, subcontractors or other third parties to channel payments to officials, as well as to their relatives, friends or business associates.

The intent of Article 1 is clear: corporate policies should prohibit all forms of bribery and extortion, regardless of the method used. Companies should build on Article 1 to prohibit the techniques for paying bribes most likely to be used in the industries in which they do business. Continuing vigilance will be required because bribe payers and bribe takers are persistent and innovative. When the more common techniques are barred, they can be expected to develop alternative techniques and new subterfuges. Chapter Four deals in detail with the use of agents, probably the most common technique for transmitting bribes.

OECD Convention

The OECD Convention is narrower in scope than ICC Rules, being directed only at prohibiting the bribery of foreign *public* officials. The Convention does not cover domestic bribery, private-to-private bribery or extortion, though the Convention's preamble recognizes "the role of governments in the prevention of solicitation of bribes from individuals and enterprises in international business transactions". However, within the Convention's area of focus, its prohibitions are clear and specific. Both "bribery" and "foreign officials" are broadly defined. Among the key points are the following:

- Bribery is prohibited "to obtain or retain business or *other improper advantage* in the conduct of international business" [emphasis added]. Thus, the prohibition applies not only to bribery in the procurement of orders, but also in such areas as regulatory permits, taxation, customs, and judicial and legislative proceedings;
- Bribery is prohibited regardless of the form it takes: ("any undue pecuniary or other advantage"), or whether the bribe is offered or paid "directly or through intermediaries";
- The breadth of the prohibition is reinforced by Commentary 7, which provides that bribery is prohibited: "irrespective of, inter alia, the value of the advantage, its results, perceptions of local custom, the tolerance of such payments by local authorities, or the alleged necessity of the payment in order to obtain or retain business or other improper advantage";
- The foreign officials who may not be bribed are also broadly defined to include "any person holding a legislative, administrative or judicial office ... whether appointed or elected". Furthermore, "all levels and subdivisions of government, from national to local" are covered. Bribery of officials or agents of international organizations is also barred;
- The prohibition against bribery also applies to "any person exercising a public function for a foreign country". This covers the situation where a government delegates a public function to a private organization, for example, the evaluation of bids in public procurement or the collection of customs duties;
- No bribes may be paid to employees of "public enterprises". This covers "any enterprise ... over which a government ... may, directly or indirectly, exercise a dominant influence". Included are companies in which governments own a majority of the stock or can appoint a majority of the board. (The only exception is for a public enterprise which "operates on a normal commercial basis ... substantially equivalent to a private enterprise, without preferential subsidies or other privileges".)

It should be noted that the definition of bribery of foreign public officials incorporated in national legislation passed by some OECD parties may differ from the language of Article 1 of the Convention. For enforcement purposes, the text of the national laws will be controlling. The OECD monitoring process seeks to ensure that national laws meet the requirements of the Convention and that any deficiencies are corrected.

Problem Areas

Facilitation payments

There has been a substantial evolution in thinking about facilitation payments since the 1990s. The traditional view, tolerating facilitation payments as a necessary evil, was reflected in the 1999 edition of ICC Rules and in the Commentary to the OECD Convention adopted in 1997.

- The Introduction to ICC Rules (1999) stated that "under current conditions in some parts of the world, an effective programme against extortion and bribery may have to be implemented in stages. The highest priority should be directed to ending large-scale extortion and bribery involving politicians and senior officials ... Small payments to low-level officials to expedite routine approvals are not condoned. However, they represent a lesser problem. When extortion and bribery at the top levels are curbed, government leaders can be expected to take steps to clean up petty corruption."
- The OECD Convention's Commentary 9 (1997) provided that small facilitation payments to induce public officials to perform their functions, such as issuing licences or permits, "do not constitute payments made 'to obtain or retain business or other improper advantage' ... and, accordingly, are also not an offence." The Commentary, however, referred to facilitation payments as a "corrosive phenomenon" which should be addressed by programmes for good governance, but concludes that criminal ization by other countries does not seem practical or effective.

Resolution on facilitation payments

Adopted by the Transparency International Annual Membership Meeting, Bali, Indonesia, 28 October 2007.

"Facilitation payments are small payments made to secure or expedite the performance of a routine or necessary action to which the payer of the facilitation payment has legal or other entitlement. It has been the long standing policy of TI to oppose the use of facilitation payments and it is now proposed that the Annual Membership Meeting of TI resolve that:Transparency International – its Board of Directors, its National Chapters, its Individual Members, its Advisory Council and the representatives of TI to other organizations, reiterate its opposition to the use of 'facilitating payments.' Accordingly, TI will boldly voice its opposition to such payments. It will call on companies to cease making such payments immediately. It will also encourage all of its chapters to join with the Secretariat in campaigning for revisions in international agreements, treaties and conventions that permit 'facilitating payments' and it will also advocate, where appropriate, for revisions of national and international laws."

Changing attitudes

There is still debate about whether exceptions for facilitation payments should be continued. However, the balance has shifted in favour of those who want to eliminate the exception. This reflects the following considerations:

- The continuation of facilitation exceptions by prominent organizations such as ICC and OECD sends an unacceptable political message to the developing world and undermines Western efforts to promote anti corruption programmes in developing countries.
- Facilitation payments are often part of an organized system of extortion, with much of the money collected by low-level officials going to their superiors and politicians. They have a corrosive effect on the integrity of the country's civil service.
- Even though individual facilitation payments are small, the cumulative effect of their systematic collection has substantial adverse economic effects and particularly hurts the poor who are least able to meet pervasive demands for payments.
- On the moral level, it is impossible to distinguish between small payments to low-level officials and large payments to high-level officials.
- From the corporate compliance standpoint, a "zero tolerance" policy is clear and therefore easier to enforce than a policy that tolerates facilitation payments.

- The facilitation-payment exception can erode the company's anti-bribery policy, particularly if the company allows employees in the field to distinguish between permissible facilitation payments and improper bribes.
- If the company requires headquarters' approval of facilitation payments, such approval implicates management in payments that may well be illegal where made.
- Facilitation payments also present troublesome accounting and tax deductibility questions.

❖ Succumbing to pressure for facilitation payments can cause future problems. The company that pays will be marked as a target for further payments, and officials have an incentive to create new obstacles, so that they can be paid off to remove them.

Those wishing to retain an exception for facilitation payments make the following points:

❖ Corrupt officials often have intolerable leverage over those who refuse to meet their demands. Where collection of facilitation payments is part of an organized extortion scheme, appealing to higher officials is more likely to result in reprisals than in relief from extortion.

❖ Ending demands for facilitation payments will require major reforms in public administration, including living wages for civil service employees and the political will to root out entrenched extortion schemes.

❖ Laws prohibiting foreign bribery are unlikely to be an effective tool for combating facilitation payments. The costs of investigating and prosecuting foreign bribery are very high, and prosecutors are unlikely to pursue facilitation payments.

❖ Until national governments are prepared to prevent extortion, companies must choose among three unattractive alternatives:

  - Making facilitation payments;
  - Letting agents, such as customs brokers, make facilitation payments; or
  - Not doing business in countries where corruption is endemic,very costly option in countries where a company has already made substantial investments.

❖ In countries where petty corruption is a way of life, failure to provide a facilitation exception could undermine the credibility of a corporate anti-bribery policy. Employees may regard a "zero tolerance" policy as a public relations exercise designed for home country consumption, not as a policy they can comply with in a corrupt country.

New ICC position

In 2005, after reviewing the pros and cons, the ICC adopted the following position:

Article 6 **Facilitation payments**

a) Enterprises should not make facilitation payments. In the event that an enterprise determines, after appropriate managerial review, that facilitation payments cannot be eliminated entirely, it should establish controls and procedures to ensure that their use is limited to small payments to low-level officials for routine actions to which the enterprise is entitled.

b) The need for the continued use of facilitation payments should be reviewed periodically with the objective of eliminating them as soon as possible." The new Article recognizes that, in the view of the ICC (Commission on Anti-Corruption), the arguments for ending facilitation payments clearly outweigh the arguments for retaining the exception. Where facilitation payments cannot be eliminated entirely, they should be subject to strict corporate controls. Their continued use should be reviewed periodically and they should be eliminated as soon as possible.

OECD position

The OECD Working Group on Bribery is conducting a systematic review of its instruments, which is scheduled for completion in the first half of 2009. Whether to continue the exception for facilitation payments provided by Commentary 9 is under consideration.

Notwithstanding the permissive approach of Commentary 9, at least 12 countries do not provide an exemption for facilitation. These include France, Germany, Italy, Japan, Korea, Mexico and the UK. Facilitation payment exclusions are provided by Australia, Canada, Sweden, Switzerland and the US. A number of countries, including the Netherlands and Norway, leave the treatment of facilitation payments to prosecutorial discretion.

The number of companies adopting a zero tolerance approach is increasing and includes major companies such as BP, Shell and Telekom Austria Group. The UN Convention Against Corruption does not provide a facilitation payments exception.

Proposed guidelines

We offer the following guidelines to companies:

- The guiding principle should be to eliminate facilitation payments as soon as possible. Companies that are well established in a country, or are providing essential equipment or services, should be in a position to turn down requests for facilitation payments.
- Whether facilitation payments must be continued should be determined by senior management based on country-by-country reviews. Information should be obtained from knowledgeable local sources, such as commercial attachés and chambers of commerce, and not only from local sales representatives, who may be predisposed in favour of continuing facilitation payments. Even in countries where petty corruption is widespread, there often are government agencies for which facilitation payments are not customary.
- Companies must provide clear guidance to their employees, indicating under what circumstances facilitation payments may be made. Employees should be informed as to where they can turn for advice in specific cases, including advice on possible alternatives to avoid demands for payments. Situations in which companies could conclude that making facilitation payments is a lesser evil include the following:
  - When there are threats of physical harm to employees or serious damage to company property;
  - When facilitation payments are required to receive essential public services, such as mail, telecommunications, power, water and police protection.
- A facilitation payment exception should only apply to small payments to low-level employees. It is essential that management controls be in place to assure that the facilitation payment exception does not undermine the company's anti-bribery policy. Some companies have specified limits for individual payments, as well as limits on the total amount of facilitation payments than can be paid on a project.
- Companies should work with local business groups, civil society and the media to encourage government reforms to eliminate facilitation payments.

Gifts, entertainment and travel expenses

ICC Rules

Article 5 Gifts, hospitality and expenses

"Enterprises should establish procedures covering the offer or receipt of gifts, hospitality or expenses in order to ensure that such arrangements (a) are limited to reasonable and bona fide expenditures, and (b) do not improperly affect, or might be deemed to improperly affect, the outcome of a procurement or other business transaction."

OECD Convention

The OECD Convention does not deal specifically with gifts, entertainment and the reimbursement of travel expenses of government employees. However these can become an issue when they reach a level where allegations can be made that they represent the giving of "any undue pecuniary or other advantage" (to use the OECD language) in order to influence the behaviour of a public official.

Guidelines

Corporate policies should provide guidelines establishing appropriate limits for gifts, entertainment and travel expenses. Decisions should not be left to the unfettered discretion of sales personnel or agents. A readily accessible help desk should provide guidance for specific cases. The following points are pertinent:

- In determining proper levels for gifts, entertainment and travel expenses, the key is whether the amounts involved are reasonable and whether there is a legitimate business purpose. Covering expenses for a visit to the company's factories and laboratories would be on the right side of the line. Paying for visits to gambling casinos or reimbursement of shopping expenses of spouses would be on the wrong side of the line.
- Timing is sensitive. Gifts and entertainment that might be acceptable at other times, could well become questionable if they come at a time when contract awards or other important decisions are about to be made.
- Government agencies, as well as major companies, are increasingly promulgating regulations and rules defining what gifts, entertainment and travel expenses their officials and employees are allowed to receive from suppliers or others. Where such rules exist they should be observed.

- Where there are no applicable rules, the best test is: how would it look on the front page of a newspaper or on the evening news? A gift that can be accepted in public is likely to be on the right side of the line. Any gift that cannot withstand the light of day should be prohibited.

Bribes versus gifts: one company's view

"When it comes to distinguishing between bribes and gifts, the perceptions of the donor and recipient often differ. A recipient may believe that what he is receiving is a gift because it in no way binds him to the donor. This applies particularly when he receives a benefit rather than cash. The donor's intentions, however, might be very different. A gift may become a bribe if it is not declared.

However, there are some useful distinguishing features:

- Bribes have to be made in secret, as they are neither legally nor morally acceptable;
- Gifts are generally made openly as a gesture of goodwill or affection;
- Bribes are often made indirectly through a third party;
- Gifts are usually made directly;
- A bribe creates an obligation on the recipient, who becomes sub-ordinate to the donor and who is encouraged to alter his or her behaviour in some way;
- A gift comes with no such conditions and is intended to identify the donor with the recipient to seal a relationship or frienship."

Dealing with Bribery and Corruption: A Management Primer, Shell, Second Edition, 2003.

Parent company responsibility for foreign subsidiaries and joint ventures

ICC Rules

Article 7 (d) provides that corporate anti-corruption policies should "apply to all controlled subsidiaries, foreign as well as domestic".

The credibility of a corporate anti-bribery policy will be compromised if the policy is not applied consistently. Employees are increasingly transferred back and forth between the parent company and foreign subsidiaries. If bribery is tolerated at the subsidiary, employees may not comply with the parent company's policy when they are transferred to the parent company.

To compete in a global economy, companies find it increasingly necessary to operate in a coordinated way. Particularly on large projects, the parent company and its subsidiaries are likely to work together, utilizing resources from different components. Corporate financial planning and allocation of resources also result in parent company involvement with subsidiaries.

Communication by e-mail among corporate components has become so widespread that it will be increasingly difficult for parent companies to claim that they do not know what their subsidiaries are doing. Even though parent companies differ in the degree of independence with which foreign subsidiaries operate, the overall trend is toward greater integration, particularly on the accounting and financial side.

Bribery scandals involving a foreign subsidiary can seriously damage a company's reputation for integrity and drive down stock prices. Legal defences based on the corporate separateness of subsidiaries do not overcome the public relations damage: "bad reputation pierces the corporate veil".

The position taken by ICC Rules is fully consistent with the efforts of the corporate-governance movement to promote greater accountability of corporate boards of directors for actions which could adversely affect a company's financial results or reputation. Failure to provide adequate supervision has increasingly become a legal charge levelled against directors, CEOs and top officers.

Exercising the parent company's controlling interest to assure that the subsidiary adopts and enforces the same anti-bribery policies as the parent is an obvious step. Negligent failure to supervise the conduct of subsidiaries has already been used by the US Securities and Exchange Commission (SEC) as a basis for civil penalties. It has been raised in Germany in the Siemens case. This trend is likely to spread to other countries. Prudent companies should anticipate the trend of legal developments and avoid the risk of being overtaken by them.

OECD Convention

The OECD Convention does not expressly address the parent-subsidiary issue. It is one of the "unresolved issues" on which the Working Group on Bribery may take clarifying action as part of their current review of OECD instruments. Several points are pertinent:

- Parent companies based in countries which have ratified the Convention cannot use their foreign subsidiaries as conduits for bribing foreign officials. Article 1, paragraph 1, of the Convention prohibits bribery "whether directly or through intermediaries";
- Article 1, paragraph 2, goes further and requires that "complicity in, including incitement, aiding and abetting, or authorization of an act of bribery of a foreign official shall be a criminal offence". This language is sufficiently broad to make extremely dangerous any involvement by the parent in the subsidiary's bribery scheme;
- Only in the case of a completely independent act of bribery by a subsidiary can the parent company expect to avoid liability. Even then, failure to supervise subsidiaries may be raised;
- A subsidiary based in a state that has ratified the Convention is prohibited from paying bribes;
- Bribes by a subsidiary may be subject to prosecution in the state where the parent is based "when the offence is committed in whole or in part in its territory" (Article 4, paragraph 1). Commentary 25 to the Convention declares that "the territorial basis for jurisdiction should be interpreted broadly, so that an extensive physical connection to the bribery act is not required";
- That will also be the case if that state utilizes nationality jurisdiction and if its nationals were involved. This possibility exists when parent companies place their own nationals in responsible positions in their foreign subsidiaries a common practice.

Joint ventures and out-sourcing agreements

ICC Rules

Article 3 Joint ventures and out-sourcing agreements

Enterprises should take measures within their power to ensure that anti-bribery provisions consistent with these Rules of Conduct are accepted by joint-venture partners as applicable to the joint venture and by parties to out-sourcing agreements.

The same considerations discussed above with respect to parent company responsibility for subsidiaries arise in the context of joint ventures and outsourcing agreements. Companies should make sure that joint ventures in which they participate and companies with which they make outsourcing agreements adopt and enforce effective anti-bribery policies. It would be foolhardy to assume that a local partner can be allowed to "do the dirty work" without implicating other joint-venture partners. Company responsibility for preventing corruption by parties to outsourcing agreements follows a trend that has long been recognized in connection with supply chain responsibility for labour standards and human rights.

Offset Programmes

Offset programmes have become a common element in large international business transactions. They are most frequently used in defence and aerospace projects, but are also used in other projects involving large procurement costs and advanced technology.

From the perspective of the purchaser, often a government agency, offsets serve two important objectives: (a) they reduce ("offset") hard currency requirements, and (b) they provide technology transfers or otherwise strengthen the local economy. Both are legitimate and beneficial to the purchaser.

Offsets can take many different forms. They can be closely related to the equipment being ordered, for example, establishing a local service shop to maintain the equipment or a spare parts manufacturing plant. Purchasers may specify that a fixed percentage of the purchase price must be spent on locally manufactured components and materials. Offsets can be completely unrelated to the contract work. Contractors may be required to buy local products for which they have to find a market in a third country.

From the perspective of the seller, offsets add burdensome and often undesirable complications to the deal. Sellers would prefer to receive the full selling price in euros or dollars, not be committed to onerous local procurement requirements and not be obligated to transfer technology that diminishes future sales. However, the commercial reality is that offsets are frequently a necessary condition for winning orders.

From the perspective of curbing corruption, offsets can involve sellers in complex arrangements where it may be difficult to distinguish between legitimate and improper practices. It is critical to determine the real beneficiary of the offset. The local service shop which must be established should not be owned by the brother of the minister who awarded the contract. The suppliers of locally manufactured components should be chosen through competitive bidding.

The legitimate reasons for offsets are sufficiently compelling to make it unrealistic to expect offsets to disappear. Regulation of offsets through international agreements seems impractical in view of the wide variety of offset arrangements. Given the potential for abuses, it is essential that companies entering into offsets exercise a high level of due diligence with respect to the participating parties. Offset arrangements should be made as transparent as possible. That may be difficult in the case of military projects. There full disclosure by the company to its home country's government officials may serve as a substitute to public disclosure.

Gifts, bribes and reporting

In its code of conduct, a major company has this language about invitations, gifts and payments:

" ... employees must not accept gifts and gratuities from suppliers or potential suppliers except for promotional items of limited value (such as inexpensive pens, mugs and calendars that bear the company's name). The same standards apply to the corporation's dealings with its customers: [The company] does not offer gifts and gratuities to employees of customers or potential customers, except for modest items for promotional purposes. All such gifts must be properly reported on expense statements. Business entertainment must also be moderately scaled and clearly intended to facilitate business goals. If, for example, tickets to a sporting or cultural event are offered, then the person offering the tickets must plan to attend the event as well.

As a general guideline, business entertainment in the form of meals and beverages is acceptable, as long as it is modest, infrequent, and as far as possible on a reciprocal basis. 'Everyone else does it' is not sufficient justification. If you are having difficulty determining whether a specific gift or entertainment lies within the bounds of acceptable business practice, ask yourself these guiding questions:

- Is it clearly related to the conduct of business?
- Is it moderate, reasonable, and in good taste?
- Would I feel comfortable owning up to the giving or receipt of this gift in front of other customers and suppliers? Other employees? My manager? My family? The media?
- Am I certain the gift does not violate any law or business regulation?

If you have any concerns or uncertainties, contact your manager or the Business Ethics function."

Summary of the ICC Recommendations and OECD Provisions

ICC Rules and the OECD Convention are complementary texts. Even though ICC Rules are broader in scope – applying to private as well as public bribery and to the demand side as well as the supply side of bribery – there is no contradiction between the two documents, and companies should adhere to the principles in both.

The laws implementing the OECD Convention carry the force of national law, while ICC Rules are voluntary and based on self-regulation. There is a need for both approaches. As ICC Rules point out, the "major responsibility" in this field rests with governments, but business also has the responsibility to police itself and to fill in the broad principles of the OECD Convention with specific steps at the company level.

Therefore companies should:

- Establish policies which adhere to the provisions in ICC Rules prohibiting the taking as well as the paying of bribes;
- Adhere to the letter and spirit of the broad OECD prohibitions against bribing public officials, whatever form such bribes may take;
- Exercise vigilance to forestall bribe payers and the bribe takers from developing alternative techniques to get around company rules;
- Eliminate facilitation payments as soon as possible and establish clear procedures and limits for employee when facilitation payments may be made;
- Provide clear guidance to employees with regard to the giving of gifts or entertainment expenses;
- Establish a consistent anti-bribery policy which will apply to foreign subsidiaries as well as to the parent company.

Fritz Heimann is Vice-Chair of the ICC Commission on Anti-Corruption. Fritz Heimann is also the author of chapters 1, 2 and 14 in this handbook.

Chapter 4

The Role of Agents and other Intermediaries

By Michael N. Davies, Q.C.

RELEVANT PROVISIONS OF THE ICC RULES AND THE OECD AND UN CONVENTION

There are three references to the use of agents or other intermediaries in ICC Rules. The principal provisions can be found in Article 2, which is devoted exclusively to the use of agents. It reads:

> "Enterprises should make their anti-corruption policy known to all agents and other intermediaries and make it clear that they expect all activities carried out on their behalf to be compliant with their policy. More particularly, enterprises should take measures within their power to ensure:

a) That any payment made to any agent represents no more than an appropriate remuneration for legitimate services rendered by such agent;

b) That no part of any such payment is passed on by the agent as a bribe or otherwise in contravention of these Rules of Conduct;

c) That agents agree explicitly not to pay bribes. Enterprises should include in their contracts provisions to terminate agreements with agents if a bribe is paid, except for agreements with agents performing routine administrative or clerical tasks.

d) That they maintain a record of the names, terms of employment and payments to all agents who are retained by them in connection with transac tions with public bodies, state or private enterprises. This record should be available for inspection by auditors and by appropriate, duly authorized governmental authorities under conditions of confidentiality.

The foregoing provisions should be applied to all agents or other intermediaries used by the enterprise to obtain orders and permits, including sales representatives, Customs agents, lawyers and consultants."

Another provision is found in Article 1, which states that

> "Enterprises should prohibit bribery and extortion at all times and in any form, whether direct or indirect, including through agents and other intermediaries." Further, Article 1 c) states:
>
> "Enterprises should not .... (ii) utilize intermediaries such as agents, subcontractors, consultants or other third parties, to channel payments to government officials, or to employees of the other contracting party, their relatives, friends or business associates."

The OECD Convention, which is concerned with the use of agents to bribe *foreign public officials*, employs much the same language and also prohibits indirect as well as direct offers of bribes. Under the Convention's Article 1.1, all signatories have agreed to enact laws as may be required to establish "that it is a criminal offence for any person intentionally to offer, promise or give any undue pecuniary or other advantage, *whether directly or through intermediaries*, to a foreign public official, for that official or for a third party, in order that the official act or refrain from acting in relation to the performance of official duties, in order to obtain or retain business or other improper advantage in the conduct of international business" [emphasis added].

The parties to the OECD Convention further agreed, in Article 1.2, to establish "that complicity in, including incitement, aiding and abetting or authorization of an act of bribery of a foreign public official, shall be a criminal offence".

The UN Convention (UNCAC), in Articles 15, 16 and 21, criminalizes all forms of corrupt practices (national or foreign, active or passive, public or private) when committed directly or *indirectly*.

If, therefore, a company employee knows of proposed illegitimate activities by the company's sales agent (or deliberately ignores indications thereof), the employee may be considered to have *implicitly authorized* the subsequent payment of a bribe and, in those countries where criminal responsibility of legal persons exists, the company may be held criminally liable in its own country. A "head in the sand" approach to managing the sales agent is not acceptable.

However, if the company can demonstrate that it did not authorize or approve the payment, that it had conducted adequate due diligence to satisfy itself that its agent would not pay a bribe and aggressively investigated and resolved any "red flags" relating to the sales agent, the risk of the company's being held criminally responsible for the transgression of its representative will be significantly reduced.

There is an increasingly recognized affirmative obligation on a company to supervise its agents. In fact, a number of major companies, including Siemens and BAE, have, in recent years, announced a substantial reduction in the number of agents employed.

The issues

The agent's role

Independent sales agents or sales representatives (the term "agent" being used in this chapter to include agents and other intermediaries) often constitute a key element in a company's international marketing and sales structure. They promote the sale of products and may be instrumental in establishing a favourable image of the company in world markets. These agents are generally independent organizations or individuals engaged to help the company solicit business for specific products and services. Moreover, the use of independent local agents may be required by certain host-country laws.

The agent provides services to promote orders for products and services and to facilitate the company's performance of its obligations under resulting orders. Orders are, however, normally placed by the customer directly with the company as supplier (although occasionally the agent may be granted authority to contract on behalf of, and in the name of, the company). The agent is commonly compensated by either a fee or a commission, which is usually determined by a percentage of the sales price of the products or services sold with his assistance.

When company sales personnel are not stationed full time in a sales territory, the agent provides an important local liaison with customers and continuous sales service, both before and after the submission of bids, during negotiation of contracts and throughout the performance of the company's obligations. The agent usually lives in the country where the customer resides, speaks the local language and is familiar with local laws, regulations and customs. Generally, he is an asset to a company in securing and fulfilling business contracts in the foreign country. That said, the use of international sales representatives can create unique problems, so much so that many multinational companies now locate their own employees in the country either permanently or on a temporary part-time basis whenever possible, in order to avoid the risks involved in retaining a local sales representative.

The risks

One reason why international sales agents can create problems is that they do not necessarily share the same ethical standards as the company and may not be trained in its code of conduct. They are usually nationals of the country where the proposed contract is to be performed and, in some of these countries, it may not be uncommon for bribes to be paid. Therefore, to secure business, agents are more likely to be susceptible than company employees to the temptation to pay a bribe.

In addition, the commission payable to a sales representative on the award of a major project is often so large that it may not only present the temptation, but also an opportunity for him to pay a significant bribe to obtain the contract, and still be left with a large sum of money in his own pocket.

Consequently, there is a serious risk that, if not carefully selected and trained and appropriately monitored, a sales representative, through his illicit activity, may not only tarnish the reputation of the company he represents, but may also cause the company, its management and its employees to be subject to criminal prosecution in their own country under the laws prohibiting foreign bribery that have been passed to implement the OECD Convention. Today a company is regarded as failing in its obligations if it fails to train its agents and, even if trained, an agent may not necessarily comply, since an agent, compared to a company employee, is much less likely to believe that the old-fashioned way of paying a bribe to secure a contract is no longer acceptable.

Remedial actions: the code of conduct

What measures, then, should a company take to ensure that its agent will refrain from paying bribes in connection with the company's business and will abide by the provisions of the company's code of conduct prohibiting payment of bribes?

First, a company should provide, as a directive to its own personnel, that in utilizing sales representatives the company will employ only reputable, qualified individuals or firms. Second, it should be made clear that such third parties will be bound by the anti-bribery provisions of the company's code of conduct and that they must represent the company in a manner consistent with its commitment to integrity. Third, the company should ensure that compensation arrangements for agents are reasonable in relation to the services performed.

In sum, a company should establish specific criteria and procedures regarding agents' selection, compensation and engagement, and the criteria and procedures should be provided for in the company's code of conduct.

Agents: Three Company Codes

WellCare Healthcare Plans, Inc.

"To ensure compliance with all marketing guidelines and the Code of Conduct, all Sales Agents should understand that WellCare undertakes the following initiatives:

- Completion of mandatory training and testing for all sales agents
- Revocation of selling privileges for sales agents who do not complete this training and score 100% on the required testing
- Mandatory new member call-backs to 100% of new enrollees to confirm that their sales experience was positive and that they understand their benefits
- Follow-up calls to all beneficiaries enrolled by any terminated sales agent to confirm their enrollment decision or facilitate disenrollment
- Monitors sales data for potential issues and to educate or even terminate agents based on our findings, with emphasis on proactive resolution of issues
- Monitors a confidential compliance Hot Line where members, associates and government regulators can report concerns about potential marketing misconduct."

Fruit of The Loom

"To assist Fruit in assuring compliance with this Code of Conduct, Contractor agrees to:

(i) Require all of its officers and employees who will be responsible for or involved with the implementation of procedures designed to ensure compliance with this Code of Conduct to review and familiarize themselves with this Code of Conduct;

(ii) Require all of Contractor's suppliers, subcontractors and agents to execute and deliver to Fruit a Code of Conduct on or before execution of an appli-cable agreement or purchase order with Fruit;

(iii) Provide Fruit with access to its and any Fruit authorized Contractor supplier, subcontractor or agent production facilities to conduct inspections;

(iv) Provide, upon request, Fruit with proof of production, including without limitation, shipping documents, cutting and sewing reports and similar documentation;

(v) Provide, upon request, Fruit with proof of compliance by Contractorand its suppliers, or agents with applicable labor laws and including, without limitation, proof that all employees meet minimum legal working age and pay requirements and the right to, interview such employees regarding the same. Fruit intends to make every available effort to assure the veracity of all documents it receives and reviews and the authenticity of Contractor's sources of supply."

Honeywell International

" When it is necessary to engage the services of an individual or firm to consult for or otherwise represent the Company, special consideration must be given to avoid any situation that may create, or appear to create, a conflict of interest between Honeywell and the person or firm employed ".

- The Company will enter into representation or supplier agreements only with companies believed to have a record of and commitment to integrity. Efforts will be taken by Honeywell to ensure that suppliers, agents, consultants, independent contractors and representatives are aware of this Code.

- The Company will seek to inform our suppliers, agents, consultants,independent contractors, and representatives of their responsibility to act on behalf of Honeywell consistent with the Code, other Honeywell policies and any applicable law or regulation."

The selection process

In selecting agents, it will normally be the responsibility of the sales manager for a particular geographical area, or for a particular business component of the company, to determine whether there is a need to appoint an independent agent for a given market, product or service. The manager should also determine the agent's required qualifications to accomplish planned sales results and recommend candidates for the job. Increasingly, however, because of the severity of the risks involved, responsibility for the decision to retain a sales agent is taken at a higher level of management.

As part of the selection process, the sales manager should carry out a thorough documented due diligence background check of each candidate. Detailed information should be obtained so that the company can evaluate, not only the candidate's financial standing, but also his commercial and technical competence to discharge the required services and his reputation for business integrity. The latter can be demonstrated by:

- A good standing in the business community;
- Sound business-practice standards;
- The absence of conflicts of interest;
- Good relationships with potential customers;
- Good government relations;
- Favourable embassy and other appraisals.

Considerable information may be obtained by having the prospective candidate complete a written application form for appointment as an international sales representative. This document should elicit information concerning:

- The nature and history of the applicant's business;
- Details of the ownership and principal officers and managers of his firm;
- Information about his representation of other companies (with a principal contact for each);
- Office facilities and staff;
- Technical, financial and educational background;
- Knowledge of the company's products and environment;
- Affiliated companies;
- Business or personal relationships with the proposed customer;
- Principal product lines currently handled for other enterprises; and
- Any litigation involving the applicant's activities.

The completed application form should also include pertinent market information, financial statements, financial references (including banks and principal suppliers) and general references (such as other companies that the applicant has represented). It should be accompanied by an authorization for the release of information from the references the candidate has provided.

The sales manager should be satisfied that the applicant understands the company's "no bribery" policy. He should also obtain the applicant's written acknowledgement of the policy and an undertaking to comply.

In many companies, there has been a recent shift to much greater management responsibility and involvement in the decision-making process relating to the selection and appointment of agents. Sales managers alone should definitely not be allowed to make the final decision on the appointment of a sales representative.

Having selected a suitable candidate, the sales manager should be required to submit a written recommendation to senior management of the company (usually the business manager, finance manager and company counsel) for their approval. This field recommendation form should clearly establish the business need for employing an agent and set forth the sales manager's comments, not only on the commercial and technical competence of the applicant, but also on his reputation for business integrity (including a summary of comments received from the local embassy, customers and other enterprises represented).

This document should set out the proposed compensation and the justification thereof and should include a copy of the application. The field recommendation form should also contain a certification by the sales manager that in his opinion the candidate firm is reputable, qualified and suitable for appointment and consistent with the company's standards of business integrity. It should also stipulate that the agent is fully aware of, and will comply with, the company's code of conduct and with the anti-bribery laws enacted under the OECD and UN Conventions and that his compensation arrangements are reasonable in relation to the services to be performed.

Agents: sample best practices

A survey of 15 multinational companies revealed some of the following best practices for hiring and dealing with agents:

- One company conducts a formal review process not only of its prospective agents, but also of its business partners' agents. This ensures that agents who may be acting indirectly on the company's behalf also go through a formal review process and that the company does not rely on their business partners' review;
- One company requires a face-to-face meeting between principals before approving a third-party agent. The company's executive vice-president (or other senior official) meets with the proposed new foreign business representative when the contract is "significant";
- When assessing the legality of a questionable contract, one company requires its own legal staff to investigate the host country's laws and to solicit an official opinion instead of relying solely upon the legal verification of their prospective agent;
- One company compensates its agents in a lump-sum payment and refuses to reimburse costs not included in contractual compensation arrangements. The rationale for this practice is to prevent agents from adding unnecessary or illegal payments or expenses to secure the contract;
- One company refuses to pay commissions to its agents until the contract is complete. While these agents may still be able to make illegal payments to secure the contract, it provides another disincentive for doing so and can provide the company with additional time to assess the agents'

It is recommended that guidelines and procedures be established relating to the method, currency and place of payment of sales-agent commissions. All payments should be by bank transfer or cheque payable to the agent and should be made in strict conformity with the written agreement. Also, save for exceptional circumstances, payments should be made in the country where the agent is active or registered. No cash payments should be made under any circumstances, and the company's financial managers should ensure that accurate records are kept, showing details of all commission payments. It is also advisable that a company conduct annual reviews of all payments made to sales representatives.

Engagement

Each foreign sales agent arrangement should be covered by a written agreement signed by an authorized representative of the company. The agreement should be for a fixed term, preferably of limited duration and should provide for periodic review. It should contain an undertaking on the part of the agent to comply at all times with all relevant laws and with the company's policy prohibiting the payment of bribes (the relevant parts of which might be incorporated into the agreement or attached as a schedule). It should also allow for a right of immediate termination by the company in the event of a breach of this provision. A provision for audit rights, verification programmes and periodic compliance reviews should also be included.

The agreement should specify the amount of compensation, and no payment should be made unless it conforms to the written agreement. Moreover, the agent should not start work for the company until all required company approvals have been obtained and the written agreement executed. The agent should report to the company regularly and on a continuous basis on the accomplishment of the assigned tasks.

It is recommended that the company establish *a standard form of international sales representative agreement* and that no modifications to the standard form be permitted without the approval of appropriate senior management or the legal department.

"Red flags"

When evaluating a prospective agent, it is very important to watch for "red flags" which could serve as advance warnings of potential illegal activities or violations of company policy. Specifically, the company should be on guard if a proposed sales representative:

- Does not reside in the same country where the customer or the project is located;
- Does not have any significant business presence within the country;

- Represents any companies with a questionable reputation;
- Requests that commissions be paid in a third country or to a numbered bank account or to some other person;
- Requires payment of the commission, or a significant portion thereof, before or immediately upon award of the contract by the customer to the company;
- Claims that he can help secure the contract because he knows all the right people;
- Has a familial or other relationship that could improperly influence the customer's decision; or
- Arrives on the scene just before the contract is to be awarded.

Other signs of questionable activity can be:

- A customer who suggests that a bid be made through a specific sales agent;
- A commission that seems unusually high in relation to the services provided;
- A request for an increase in the agreed commission in order for the agent to "take care" of some people.

If these or any other red flags are identified, the company should thoroughly investigate and satisfactorily resolve them before proceeding with the appointment of the sales representative. Any red flags that arise following appointment of the agent should be similarly investigated, reviewed and either be appropriately resolved or result in termination of the agent's contract.

Summary of the ICC Recommendations on agents and sales representatives

Foreign sales agents or representatives can be an important component of a company's successful sales performance, and there is no suggestion, either in ICC Rules or in the OECD Convention, that these individuals' services should be dispensed with. There is a recognition in both documents, however, that much care must be taken in the selection of a sales representative and that the role of sales agents must be carefully supervised. If these measures are not taken – and the company becomes involved in illegal activities because of an agent's actions – the company may be held liable for the consequences.

Therefore companies should:

- Write into their codes of conduct provisions requiring responsible company personnel to hire only qualified and reputable agents;
- Make clear in the code that all agents are bound by its anti-bribery provisions and by those of the OECD Convention;
- Before hiring an agent, conduct a detailed background check on his professional competence and personal integrity;
- Require prospective agents to fill out a detailed application form listing their business details, product lines and references;
- Discuss the company's "no bribery" policy with the proposed agent and be satisfied that he will comply;
- Establish specific compensation guidelines to ensure that an agent's compensation is not excessive in relation to the services he renders;
- Require senior management's approval of all sales-representative appointments;
- Pay all agents' commissions by cheque and not in cash;
- Require agents to sign a written agreement containing, among other provisions, a commitment not to pay bribes;
- Be alert to red flags which can signal questionable integrity on the part of an agent;
- Avoid, wherever possible, appointing agents in high-risk countries were bribery is prevalent.

Michael Davies is a member of the ICC Commission on Anti-Corruption. He is also the author of Chapter 7 in this handbook.

Part II
Management Initiatives

Chapter 5

Responsabilities of Enterprises

By François Vincke

RELEVANT PROVISIONS OF ICC RULES OF CONDUCT AND OF THE OECD CONVENTION

Article 7 of ICC Rules of Conduct sets out the corporate policies companies should adopt:

> "In order to prevent bribery and extortion, enterprises should implement comprehensive policies or codes reflecting these Rules of Conduct as well as their particular circumstances and specific business environment".

These policies and codes should:

- Provide guidance and training in identifying and avoiding bribery and extortion in the daily business dealings of the enterprise;
- Offer confidential channels to raise concerns, seek advice or report violations without having to fear retaliation;
- Include disciplinary procedure to sanction misconduct;
- Apply to all controlled subsidiaries, foreign and domestic.

Article 9 of ICC Rules of Conduct sets out the responsibilities of enterprises:

" The board of directors or other body with ultimate responsibility for the enterprise should:

a) Take reasonable steps to ensure compliance with these Rules of Conduct, including :

- Making resources available and supporting management in implementing the corporate policies reflecting them;
- Establishing and maintaining proper systems of control and reporting proce-dures, including independent auditing;

b) Sanction violations and take appropriate corrective action;

c) Make appropriate public disclosure of the enforcement of its anti-corruption policies or codes.

The audit committee of the board or other body with similar responsibility should conduct regular independent reviews of compliance with these Rules of Conduct and recommend corrective measures and policies as necessary. This can be done as part of a broader system of corporate compliance reviews."

ICC Rules of Conduct and Recommendations stress the recognition *of the need for complementary and mutually supportive action by the business community and by governments and international organizations. They further make it clear that the success of ICC Rules of Conduct in combating corruption through self-regulation will be enhanced by actions by international organizations and by national governments to strengthen the legal and administrative framework for combating corruption.* That call to self-regulation, embedded in international conventions and national legislation, is the thrust of the present chapter.

Why boards need to act

The end of laissez faire

The coming into effect of anti-corruption conventions, the advent of new norms of corporate governance and the introduction of corporate legal liability have brought home the notion that ethical concerns have to be part and parcel of a board of directors' concerns.

New corporate governance theories, while redefining the roles and powers within corporations, have imposed high standards of accountability on board members and on corporate executives in the discharge of their duties. Directors and executives have to attend to the corporation's business by adequately and efficiently performing their fiduciary duties with due diligence and care and in the best interests of their corporation and its shareholders (and/or stakeholders). They have to provide - in a spirit of transparency - timely, accurate and relevant information on material matters concerning the corporation.

In doing so, the board should apply the highest ethical standards. This will require the board pro-actively to put in place a system for preventing illegal and unethical conduct, prohibiting misbehaviour and imposing sanctions in case of infringement of those standards. Specialized committees of the board, and in particular an ethics or audit committee, will help the board regularly to oversee –in the context of general compliance reviews – the ethical policies of the company and to test them against ICC Rules of Conduct. This specialized committee should examine possible incidents and propose amendments to corporate policies. The chief compliance officer (CCO) should have unhampered contact with the chairman of the audit/ethics committee and should report on a regular basis, and at least once a year, to this committee. The compliance function can, in smaller organizations, be part time and be assumed by the general counsel or the CFO.

Lack of adequate supervision of corporate practices by the board may lead to far-reaching consequences, and courts may declare a company liable for non-compliance if this is the case. In certain jurisdictions, courts may even impose independent monitors to oversee a company's compliance and its implementation of an integrity programme.

Ethical *laissez faire* on the part of the company's top management cannot be condoned, and blaming ethical incidents on underlings can no longer be tolerated.

The OECD Principles of Corporate Governance of 2004 contain the following recommendation:

> "The Board should apply the highest ethical standards. It should take into account the interests of the stakeholders."

The Annotations to the Principles state:

> "The Board has a key role in setting the ethical tone of a company, not only by its own actions, but also in appointing and overseeing key executives and consequently the management in general. High ethical standards are in the long-term interests of the company as a means to make it credible and trustworthy, not only in day-to-day operations but also with respect to longer term commitments."

Not long ago, corporate misbehaviour resulted only in the liability of those employees, officers or executives who actively committed or participated in a prohibited act. It was commonly accepted that corporate bodies could not incur criminal (or, in certain jurisdictions, administrative) liability for prohibited acts. This has changed, and a number of international conventions and national legislations increasingly provide for the legal liability of corporations (either criminal, administrative or civil), along with the criminal liability of physical persons.

Even if legal liability is not yet regularly imposed on corporations by the courts, the mere existence of the concept underlines that corporations have to be compliant with legal and ethical norms. Not exercising sufficient oversight, not providing the necessary means to combat fraud and corruption and not designating personnel capable of monitoring effective compliance exposes corporations to severe consequences, not only financial ones but also outcomes that can affect the continuity of the corporation. It is the task of the top echelon of the corporation to make the necessary decisions to avoid these consequences.

PricewaterhouseCoopers (PwC), in its Global Economic Survey, states the continuing problem as follows:

> "Our 2007 survey reveals that fraud remains one of the most problematic issues for businesses worldwide, with no abatement no matter what a company's country or operation, industry or size. Of the 5,428 companies in 40 countries [surveyed] over 43% reported suffering one or more significant economic crimes during the two previous years [...]."

Losses incurred as a result of economic crime reach staggering figures. The PwC Survey found that for 80 per cent of the companies reporting fraud, damage during the two preceding years amounted to in excess of USD 4.2 billion, of which USD 882 million was ascribed to bribery and corruption.

Tone at the top

If companies are confronted with the problem of economic fraud, the duty of their boards and CEOs will be to demonstrate, in words and deeds, an example of preferred ethical behaviour and to indicate what should be done at all levels of the company to address ethical lapses.

In corporate messages from top management to co-workers, it is important to set forth the values of the company, the prohibitions on unethical behaviour and recommended best practices. The board and/or the CEO should fully endorse the company's code of conduct and its integrity programme and demonstrate their determination to act themselves in compliance with the code's provisions and to emphasize their commitment to allocate the necessary resources to create a genuine compliance culture.

The corporate compliance policies must indicate that all those who are working for the company – executives, officers and employees alike – will have to act in compliance with the code's norms and that all could be disciplined in case of infringement. It should be made clear that there is no place for exceptions or privileges.

In March 2007, Ernst & Young (E&Y) surveyed a large number of multinationals in 13 European countries and found that

> "Employees are not hostile to corporate anti-fraud measures and would welcome clarity and encouragement to act positively in the best interests of the company".

E&Y further noted that

> "Most people would prefer to work in an environment which has a code of conduct. Most respondents [to the survey] believe that people in their companies need a unified and agreed set of guidelines on what is right and wrong in the company [...]. Without a code of conduct, employees are left to work it out for themselves, and there is no clear set of standards other than their own personal ethics against which behavior can be measured.

Words will not suffice

Integrity cannot be decreed, it must be organized. The ICC Rules of Conduct recommend that the board make resources available to carry out a genuine integrity policy. This will require extensive information for, and training of personnel, the appointment of compliance officers, the putting into place of communication channels to raise ethical concerns and the sanctioning of misconduct. Admittedly, this approach involves considerable cost, but it is necessary to weigh this cost against the potentially huge reputational and other damage resulting from a corporate ethics scandal.

Group-wide compliance

The Board of Directors should not devote attention only to what happens within the parent corporation. On the contrary, the ethical policies put in place by the parent company's board should be applied in the economic group in its entirety, at home as well as abroad, in all of the group's divisions, branches, controlled subsidiaries and majority-held joint ventures, as well as in the affiliates in which the group exercises *de facto* control. Moreover, as far as feasible, they should be applied in all non-controlled entities working closely with the corporation. A special effort will be required to make subcontractors, outsourcing partners and intermediaries aware of, and compliant with, company standards. In particular, slush funds in offshore jurisdictions or tax havens in far-away affiliates, protected by bank secrecy rules, should be eliminated.

No more "business as usual"

Enterprises now have – and in the future will have – a pivotal role in determining, within the existing legal context, the integrity of their business conduct. Admittedly, the provisions contained in the OECD Convention and UNCAC have to be incorporated in the signatory countries' legislation and do not, in themselves, create rights and obligations for individuals or enterprises. Failing to comply with the provisions of both Conventions, however, would be unwise.

First, the signatory states have, within a short period of time after the signing of the OECD Convention, adopted effective legislation implementing it and have introduced in their national laws prohibitions and criminal sanctions against international corruption. The states having ratified UNCAC have, to a large extent, done the same or are in the process of doing so.

Second, notwithstanding an isolated case in one major European exporting country – which can only be deplored and cannot serve as a precedent – it is illusory to expect exceptions based on national interest considerations by a sympathetic local administration to prevent prosecution of offences, since such discriminatory treatment is specifically forbidden by the OECD Convention.

Third, the OECD Convention is not going to fade away, disappear or become obsolete. The monitoring system, which is built into the Convention, has introduced an element of mutual review of the states' anti-corruption performance by their peers. In this process, national implementing laws are being examined for their effectiveness, and the resources are being made available for their application, as well as for the prosecution of offences within an individual state. This monitoring system is the best guarantee of the Convention's continued effectiveness. It is expected that UNCAC will, over time, be monitored in the same way.

With both the OECD Convention and UNCAC in effect, it would be a mistake to believe it is possible to do "business as usual". Hoping that these instruments will become obsolete is wishful thinking.

Responsibilities of the Board

Self-regulation

The prohibition of international corruption is here to stay, and the best way to respond is to comply with it. Self-regulation within an enterprise or between enterprises of a sector (under the aegis for instance of a business or sector organization) is the surest way for a board to act responsibly and to attain maximum compliance.

Enterprises from the same sector will benefit from assessing the risks they are facing, from benchmarking their practices and from defining common standards. These standards should go beyond general recommendations and reduce or eliminate suspicions raised as the result of illicit competition.

Examples of sector-wide ethical self-regulation:

- The Wolfsberg Anti-Money Laundering (AML) Principles;
- The Extractive Industries Transparency Initiative (EITI);
- The Policy Statements on Corruption of FIDIC (the International Federation of Consulting Engineers);
- The Sustainable Development Charter of the International Council on Mining and Metals (ICCM);
- The Guidelines on Reputational Damage of the International Association of Oil and Gas Producers (OGP);
- The Equator Principles adopted by banks on project financing; and
- The Common Industry Standards of the Aerospace and Defence Industries Association of Europe (ASD).

ICC has always been convinced that self-discipline, based on the values the enterprise has defined, is the most effective means of encouraging ethical conduct in business. Self-regulation also helps integrate the values into a sector and into an individual enterprise. In addition, rules developed within or between enterprises and based on the values a company has defined, have a more educational and convincing impact, because they are adapted to a company's particular circumstances.

The aforementioned E&Y Survey records that 88 per cent of the responding employees consider that companies need to have a code of conduct but found *that only just over half of respondents in Central & Eastern Europe, and two thirds of those in Western Europe work for companies that have a code of conduct or where they are aware of the code of conduct.*

Benefits of a code

Self-regulation, based on a careful assessment of the risks a company is facing, can address, with sufficient detail and precision, the particular issues confronting an individual business activity

Take the case of "facilitation payments". The OECD Convention, in Commentary 9, excludes small facilitation payments from the scope of the Convention. By contrast, a carefully drafted self-regulatory code can (i) either prohibit all facilitation payments or (ii) provide, if it is determined that such payments cannot be avoided altogether, appropriate guidance and establish the strict conditions under which such payments could be permitted – by confining them, for example, to those qualifying fully as a facilitation payment.

ICC Rules of Conduct of 2005 make it clear that, as a general rule, "Enterprises should not make facilitation payments". The Rules of Conduct go on to say that: "In the event that an enterprise determines, after managerial review, that facilitation payments cannot be eliminated entirely, it should establish controls and procedures to ensure that their use is limited to small payments to low-level officials for routine actions to which the enterprise is entitled."

It is in this spirit that ICC Rules of Conduct provide that "enterprises should implement comprehensive policies or codes reflecting the Rules of Conduct as well as their particular circumstances as well as their specific business environment."

ICC does not believe that all codes have to be the same or even that they have to look alike. On the contrary, a code should reflect the specific culture and spirit of an individual enterprise or a sector of activity. Clearly, the basic principles will always have to be the same, but the approach may be different.

Drafting a code

In view of the foregoing, responsibility for drafting a code of corporate practice should not be delegated to outside consultants or specialists unaware of a company's culture. On the contrary, every effort should be made to bring together around the drafting table all those segments of an enterprise which can bring a distinctive contribution to the development of this important document. While the final responsibility for adopting the text will lie at the board of directors' level, all divisions of a company should be involved and/or consulted during the drafting process. Those in charge of human resources and legal matters should have a decisive role, but this should not inhibit contributions from managers of local affiliates, marketing operatives, internal auditors, accountants, treasury staff and all parts of the organization which deal, on a day-to-day basis, with matters concerning integrity.

If, at the outset, people of various professional, cultural and educational horizons are brought together to identify the risks a company is facing, the final code will have an enhanced legitimacy and gain greater acceptance. The drafting process will take time and may involve difficult discussions. Some drafters may opt for a hard line and may want to impose stringent rules, while others may prefer a more lenient course. There could be a confrontation between those who want to cover as many details as possible (to avoid future problems of interpretation) and others who prefer broader, more open principles.

Finally, there can be opposition between those who want to concentrate on the drafting of the rules, leaving compliance more or less open, and those who want to install an elaborate compliance system. Depending on the diverse regulatory provisions, local customs or practices, it may be required, convenient or simply desirable to associate trade union representatives with the common effort, for instance in matters concerning sanctions in case of non-compliance, or on the introduction of a whistleblowers' hot line. A discussion with he unions and their acceptance of the agreed rules will increase the credibility of the texts, around which everyone will be able to unite.

Cultural differences, corporate sensitivities and distinct legal approaches will result in unavoidable but acceptable differences between companies. It is typical of self-regulation that each entity (enterprise, corporation, internationally operating group or business organization) brings to the process its own predilections. One can, for instance, imagine that an organization based in a "Latin" environment may give preference to broad principles, while "Anglo-Saxon" entities may favour detailed and technical provisions that could cover every specific circumstance. It will be important, though, to have a single policy for the company and not several policies for each of the company's operations in different cultures.

The importance of a corporate practice manual is not whether it follows a prescribed form. A code of conduct is a document that should have a genuine credibility in order that all parts of the organization can accept it as a guide to their daily business behaviour. Compliance with it should be natural in every circumstance. In short, all members of an organization should become owners of "their" code.

Incorporating an ethics clause

The credibility of a code will be further enhanced by the inclusion of an ethical or anti-corruption clause – containing an explicit reference to a code's provisions – in the agreements a company concludes with its business partners. Such a clause can be drafted in several ways and can either cover all ethical issues for which the company wants to see strict observance of its values (e.g., human rights, labour conditions, environment, sustainable use of resources and ethics), or the drafting of the clause can be focused only on the fight against corruption. In the latter case, a straightforward reference to ICC Rules of Conduct provides an easy solution.

What about SMEs?

If a company is a small or medium-sized enterprise (SME), it may question whether the drafting of a code is an insurmountable obstacle. Indeed, where will the company find the resources and time necessary to organize the drafting? Can it rely on internal expertise to set up a credible and complete code of good practices, applicable in most circumstances?

The answer to these difficult questions will probably be "no". Very small-scale companies generally do not have this expertise available. That should not, however, lead to the conclusion that the company in question should not have its own standards and its own compliance system to regulate and oversee its practices in often complicated markets. On the contrary, small-size enterprises, even more thanlarge corporations, need direction – in particular because of their lack of experience in international markets and the exposure they will be subject to in moving into these markets. In addition, all enterprises, whatever their size, should have a compliance function, but this function may very well be discharged in an SME as a half or part-time function or as part of the responsibilities of the general counselr the CFO.

An SME's lack of internal expertise can be overcome by participating in various forms of "collective action" against bribery or by receiving help and support from larger business organizations (either organized by sector or on a national or regional basis), of which the company is a member, or from larger companies it has a close association with, for instance as subcontractor, supplier or customer. The drafting of a code with the aid of a business organization, or by a friendly larger corporation, can help meet most of the needs of a smaller-scale company and give it the necessary "weapons" to face challenging new international markets.

Codes and useful examples

A company code of conduct may usefully include examples of situations that present difficult ethical dilemmas to managers or employees. In a number of company codes one can find concrete cases indicating how employees should act under certain conditions. Consider the following excerpts from one company's code, which "put flesh on the bones" to back up the code's provisions:

Question: A representative of a customer, supplier or vendor has invited my spouse and me to dinner or to attend a sporting event. May we attend?

Answer: You should obtain the approval of the manager who is authorized to approve your business expense reports before accepting. Company policy does not strictly prohibit accepting these types of business courtesies, but be sure it doesn't appear that business discussions are secondary to the personal benefit.

Question: It is the holiday season and I have just received at home a 10-pound box of prime steaks from a supplier with a card that says "Merry Christmas". May I keep the steaks?

Answer: No, return the steaks to the donor or send them to the corporate vice president of industrial relations for donation to a food bank. A polite thank-you letter and explanation of company policy on accepting business courtesies of appreciable value would be appropriate.

Question: A vendor offers to provide free air transportation between his company's separate plant locations. May I accept?

Answer: Your company will pay the cost of business travel that it deems necessary. Approval of the vice president responsible for the organization would be necessary to grant exceptions to this rule.Budget constraints or convenience are not acceptable reasons for accepting this business courtesy.

ICC's four recommendations

In practical terms, ICC Rules of Conduct, although not imposing uniformity, make four recommendations as guidelines in drafting a code and establishing corporate policies:

1. Provide guidance in identifying and avoiding bribery and extortion.
2. Establish and maintain proper systems of control and reporting procedures, to prevent misconduct.
3. Put into place a genuine compliance program (the "Seven Steps" described below).

4. Disclose regularly appropriate information about the corporation's compliance.

These recommendations are discussed below.

Guidance by top management

Drafting a code of conduct, while it may be the work of a number of different company divisions, will ultimately be the responsibility of the top executives. In concrete terms, this means that the board of directors will have to give effective guidance to officers and employees and be accountable, as the last resort, for a company's behaviour.

Control and reporting procedures

However, the mere promulgation of a document full of good intentions will not suffice. A company's board of directors should also select and endorse the proper control and compliance methods to make the rules a living part of the company's daily life. The enterprise's governing body cannot establish a number of rules, then appear uninterested in their effective application. If it were to do so, it could be criticized for using a corporate code as a mere public relations or marketing tool, or worse, as a device primarily designed to shield senior management from responsibility for the actions of subordinates.

In implementing the corporate code, the board should designate the departments or individuals who can best ensure effective day-to-day control. This should be done taking into consideration the nature of the organization. No two companies are alike; some may have stronger controlling bodies than others, i.e., external and internal auditors, corporate or outside lawyers and extensive human resources departments.

In general, control over proper accounting and financial recording will be entrusted to financial managers and auditors, while behaviour as it relates to compliance with ethical standards is more likely to be the province of management or corporate lawyers.

Having designated the specific departments and individuals, the board will have to determine, and its audit/ethics committee will have to oversee, the systems or procedures for control and decide how and with what frequency the controls will be exercised. Such procedures should be devised with the aim of preventing violations of the code. The greater the risk of violation, the more stringent the procedures will have to be. As always in business, the means to be used should be adjusted to specific situations.

Control systems or procedures are a prerequisite, but no enterprise can expect that a control function alone will promote full adherence to a corporate code. Such adherence can only be achieved through the establishment of a genuine compliance programme.

Putting in place a compliance programme

Setting up a compliance programme will help an enterprise make its code a reality, and it will also be in its self-interest. For example, in a number of countries, a fully fledged compliance plan can help the enterprise show that it has used all reasonable means to avoid prohibited behavior. Under the US Federal Sentencing Guidelines, as well as the Thompson Memorandum and the Italian Legislative Decree no. 231 of 8 June 2001, it is possible to obtain reductions in fines if a corporation can prove that it has put in place an effective corporate compliance programme with sufficient resources to uphold it.

The G8 Summit in Evian, France said the following about compliance programmes:

> "We encourage the private sector to develop, implement and enforce compliance programs relating to our domestic laws criminalizing foreign bribery".

What does a compliance programme require in order to be effective It is impossible to recommend universally applicable formulae; the enterprise will have to formulate for itself the measures that - according to its history, culture and practical circumstances - are most conducive to bring about a compliance culture?.

A compliance programme should consist of a number of different measures aimed at (i) making the provisions of the code and the values of the enterprise known (education and training function); (ii) seeing to it that the company's code is effectively implemented (compliance function); and (iii) imposing sanctions in the event the rules are contravened (disciplinary function).

These functions can be broken down into seven steps:

1. **Setting up compliance standards that are capable of preventing illicit acts**

   The code will often only put forward general prohibitions of forbidden behavior. These are unlikely to answer all potential questions. Take the example of gifts. A code may prohibit receiving any gifts having a substantial value. But the setting of a more precise and specific standard will greatly assist the personnel in their understanding of the code; consequently, it will be useful to delineate, for example, in which circumstances a gift may be received, what maximum monetary value it may have, when it should be declined and whether it should be returned or given to a charity. Setting a compliance standard amplifies and makes a code provision more specific. It also eliminates questions and reduces the instances of acts contravening the rules.

2. **Assigning high-level personnel to oversee compliance**

The personnel overseeing compliance may or may not be the controllers referred to previously. They may or may not have compliance as their full-time job. When they do, they will often be referred to as "compliance officers".

An enterprise may not have the means and the organizational strength necessary to have one or more compliance officers. It is not simply a question of having a large enough work force to designate someone to carry out compliance overview; for any enterprise, it is important to find dedicated, high-level, competent and experienced persons who can give appropriate counseling about what and what not to do.

Compliance officers have an educational, as well as a supportive function. Their role is not that of a prosecutor or a police officer, but an advisor. They should be able to interpret a company's code and the rules without complacency or exaggerated zeal. For example, the company's compliance officer should be ready to answer questions about the designation of an agent or other intermediary in a new market. What kind of person or organization would be acceptable for fulfilling this job? What kind of clauses should be contained in the contract hiring the agent? What kind and level of consideration may be paid by the company, so that the contract cannot be considered a conduit for bribe payments? For all such questions, the compliance officer should have appropriate answers.

3. **Avoid hiring and promoting individuals unlikely to be compliant: ensure that human resources policies and practices are compatible with the company's code of conduct**

It is clear that no effective self-regulation will be possible if a company hires and/or gives important authority to individuals who are not trustworthy. Such personnel will never, even with extensive education and training, comply with self-regulatory codes.

More generally, a company's human resources policies should integrate an ethical dimension. The job evaluations and performance interviews performed should take into account compliance and, as suggested in the Annotations to the OECD Principles on Corporate Governance, "the incentive structure of [your] business needs to be aligned with its ethical and professional standards so that adherence to the values [of your company] is rewarded and breaches of law are met with dissuasive consequences or penalties."

4. **Communicating standards and procedures to employees**

Communication is a key element in all self-discipline exercises. Members of an enterprise will not adhere to a code if management has not made a strong effort to communicate with all concerned. "All concerned" does not only mean staff working for the enterprise; it can also mean the personnel working for subcontractors, suppliers and customers. Policies and standards on gifts and entertainment, for example, may have to be made known beyond the limits of a company's payroll.

The most formal and well-established means of communication is the written one, and it will continue to play an important role. But electronic, visual, video and other forms of communication are often a more direct, lively and appropriate means for conveying a company's ethical message. Cultural and corporate preferences must be taken into consideration in creating the best communication tools. Organizing specialized seminars or introducing an ethical component into all professional training sessions are also options.

Finally, a company's code of conduct should be introduced into the overall corporate training program. This carries symbolic value in demonstrating that ethical training applies to everyone in the enterprise.

5. **Implementing monitoring, auditing and reporting systems**

Compliance should also include positive measures aimed at avoiding infringement of the rules. These provisions can comprise, for instance, monitoring mechanisms that allow management to closely supervise more sensitive areas, such as the selection and compensation of foreign sales representatives.

Reporting mechanisms can also enhance proper compliance. The receipt of reports may be the function of either the compliance officer(s) or the persons entrusted with control or monitoring. Responsibility for making reports should be the task of anyone aware that a contravention of the rules is about to take place or has taken place.

Such reporting, often referred to as "whistleblowing", can be made through a hot line or a mail drop; it can be made anonymously or by name but, to the extent feasible, confidentiality should be granted to the person reporting (see Chapter 7 on Whistleblowing).

A complementary approach can involve the submission of "compliance letters" by managers of the enterprise, which attest, on a regular basis, that the provisions of the code of conduct have been respected and that no action or failure to act has been observed.

There are other valuable tools for monitoring compliance; for example, periodic audits for compliance with the code and regular policy compliance reviews by business managers.

6. **Using disciplinary mechanisms to enforce standards and procedures**

When a provision of a company's code is broken, management should step in to apply appropriate sanctions and to correct the situation. Various means can be used to achieve consistency in the use of disciplinary measures and to avoid leaving a wide area open to subjective interpretation. Whenever a pattern of non-compliance is discovered, measures should be taken to prevent the pattern from recurring.

Take the example of a company discovering the existence of a network of private-to-private corruption involving personnel responsible for procurement. In such a case, it is necessary, not only to sanction the people responsible for non-compliance, but also to reform the practices which enabled the misbehaviour to occur in the first place. If these measures are taken, repetition of the act or similar behaviour will be unlikely.

Non-compliance should not remain unsanctioned. Compliance will not be sufficient if non-compliance is not punished. Sanctions should be applied consistently, without favouritism or bias. The ICC Rules of Conduct speak of the responsibilities of directors, officers and employees and makes no distinction between organizational levels. Serious and persistent breaches of the code that could seriously damage the reputation of the company should be punished by the dismissal of the people directly involved as well as those with supervisory responsibility.

7. **Taking steps to respond after an offence has been detected, including amending the compliance programme**

Self-regulation will have credibility and respect inside and outside an enterprise only if the proper conclusions are drawn from serious breaches of the rules and appropriate steps are taken to remedy them.Amending or modifying a company's code should not be undertaken lightly, and the provisions should not be altered on a too-frequent basis. But a company must accept that, in some circumstances, it may be necessary to change its code, either because practices have changed or because an ethical failure has been discovered that was not sufficiently covered by the code's provisions.

Disclosure of enforcement measures

Financial analysts, investors and the public in general want to receive precise and significant information about the way enterprises conduct their ethics policy. They will require data about the enforcement by a company of its code of conduct. More and more companies meet this demand by including in their annual or sustainability report a chapter devoted to policies they have adopted or enforcement measures they have taken. The model disclosure form prepared by the Global Reporting Initiative (GRI) can serve here as a useful guideline.

Summary of ICC Recommendations on Responsibilities of Enterprises

The OECD Convention and UNCAC are a point of no return in the fight against corruption and are stepping stones in the process of eliminating them. However, legal texts alone will not suffice and the practical day-to-day work in fighting this evil must be done by enterprises. Top management, working in tandem with several divisions in the company, is responsible for stamping out corrupt practices before they become subject to sanctions imposed by the state.

Therefore companies should:

- Develop a clearly expressed code of good corporate practice with input from a range of company sources;
- Give management and the board responsibility for devising systems for implementing the code;
- Put into place a compliance programme containing measures aimed at education and training, as well as disciplinary measures if the code is violated;
- Modify the company's code if practices change or the original document proves to be inadequate;
- Apply sanctions against code violators fairly, consistently and without bias.

François Vincke is member of the Brussels Bar and Chair of the ICC Commission on Anti-Corruption. He is also the author of Chapter 5 and 11 in this handbook.

Chapter 6

Accounting, Auditing and Financial Controls

By Jermyn Brooks and Frank Piantidosi

Introduction

Accounting, auditing and financial controls may seem somewhat marginal to the main task of fighting bribery and other forms of corruption. This is not the case, for three reasons:

- All acts of bribery trigger movements of cash or other assets, so physical and accounting controls over such transactions are key to their detection and, preferably, prevention.
- Proof of bribery is often extremely problematical, and a record of the transaction in the accounting and financial records is often the only hard evidence that can be produced in court.
- Inaccurate recording of transactions in accounting systems may itself be a violation of laws and regulations of some countries and can lead to improper treatment for tax purposes, potentially causing civil or criminal exposures for companies and personnel involved.

Rules prescribing the accurate and complete recording of all transactions, and the internal and external checks in place to help achieve this, therefore, go to the core of the fight against bribery and other forms of corruption.

The need for integrity in corporate accounting systems has been highlighted by recent investigations into allegations of large scale bribery involving a number of companies from major exporting companies. More than 2000 companies were also implicated in the UN Oil-for-Food Programme bribery scandal. Since 2002, in the wake of the Enron and WorldCom accounting frauds, reforms have been enacted in a number of countries affecting stock exchange listing requirements, corporate governance, oversight of the accounting profession and the conduct of other professionals. These include the Sarbanes-Oxley Act in the United States and J-SOX.

Change is also being driven from within corporations. Senior executives and those charged with governance are increasingly treating bribery and corruption as common business risks in an era of globalization, which need to be managed to protect the reputation and value of their companies. They are deploying techniques such as Enterprise Risk Management (ERM), Governance, Risk and Compliance (GRC) or Fraud Risk Management (FRM) to bring more sophisticated processes to this issue. They are founding their anti-bribery and anti-corruption approaches on a careful analysis of their company's specific risks, based on the nature of their business, location of operations and the reputation of their business partners on ethical issues. And increasingly they are basing their policies and the related implementation efforts on the standards provided by ICC Rules of Conduct or on the TI Business Principles for Countering Bribery or the Partnering Against Corruption Initiative (PACI) Principles of the World Economic Forum, themselves derived from the TI Principles.

Greater clarity in corporate structures and in the related recording of transactions in the books can enhance a company's credibility in capital markets, strengthen its reputation and better protect against corrupt managers enriching themselves at the expense of employees and shareholders. This is the wider dimension of the matters covered in this chapter.

RELEVANT PROVISIONS OF ICC RULES, THE OECD CONVENTION AND THE UN CONVENTION AGAINST CORRUPTION (UNCAC)

Both ICC Rules and the OECD Convention prohibit the establishment or use of off-the-books accounts to conceal the source and use of funds that are used to pay illegal bribes. They also prohibit the use of false documents and invoices; the making of inadequate, ambiguous, or deceptive bookkeeping entries; and any other accounting procedure, technique or device that would hide or otherwise disguise illegal bribery payments made by or on behalf of a company.

ICC Rules

Article 4 of ICC Rules, Financial Recording and Auditing, states:

a) All financial transactions must be properly and fairly recorded in appropriate books of account available for inspection by boards of directors, if applicable, or a corresponding body, as well as auditors.

b) There must be no 'off-the-books' or secret accounts, nor may any documents be issued which do not properly and fairly record the transactions to which they relate.

c) Enterprises should take all necessary measures to establish independent systems of auditing in order to bring to light any transactions which contravene the present Rules of Conduct. Appropriate corrective action must then be taken.

Off-balance-sheet entities

by Rick Wayman, www.investopedia.com (excerpted)

"The term 'off-balance-sheet' can refer to many things. Typically, it refers to separate legal entities (separate companies of which the parent holds less than 100% ownership) or contingent liabilities such as letters of credit or loans to separate legal entities that are guaranteed by the parent ...

Bad things happen when economic reality differs significantly from the assumptions that were used to justify the off-balance-sheet entity ... Enron exemplifies how ego can be the basis for the misuse of off-balance-sheet items. Here, off-balance-sheet vehicles appear to have been used to pump up financial results rather than for legitimate business purposes. What started as a plan to legitimately use off-balance-sheet vehicles morphed into ways to manufacture earnings as trades went bad."

The OECD Convention and 1997 Revised Recommendations adopt some of the language of ICC Rules, but are narrower in the sense that they direct sanctions against accounting frauds used to hide bribes to foreign public officials rather than reflecting the broader provisions of ICC Rules, which prohibit these practices for any reason. To more effectively combat the payment of bribes to government officials, the Convention recommends, not only that countries impose sanctions on the commission of illegal acts of bribery (Articles 1 and 3), but also that they impose similar, additional sanctions for the failure of a company to truthfully account for or adequately disclose illegal bribery payments after they have been made.

Article 8 of the Convention, Accounting, states:

> "In order to combat bribery of foreign public officials effectively, each Party shall take such measures as may be necessary, within the framework of its laws and regulations, regarding the maintenance of books and records, financial statement disclosures, and accounting and auditing standards, to prohibit the establishment of off-the-books accounts, the making of off-the-books or inadequately identified transactions, the recording of non-existent expenditures, the entry of liabilities with incorrect identification of their object, as well as the use of false documents, by companies subject to those laws and regulations, for the purpose of bribing foreign public officials or of hiding such bribery."

Under Article 8(2) of the OECD Convention, countries are called upon to establish "effective, proportionate and dissuasive civil, administrative or criminal penalties for such omissions and falsifications in respect of the books, records, accounts and financial statements" of companies subject to the country's laws and regulations governing the maintenance of books and records, financial statement disclosures and accounting and auditing standards.The OECD does not require internal controls to be legislated, but there is a strong recommendation that companies should follow the practice in this area recommended by professional bodies or required under the listing rules of many stock exchanges.

The UN Convention Against Corruption (UNCAC) which came into effect in 2005 lists in Article 12 an almost identical set of provisions regarding the integrity of the books and records of a company as noted above for the OECD Convention. Article 12 additionally calls for the business world to develop appropriate internal controls and audit procedures and to establish codes of conduct.

Corporate responsibilities and practices

The "accounting provisions" of ICC Rules and of the laws and regulations of the countries implementing the OECD Convention reflect sound standards of corporate governance in respect of the duties of accountability to a company's owners, government agencies and other stakeholders. They require the focused attention of a company's executives, the members of its audit committees and board of directors (or bodies serving similar functions), as well as its internal and external auditors.

Responsibilities of management and those charged with governance

Management should implement and periodically update written anti-bribery and anti-corruption policies that reflect a commitment to honesty in business transactions and accounting and are therefore consonant with the Convention and the respective anti-bribery laws and regulations of the home and host countries.

Management should also design, implement and periodically update the managerial and accounting processes and internal controls necessary to implement their anti-bribery and other anti-corruption policies.

Those charged with governance such as boards of directors, audit committees or other governing bodies should exercise oversight over management's actions in the fight against bribery and corruption, to help ensure that management discharges its responsibilities effectively.

Accounting, auditing and financial controls

Violations of laws, regulations, rules, standards and policies are generally a result of deficiencies in corporate governance. Unless these deficiencies are identified and corrected, compliance breakdowns will occur. *What is needed is top-level accountability ("tone at the top"); the adoption and use of a code of conduct and compliance programme, as described in Chapter Five ("The Responsibilities of Enterprises") in this manual; a clear definition of roles and responsibilities; management's reporting on effectiveness of internal controls, hiring, training, performance evaluation, compensation and incentive programmes that encourage and support compliance; and monitoring, including monitoring bodies independent of management, such as audit committees.* Without all of these, the sustained effectiveness of a company's anti-bribery and anti-corruption programme is endangered.

Companies can use published internal control frameworks to develop internal control systems to protect against non-compliance with applicable laws and regulations. Such frameworks include, *"The Combined Code: Committee on Corporate Governance"* (1998, UK); *"CoCo: Guidance on Control and Governance"* (1995, Canada); and *"COSO: Internal Control-Integrated Framework"* (1992, US). The internal control system should be customized to the specific individual enterprise and should allow exercise of reasonable judgement in its application.

Companies may also find helpful the guidance paper, "Managing the Business Risk of Fraud: A Practical Guide", published in 2008, which provides guidance concerning internal control processes for dealing with various types of fraud, including bribery and corruption.[1]

We shall now discuss the different elements of effective accounting, auditing and financial controls relating to anti-bribery and anti-corruption.

1 Institute of Internal Auditors / American Institute of Certified Public Accountant / Association of Certified Fraud Examiners, *Managing the Business Risk of Fraud : a Practical Guide, 2008.*

Risk assessment

To prevent and detect bribery and other forms of corruption, companies should first perform a risk assessment. This identifies what could go wrong, the related likelihood of such an occurrence and the magnitude of the resulting consequences. For example, to evaluate the risks of bribery and corruption in the procurement process, one might analyze the means and methods that might be employed by the engineering department to create specifications that favour specific vendors, how purchasing may unfairly award contracts and how accounting may record bribes. The risk assessment process provides a foundation for designing appropriate internal controls to accomplish the company's policy objectives to prevent and detect bribery and corruption.

This risk assessment can be performed on a stand-alone basis. However, it is increasingly common for companies to integrate it with a broader assessment of risks the company faces, such as those performed for Enterprise Risk Management (ERM) purposes. Greater detail may be required to address bribery and corruption risks than for some other areas, but integration has several advantages:

- It can avoid inconsistencies between separate risk assessments and their documentation that could otherwise arise and create legal and regulatory exposures;
- It can help to ensure the risk assessment is updated regularly, when other risks are re-assessed;
- It can help to ensure the risk assessment receives appropriate attention from senior management, the board of directors, the audit committee or others charged with governance, when they discuss the key risks identified in an overall risk assessment.

Anti-corruption policy

Accounting and auditing controls are linked to the company's overall anti-corruption policy. Chapter 5 stresses the importance of developing a clear, concise written statement of the policy. It also reviews how the company should treat gifts and entertainment. The basic question of how to employ and treat agents is discussed in Chapter 4 "The Role of Intermediaries". Chapter 10 "Political Contributions" gives concrete advice on how contributions to political parties should comply with applicable laws. All of these issues are closely linked to the need to maintain proper accounting and control procedures.

Internal controls over financial reporting

The company's accounting policy should require that it maintain a system of internal controls and record-keeping so that its books and records accurately reflect its transactions and disposition of assets. The internal control system should be supported by the establishment of a code of corporate conduct and enforced by a compliance programme as outlined in Chapter 5 of this manual. An *audit committee* composed of independent outside directors should oversee the structure of internal controls, the internal audit function, and the employment of independent auditors.

Accounting policies

The company's accounting policy should have explicit prohibitions against "off-the-books", false, or "masking" entries. Off-the-books accounts are typically funded by methods such as cash (versus credit) sales, sales of scrap, kickbacks, payments received on fictitious invoices or sales recorded on a second set of books. Records and documentation for payments/reimbursements should be maintained in accordance with a records retention and archiving policy that is consistent with tax and other applicable laws and regulations, e.g., laws against money laundering (see Chapter Nine). All transactions should be fully identified, adequately described and accurately and properly classified in the accounts. In addition, the accounting requirements should provide for an adequate audit trail for the external and internal auditors.

Precise accountability for enforcing these policies and procedures should be established at various levels of the organization (departments, divisions, locations, subsidiaries, corporate, etc.) and should be consistently applied.

Policies for approving expenses

To determine that expenses are legitimate and that they do not get out of hand, company policies on approving expenses should require that:

- There be independent approval at a higher level than the one at which the expense was incurred;
- There be limits for gifts, entertainment and business courtesies to and from clients, vendors and government officials (local and foreign);
- "High risk" expenses/payments, e.g., in ambiguous situations and exceptions, have prior senior-management approval;
- Above a specified nominal amount, no expenses be approved without complete back-up documentation, e.g., invoices, receipts, and contracts;
- The department processing the payment/reimbursement, such as the accounting or accounts payable department, verify that proper approval and documentation exists;
- There be adequate segregation of duties between the authorization, approval and payment/reimbursement processes;
- There be an account provision in the company's general ledger to segregate "facilitation payments" and "business courtesy" payments.

Channels for communication

As described in Chapter 7, companies should provide channels for communications by, and protection for, persons unwilling to violate professional standards or ethics under instructions or pressure from hierarchical superiors. For SEC-registered companies, this is now a legal requirement in relation to the manipulation of financial information.

Training

Management should provide anti-bribery and anti-corruption training to employees and agents upon hiring and refresher courses periodically thereafter. The training should explain the application of the company's policies to specific situations the employees and agents may encounter. It should note that the policy applies on a worldwide basis, at least to company-controlled entities.

Detection and monitoring

Effective detection and monitoring controls can serve as a strong deterrent for bribery and corruption as well as helping to detect such activities promptly if they occur, reducing their adverse impact on the company. Key aspects of such controls include:

- Bribery and corruption-focused due diligence prior to making acquisitions and entering into significant arrangements with business partners;
- Continuous monitoring of transactions in business areas of heightened bribery or corruption risk to identify those meriting additional scrutiny;
- Data mining in areas where continuous monitoring is not feasible;
- Focused internal auditing to detect bribery and corruption.

Evaluating internal controls

Management should periodically evaluate the design and operating effectiveness of their internal controls to prevent and detect bribery and corruption, assessing their adequacy in light of the results of the company's most recent risk assessment. When evaluating internal controls, it is important that an entity adopt a horizontal process view in addition to a vertical functional/organizational view. Since processes link functions to achieve an objective – such as procurement linking engineering, finance, accounting, and purchasing – control gaps can be overlooked when controls are viewed only from a functional (e.g., financial) perspective. Where actual bribe payments are detected, an analysis of internal controls should be part of the internal review process to identify and remedy any weaknesses disclosed.

Reporting on internal controls and on anti-corruption policies

Companies should follow the OECD's Recommendation that senior management of the organization make a statement in their annual report to shareholders about their internal control mechanisms, including those that contribute to preventing bribery. Management reporting on the effectiveness of the internal control system helps keep management and others in the company focused on the importance of such control procedures. In addition, such reporting keeps those to whom the company is accountable informed about its internal control activities.

Pressure to state publicly a company's anti-corruption policies and to report on issues around their implementation and monitoring are currently growing, driven by increased interest in this area of risk by capital market analysts (e.g., the criteria established by FTSE4Good) and by the reporting requirements of such voluntary commitments as the UN Global Compact and the PACI of the World Economic Forum.

Responsibilities of internal auditors

The internal auditors have responsibilities with respect to fighting bribery. Under the professional standards of The Institute of Internal Auditors (IIA), internal auditors must be alert to indicators of fraud, including the payment and acceptance of bribes. Internal auditors also assist in the deterrence of illegal payments through their reviews of controls and investigation of transactions. The existence of an internal audit function fosters a control consciousness. When internal auditors become aware of illegal bribery or fraud, professional standards dictate that they must inform management and/or the competent authorities and follow up on the implementation of appropriate remedial controls. Internal auditors also report to the board and senior management on significant risk exposures and control issues. Internal audit standards require the auditor to encourage the development and adoption of adequate internal controls by evaluating the effectiveness and efficiency of controls and promoting continuous improvements.

Under a proposed new Institute of Internal Auditors' standard scheduled to be approved in summer 2008, internal auditors would be required to evaluate both the potential for fraud to occur and how the company manages fraud risk. A proposed revision of an existing standard would require internal auditors to consider the probability of fraud when developing the objectives for each audit performed. If these proposed standards are approved as expected, the IIA co-sponsored guidance paper referred to earlier, *Managing the Business Risk of Fraud: a Practical Guide*, may quickly be widely used by internal auditors in their evaluations.

Managing the Business Risk of Fraud

Published by the Institute of Internal Auditors (IIA), July 2008 (excerpted)

"Only through diligent and ongoing effort can an organization protect itself against significant acts of fraud."

Key principles for proactively establishing an environment to effectively manage an organization's fraud risk include:

Principle 1 As part of an organization's governance structure, a fraud risk management program should be in place, including a written policy (or policies) to convey the expectations of the board of directors and senior management regarding managing fraud risk.

Principle 2 Fraud risk exposure should be assessed periodically by the organization to identify specific potential schemes and events that the organization needs to mitigate.

Principle 3 Prevention techniques to avoid potential key fraud risk events should be established, where feasible, to mitigate possible impacts on the organization.

Principle 4 Detection techniques should be established to uncover fraud events when preventive measures fail or unmitigated risks are realized.

Principle 5 A reporting process should be in place to solicit input on potential fraud, and a coordinated approach to investigation and corrective action should be used to help ensure potential fraud is addressed appropriately and timely."

Financial reporting and disclosure

Despite management's best efforts at designing policies, procedures, and controls to prevent illegal payments, such controls are not infallible. If such incidents arise, determinations must be made concerning: (1) the fact of the bribe or other illegal payment; (2) any direct effects that the illegal payment has on financial statement amounts; and/or (3) any resulting actual or contingent liabilities or losses (e.g., penalties assessed or assessable against the company, revocation of a government contract) arising from the illegal payment.

The company must then determine whether or not the laws (including legislation implementing the OECD Convention), governmental regulations, or generally accepted accounting principles of the applicable countries (or the company's own policies) mandate disclosure of such activities and/or any consequent actual or contingent losses or liabilities. *The safest and the most appropriate course is to provide for full disclosure.*

Disclosure is generally required when:

- The illegal payments themselves have a material and direct effect on the determination or classification of financial statement amounts;
- The fines and penalties paid or imposed on illegal activities are material;
- The allegation or determination of illegal payments gives rise to a material contingent liability for fines, penalties and/or legal expenses;
- The illegal activity exposes the company to the risk of other material contingent liabilities and losses – such as the loss of government contracts or significant business relationships and their associated revenues, losses and liabilities resulting from the enforced discontinuance of operations in another country, or the threat of expropriation of the company's assets located in that country.

In determining whether an actual or contingent amount is "material", both the magnitude (individually and in the aggregate) and the nature of the item (e.g., amounts resulting from illegal activities, may have a lower materiality threshold than other amounts) must generally be considered. Materiality may also be influenced, or even dictated, by other considerations such as legal and regulatory requirements of the home country, the requirements established by legislation implementing the OECD Convention and particularly adverse publicity and the effect on corporate reputation and the price of its shares.

If the national accounting standards followed by a company do not meet or exceed International Accounting Standards (IAS), the company should consider the disclosure requirements of the IAS as well. The accounting standards followed should include a requirement to address disclosure in the financial statements of the full range of material contingent liabilities, as described above.

False accounting: a slippery slope

From "Tackling International Corruption" by John Brademas and Fritz Heimann in the September/October 1998 issue of Foreign Affairs.

"A company that decides to bribe must engage in a pattern of deception involving off-the-books transactions and secret bank accounts. The normal control system, including auditors, lawyers, and boards of directors, must be kept in the dark. The absence of accountability will lead to additional abuses. Middlemen and even company employees will pocket money ostensibly intended for government officials. As abuses expand, exposure becomes ever more likely."

From "Tackling International Corruption" by John Brademas and Fritz Heimann in the September/October 1998 issue of Foreign Affairs.

Responsibilities of external auditors

Companies should require their auditors to follow auditing standards of high quality, which meet or exceed IAS requirements including ethics standards, particularly in those pertaining to auditor independence. For example, ISA (International Standards on Auditing) 240, 250, 260 and 400 require auditors, among other things, to consider laws and regulations in an audit of financial statements, communicate their findings on a timely basis to management and others charged with governance and understand the accounting and internal control systems.

From the perspective of the external auditor, illegal bribes generally fall into three categories:

1. *Inadequately disclosed illegal bribery payments and/or fines and penalties paid or imposed on account of illegal activities that have a material and direct effect on the determination or classification of financial statement amounts (i.e., amounts described in the first bullet point in the preceding section)*

For example, if material and non-deductible illegal bribe payments have been improperly recorded on a company's books as ordinary business expenses, those amounts would not only be mis-labelled on the financial statements (i.e., their true identity as an illegal bribe would be concealed), but they would also have a direct effect on the amount of the company's tax accrual, and hence its net after-tax income (which would be overstated).

The responsibility of a company's external auditor for detection of misstatements resulting from these types of illegal bribe payments, fines or penalties is generally the same as its responsibility for detecting fraud. Upon detection of such amounts, the auditor generally has the additional responsibility of determining whether these illegal activities might also give rise to material indirect effects that may require additional disclosures.

2. *Illegal activities, whether or not properly recorded, which have no direct material effect on the financial statements (or which have material direct effects that have been properly accounted for and disclosed), but which have material indirect effects that have not been adequately identified and disclosed.*

For example, material contingent liabilities and losses may arise when an illegal bribe has been illegally offered or promised but was never actually paid. In such cases, unless the activity has been detected by the authorities and subjected to fines and penalties, these bribes would not usually have any direct effect on financial statement amounts.

The external auditor's responsibility to detect hidden or disguised illegal payments that do not have a material direct effect on the financial statements, or those that have been offered or promised but not paid is, in general, significantly less that it is for detecting illegal payments that have a material direct effect. An external audit will generally not detect the former payments or activities unless the auditors are informed of them by the company's management, legal counsel or employees, or unless the auditors find evidence of an investigation or an enforcement proceeding in documents reviewed in the normal course of conducting an audit (e.g., directors' meeting minutes).

Although the indirect financial statement effects of such payments or activities could be material, audits conducted in accordance with the auditing standards of most countries generally do not provide assurance that such payments will be detected or that any resulting contingent liabilities will be identified and disclosed.

However, when auditors are informed by the company, or when, in the course of conducting the audit, they otherwise become aware that the company has engaged in illegal activities, the auditors must identify any contingent liabilities or losses that may result from these illegal activities, then assess the likelihood that such contingencies will ultimately mature into liabilities and losses that could have a material direct effect on the company's financial statements or on the future conduct of its operations.

3. *Illegal activities that do not have a material direct or indirect effect on the determination or classification of financial statement amounts*

Except where otherwise provided by a country's anti-bribery laws or other anti-corruption regulations, a company's external auditor generally does not have responsibility to detect hidden or disguised illegal activities that do not have either a material direct or a material indirect effect on the financial statements. An external audit will generally not detect these payments or activities unless the auditors are otherwise informed of such payments by the company's management, legal counsel or employees, or unless they find evidence of an investigation or an enforcement proceeding in documents that are reviewed in the normal course of conducting an audit.

Whether cases of bribery or fraud fall under 1, 2 or 3 above, it is reasonable to expect that in evaluating risks affecting their audit and in assessing the effectiveness of the internal control and compliance systems, auditors will have indicated to management weaknesses which might allow illegal activities to pass undetected. Such warnings can assist in the prevention of bribery and fraud.

Where the auditor becomes aware that an illegal activity, whether or not material in amount, has been paid, offered or promised, the following procedures should be considered:

- *Management involvement*: If the audit team discovers that illegal payments were disguised or hidden in the company's records, it should conduct an investigation to determine whether one or more members of senior manage ment (as opposed to low-level employees or agents) were involved in the payment or in its cover-up. Involvement of senior management has much broader implications for the audit engagement.

- *Corrections and adjustments:* When the effect of illegal payments on one or more of the company's account balances (and/or other quantified disclosure data) becomes known, the audit team should propose the appropriate adjustments, and the client should make the entries required to correct its accounting books and records. If the direct effects of all such corrections and adjustments on amounts set forth in the financial statements are material, the auditors should propose, and the client should make, the necessary revisions to them. Note also that disclosure is generally required when a material misstatement is discovered in previously issued financial statements.
- *Other financial statement disclosures*: The auditors and the company, usual ly with the assistance of legal counsel, should identify and attempt to quantify any loss or liability contingencies that might reasonably be expected to result from the company's illegal payments, offers or promises. The auditors and the company must then evaluate the adequacy of disclosure in the financial statements of the identified loss contingencies and other potential effects of the illegal payments on the company's prospective operations. Whether the illegal payments or the existence of material loss contingencies must be disclosed in the financial statements will be determined by reference to any applicable laws or governmental regulations of the country involved, or by reference to that country's generally accepted accounting principles.

In this regard, it should be noted that payment of an illegal activity in violation of management policy may be indicative of a significant deficiency or material weakness in the company's internal control systems, which itself may constitute a vio lation of the country's anti-bribery or other anti-corruption laws and give rise to penalties or sanctions. For example, in the United States under amendments to securities law enacted as part of the Foreign Corrupt Practices Act of 1977, severe penalties may result from a company's failure to "devise and maintain a [sufficiently reliable] system of internal control ... ". The US Federal Sentencing Guidelines for Organizations provide for a significant reduction in punishments and fines for organizations found guilty of crimes should they have an effective programme to detect and prevent violations of laws and regulations.

- Effects on auditors' report: If the auditor concludes that the company's financial statements are materially affected by illegal payments, the company should revise its financial statements and make any necessary disclosures. If it refuses to do so, the auditor should issue a qualified or adverse opinion, disclosing all of the substantive reasons for doing so. Conversely, if the external auditor is prevented by the client from obtaining sufficient evidence to evaluate whether material illegal payments have been made or how such payments may affect the financial statements, the auditor should ordinarily:
  - Disclaim an opinion because of a scope limitation;
  - Report its findings to the audit committee, board of directors or similar body;

- Determine whether other actions, such as resignation, may be required to comply with his professional responsibilities or with the country's laws and regulations.

Communication with the company's audit committee, board of directors or similar bodies may also be required or advisable when:

1. The auditor has uncovered evidence indicative of senior management's involvement in illegal bribery and/or its cover-up;
2. Management refuses to properly investigate unresolved issues regarding the possible illegal payments and/or the propriety or legality of the accounting procedures used to record such amounts;
3. Scope limitations are imposed by circumstances beyond the company's control;
4. The company refuses to make the revisions to the financial statements and financial statement disclosures which the auditor concludes are required in order to properly account for illegal payments;
5. The auditors have found illegal payments that have material direct and/or indirect effects on the financial statements and related disclosures. The assessment of the implications that such payments have for the company's internal control system should also be communicated.

Management and the board of directors typically have the primary responsibility for determining the extent to which illegal payments and/or the failure to properly account for them must be reported to government regulatory agencies or other outside parties. However, when the company fails to adequately meet this obligation, the independent auditor may, in some countries, have a legal or a professional responsibility to report the improprieties to third parties.

Summary of the ICC Recommendations on accounting, auditing and financial controls

The provisions on auditing and accurate record-keeping are among the most important sections of ICC Rules and the OECD Convention. These provisions deal, not only with putting proper financial controls in place, but also with what to do if incidents of bribery nevertheless arise. The results of bribery and other illegal activities can remain masked and pose a threat to a company for an extended period if proper supervision of financial transactions is not implemented. A failure to account for illegal practices can have grave consequences for a company and its auditors.

Therefore companies should:

- Have an accounting policy with explicit prohibitions against off the books or false entries;
- Establish accountability for enforcing these prohibitions at various levels of the organization;
- Require that expenses be approved at a higher level than the one at which the expenses were incurred;
- Adhere to international, national and local laws and regulations regarding disclosure of illegal bribes or other illegal payments;
- Develop and maintain adequate internal controls, including a code of conduct and compliance programme;
- Adopt and maintain an internal audit programme;
- Report on internal controls in their annual report;
- Consider reporting on the company's anti-bribery and other anti-corruption policies and their effectiveness in the annual report.

External auditors should:

- Determine whether illegal practices, such as the paying of bribes, have a material effect on companies' financial statements;
- Investigate whether senior management were involved in any hidden illégal payments;
- When illegal payments are discovered, propose appropriate adjustments to correct a company's accounts and financial records;
- Evaluate the adequacy of disclosure in the company's financial statements;
- Give a qualified or adverse opinion of the company's practices if the company fails to respond to suggestions to revise its financial statements or to provide disclosure;
- In certain countries, report the company's violations to third parties, such as government regulatory agencies or other outside parties.

Jermyn Brooks was previously a Global Managing Partner of PricewaterhouseCoopers and is currently Director of Private Sector Programmes for Transparency International.

Frank Piantidosi is the Chairman and CEO of Deloitte Financial Advisory Services LLP.

The authors have revised and updated the chapter by Mritunjay Singh and David W. LaRue, as updated for the 2003 edition by Jermyn Brooks and Tom Milan.

Chapter 7

Whistleblowing

By Michael N. Davies, Q.C.

Changing perceptions

Numerous corporate scandals in the United States and elsewhere since the turn of the century have resulted in a growing distrust of corporate management. This change has brought with it a new perception of the importance of whistleblowing. The public perception is that, if whistleblower concerns had been heeded, some of the recent corporate disasters could have been avoided, and that in order to prevent future misconduct, whistleblowers should be encouraged to come forward and should be protected from retaliation. This increasing recognition that whistleblowers can play a critical role in disclosing corporate, as well as governmental, misconduct has also led to considerable legislative activity in many countries designed to protect whistleblowers and to encourage them to raise concerns.

Implications for companies: encouraging internal whistleblowers

In this new environment, companies have come to recognize that whistleblowers are more likely to come forward. If whistleblowers face a hostile internal environment, the whistleblower may go public – to regulators, prosecutors, union management or the media. Thus, the prudent course for management is to establish a positive climate for whistleblowers that encourages them to report internally without fear of retribution.

An *internal* whistleblowing system has major advantages for an enterprise. It usually gives it the opportunity to address the problem and take corrective and other remedial measures and thereby avoid the adverse publicity, investigation and prosecution that usually follow "after-the-fact" external whistleblowing. If the whistleblower reports early enough, when the problem is still in the planning stage – and ideally that will happen if the company encourages whistleblowers – this should allow the company to prevent bribery or other wrongdoing from taking place. Even if the company finds out about a problem too late to prevent it from happening, it will still be in a position to take disciplinary and other remedial measures designed to prevent a recurrence. That will also put the company in a better position to deal with the authorities and the media.

From the employee's standpoint, if the company deals responsibly with the issues disclosed and provides meaningful protection and support, a good relationship can likely be maintained between the company and the whistleblower. This is seldom the case when the whistleblowing is external.

External whistleblowing can be very detrimental to a company, often leading to investigation and prosecution, resulting in bad publicity, the imposition of fines and possibly jail terms for executives and employees. It is also usually very detrimental to the whistleblower, severely impairing his or her ongoing relationship with the company and other employees. Frequently, it leads to the whistleblower deciding to leave the company (even if protected by statute) and seeking other employment, which may be difficult to find. Having an internal reporting system in place does not eliminate, but certainly reduces, the risk that an employee will blow the whistle outside the company.

It is important to recognize that a whistleblowing system inevitably raises tensions. For the whistleblower there may be conflicting feelings of loyalty towards fellow employees and a sense of obligation to broader corporate interests, as well as to the overall public interest. Potential whistleblowers are likely to be in a very sensitive and potentially precarious position vis-à-vis those whose conduct they criticize. They are often harassed or ostracized by their fellow employees and are susceptible to being demoted or fired by hostile managers. Quite often there will be disagreements about the propriety or the legality of the actions challenged by the whistleblower, and his or her views may prove to be incorrect.

There are also some countries (such as those in central and eastern Europe), where the memory of state-organized eavesdropping and the historical stigma attributed to whistleblowing still prevail. Notwithstanding all of these concerns, it is in the corporate interest to deal pro-actively with whistleblowers.

Establishing a whistleblowing culture

Responsible enterprises need to be made aware of actual or potential wrongdoing – such as bribery, fraud and accounting improprieties – by one or more of their employees or agents. It is other employees within the enterprise who are most likely to become suspicious or aware of any proposed or actual unlawful activity and who are therefore in the best position to bring it to the company's attention. However, potential whistleblowers will not report internally if they fear reprisals from within the enterprise or suspect that management may condone or may even have participated in or approved the illegal activity. In that event, the company's ability to take appropriate remedial measures will be severely impaired. If it is not perceived as "safe" to blow the whistle internally, a conscientious employee with concern for the public interest will report the wrongdoing to the authorities or the press. When unlawful activity has occurred, internal reporting enables the company to notify the authorities and to be perceived in a more favourable way in any investigation or prosecution that could ensue.

RELEVANT PROVISIONS OF THE ICC RULES AND THE OECD, UN AND OTHER CONVENTIONS

Article 7 of the 2005 ICC Rules of Conduct and Recommendations on Combating Extortion and Bribery provides that enterprises should implement comprehensive policies or codes which, (among other things), should "b) offer confidential channels to raise concerns, seek advice or report violations without having to fear retaliation". ICC followed this up by developing guidelines on whistleblowing (see below).

The OECD Convention does not deal with whistleblowing, but the OECD Guidelines for Multinational Enterprises, adopted by the OECD in June 2002, explicitly caution companies not to punish those who report suspicious practices. The Guidelines set out what OECD governments have agreed constitute good corporate behaviour. Section II, entitled "General Policies", provides that enterprises should "refrain from discriminatory or disciplinary action against employees who make bona fide reports to management or, as appropriate, to the competent public authorities, on practices that contravene the law, the Guidelines or the enterprise's policies".

The United Nations Convention against Corruption (UNCAC) of 9 December 2003 (Article 33) requires each state party to consider incorporating into its domestic legal system: "appropriate measures to provide protection against any unjustified treatment for any person who reports in good faith and on reasonable grounds to the competent authorities any facts concerning offences established in accordance with [the] ... Convention".

The Council of Europe Criminal Law Convention on Corruption of 27 January 1999 (Article 22) obliges member states to adopt: "such measures as may be necessary to provide effective and appropriate protection for those who report the criminal offences established in accordance with [the] Convention".

The Council of Europe Civil Law Convention of 4 November 1999 (Article 9) requires that each Party provide: "in its internal law for appropriate protection against any unjustified sanction for employees who have reasonable grounds to suspect corruption and who report in good faith their suspicion to responsible persons or authorities".

The Inter-American Convention Against Corruption of 29 March 1996 (Article III, Section 8) requires signatories to consider creating, monitoring and strengthening "systems for protecting public servants and private citizens who, in good faith, report acts of corruption, including protection of their identities".

The African Union on Preventing and Combating Corruption of 11 July 2003 (Article 5) requires State Parties to adopt: "measures that ensure citizens report instances of corruption without fear of consequent retaliation".

The European Commission has not imposed any obligation on member states to enact whistleblower protection legislation. It has, however, taken steps to encourage internal whistleblowers among its own employees and, in April 2002, it adopted rules under which Commission employees have a duty to report concerns about serious wrong doing, and managers have a corresponding duty to follow up. Protection against retaliation is provided so long as the disclosure is made in good faith.

ICC Whistleblowing Guidelines

In 2008, ICC issued its *"Guidelines on Whistleblowing"*, the first world business organization of its kind to establish a global standard for facilitating the set up of these programmes. In publishing the guidelines, ICC noted that internal fraud reporting systems are not widespread throughout the world. An Ernst & Young survey of 13 European countries in 2007 showed that only 33 per cent of the company respondents said they had a hot line for employees to report incidents of possible fraud.

The ICC guidelines, aimed at helping companies establish and implement internal whistleblowing programs, recommended the following practical steps:

Enterprises should create a whistleblowing programme as part of internal integrity practices, which should:

- Handle reports early on, in full confidentiality;
- Appoint a high-level executive to manage the whistleblowing unit;
- Communicate in as many languages as there are countries of operation;
- Abide by external legal restrictions;
- Determine whether reporting should be compulsory or voluntary and whether reporting can be on an anonymous basis;

- Acknowledge, record and screen all reports; and
- Enable employees to report incidents without fear of retaliation, discrimination or disciplinary action.

ICC Guidelines on Whistleblowing (excerpted)

1) Enterprises are encouraged to establish, within their organization and as an integral part of their integrity programme, a whistleblowing system, commensurate with their size and resources.

Such whistleblowing system should aim to:

(i) Receive and entertain, in full confidentiality, all reasonable requests for advice and guidance on business conduct matters and ethical concerns raised by the employees of the enterprise and of its subsidiaries or affiliates (the group), but also, to any extent possible, by any of the group's agents, suppliers and customers; and to;

(ii) Receive and handle, at the earliest stage possible, by the same categories of persons, all reports made about any occurrence, whether established or soundly suspected, of a breach of applicable laws and regulations, the enterprise's code of conduct or the ICC Combating Extortion and Bribery Rules of Conduct and Recommendations, which could seriously harm the enterprise or the group, if no remedial action is taken.

2) Enterprises should appoint high-level personnel of undisputable repute and extensive work experience to be in charge of the management and administration of their whistleblowing units or ombudsservice. These personnel should be given a large autonomy within the enterprise and report to the highest echelon possible within the group. As part of these arrangements, an enterprise may designate a firm, external to the group, specialized in receiving and handling whistleblowing reports. Such firm should be independent, of undisputable repute and should offer appropriate guarantees of professionalism and secrecy."

(For the full text of the Guidelines, go to www.iccwbo.org and click on "Anti-Corruption".)

Evolution of whistleblower protection legislation

Only in recent years has the potential value of employees' raising concerns about wrongdoing in the workplace given rise to legislation designed to protect whistleblowers from reprisal. Initially, such legislation (for example, the US Whistleblower Protection Act of 1989) only applied to public sector employees, encouraging them to report wrongdoing and protecting them from retribution, irrespective of the disclosure route used.

Legislation in the United Kingdom (the Public Interest Disclosure Act of 1999 (PIDA) – responding in part to a variety of serious accidents (such as the Clapham and other train crashes in the UK that might have been prevented had employees come forward with their concerns regarding safety issues) – provides protection for both public and private sector employees with respect to disclosures made in good faith. Some of the recent legislation also recognizes the potential benefit to all concerned of internal versus external disclosure and creates incentives for employers to put into place internal reporting procedures. The UK statute, for example, protects whistleblowers when in good faith they raise concerns internally or to prescribed senior government officials. Wider disclosure (to the media, MPs or police, etc.) is protected if "reasonable" and where the matter:

- Is exceptionally serious;
- Is not raised internally or with a prescribed regulator because the worker fears that he/she would be victimized;
- Is not raised internally because of reasonable belief that there would be a cover-up and there is no prescribed person; or
- Was raised internally or with a prescribed person but was not dealt with properly.

Similar New Zealand legislation, enacted in 2001, conditions external disclosure on the perceived failure of internal disclosure mechanisms – i.e., where they do not exist or where the person to whom the employee must report is believed to be involved in the wrongdoing.

The UK Public Interest Disclosure Act of 1999 (excerpts)

"Section 43(H)(1) A qualifying disclosure is made in accordance with this section if –

(a) The worker makes the disclosure in good faith,

(b) He reasonably believes that the information disclosed, and any allegation contained in it, are substantially true,

(c) He does not make the disclosure for purposes of personal gain,

(d) The relevant disclosure is of an exceptionally serious nature,

(e) In all the circumstances of the case, it is reasonable for him to make the disclosure".

47B(1) A worker has the right not to be subjected to any detriment by any act, or any deliberate failure to act, by his employer on the ground that the worker has made a protected disclosure."

Legislation in the United States – the Sarbanes-Oxley Act of 2002, Section 806 (see Chapter 6), enacted in the wake of the Enron and WorldCom scandals – calls for rules to be developed that will require attorneys to report violations "up the ladder" to the most senior levels of management and ultimately to the audit committee or the board if management fails to take appropriate remedial action. In the field of money laundering, recent legislation requires banks and lawyers to disclose suspicious transactions to the authorities. Sarbanes-Oxley has also stimulated an ongoing debate regarding possible limitations on the confidentiality provided by the traditional attorney-client privilege.

Sarbanes-Oxley Act of 2002 (excerpts)

Sec. 1514A. Civil action to protect against retaliation in fraud cases

(a) WHISTLEBLOWER PROTECTION FOR EMPLOYEES OF PUBLICLY TRADED COMPANIES

No company with a class of securities registered under section 12 of the Securities Exchange Act of 1934 (15 U.S.C. 78 l), or that is required to file reports under section 15(d) of the Securities Exchange Act of 1934 (15 U.S.C. 78 o) (d), or any officer, employee, contractor, subcontractor, or agent of such company, may discharge, demote, suspend, threaten, harass, or in any other manner discriminate against an employee in the terms and conditions of employment because of any lawful act done by the employee .

(1) To provide information, cause information to be provided, or otherwise assist in an investigation regarding any conduct which the employee reasonably believes constitutes a violation of section 1341, 1343, 1344, or 1348, any rule or regulation of the Securities and Exchange Commission, or any provision of Federal law relating to fraud against shareholders, when the information or assistance is provided to or the investigation is conducted by

  (a) A Federal regulatory or law enforcement agency;

  (b) Any Member of Congress or any committee of Congress; or

  (c) A person with supervisory authority over the employee (or such other person working for the employer who has the authority to investigate, discover, or terminate misconduct);

(2) To file, cause to be filed, testify, participate in, or otherwise assist in a proceeding filed or about to be filed (with any knowledge of the employer) relating to an alleged violation of section 1341, 1343, 1344, or 1348, any rule or regulation of the Securities and Exchange Commission, or any provision of Federal law relating to fraud against shareholders."

The New York Stock Exchange Listing Manual (Section 303A.10) provides that listed companies must adopt a code of ethics for directors, officers and employees. The commentary stresses that each code of ethics must contain compliance standards and procedures that will facilitate the effective operation of the code and, *inter alia*, whistleblowing procedures and whistleblower protection.

France Act nt. 2007 – 1598 of 13 November 2007 (Article 9) amends the Labour Code and prohibits any discrimination against a person who has reported or brought a witness report to an employer or to the authorities about corruption. Any discriminatory act is to be declared null and void.

Problems implementing an internal whistleblowing system

Experience with the development of internal whistleblowing systems has shown that concerns reported by employees pursuant to the system generally fall into one of four categories:

Real problems

First, there is the reporting by an employee of a concern that turns out to be a real problem, which the company is then able to deal with in a responsive and responsible manner. The reporting of genuine problems is likely to happen often enough to make the existence of an internal whistleblowing system worthwhile.

Perceived problems

Often an employee, on the basis of limited information, will in good faith report a concern which, upon further investigation by the company, turns out not to be a problem. In these circumstances, it is most important to communicate the conclusions back to the reporting employee in order to preserve the credibility of the programme and to ensure there is no perception of a cover-up by the company.

Employee grievances

Employees may try to utilize an internal whistleblowing system as a means of securing redress for personal employee grievances that have nothing to do with a breach of laws or the company's code of conduct. These grievances may include issues relating to promotion or compensation or other job-related disputes with managers or fellow employees. These should be appropriately dealt with by some other process, usually within the Human Resources Department. Initially, a large number of calls may fall into this category, but the problem should decrease rapidly as employees come to understand the real purpose of the whistleblowing process.

Abuse of process

Finally, although this doesn't happen very frequently, complaints are sometimes made under an internal whistleblowing system which constitute a clear abuse of the process. First, where the local legal system provides protection for whistleblowers, employees, for example, may invent or exaggerate to try and protect themselves from an anticipated lay-off or discharge. Due care needs to be taken to diligently investigate these complaints in order to identify their true purpose. Second, false or malicious reporting of a problem can be used by an unscrupulous employee who has a personal grudge against a manager or another employee or for other improper personal purposes. Appropriate disciplinary action needs to be taken against such an employee to effectively deter this type of abuse.

For a whistleblowing system to work effectively, it is important that the ombudsperson and others responsible for administering the internal reporting system be of indisputable integrity and have the requisite knowledge, experience and training to be able to distinguish between these various categories of employee complaints and to deal with them appropriately. Selecting highly respected local employees to perform and explain the ombudsperson role contributes significantly to the success of the program, particularly in countries where there is a cultural sensitivity with regard to reporting concerns about fellow employees.

Concern that the system can be abused applies to external as well as to internal whistleblowing. In evaluating whistleblower complaints, government officials and the media should exercise care to determine whether the complainant may be misusing the process because of personal animosity or to serve political objectives.

Evaluating the bona fides of whistleblower charges is made more difficult when dealing with anonymous allegations. While anonymous complaints should not be rejected out of hand ? because whistleblowers may well have legitimate concerns about reprisals ? it is also true that the validity of allegations can be determined much more readily when the identity of the whistleblower is known.

In addition, company employees against whom allegations are made are also entitled to fair play. Their rights to defend themselves may be impaired when they have to respond to allegations by unidentified accusers. In medieval Venice, there was a long-standing controversy concerning the legitimacy of acting on anonymous accusations deposited into the mouth of the bronze lion on the steps of the Doges' Palace. The Venetian authorities justified the process as one serving the public interest. Some historians, however, have regarded it as a dangerous abuse.

Whistleblowing: two company codes

3D Systems

"We believe that communication and 'whistleblowing' perform a valuable function in maintaining high ethical standards of conduct and reducing the risks to the Company, its employees and stockholders from conduct that does not meet our high standards. Accordingly, in the unlikely event that you become aware of circumstances that appear inconsistent with our Code of Conduct or if you are instructed by a supervisor or manager to act in a manner inconsistent with our Code of Conduct, you are expected to inquire into the matter to assist the Company in avoiding violations of the Code of Conduct. Initially, we encourage you to review the matter with your supervisor, but if the matter is not resolved as a result of those discussions or you are uncomfortable in discussing the matter with your supervisor, you should contact the Chief Executive Officer or the General Counsel of the Company to explain the facts. If the facts reveal that such a violation may have occurred, the Company will investigate the situation and take appropriate action."

Honeywell International

" ... all employees shall have access to one or more telephone help-lines, which will be monitored on a 24-hour basis by a professional, independent contractor, through which suspected violations of laws, regulations, Company policies, or the Code of Business Conduct may be reported. This help-line is not intended to replace normal supervisory channels for reporting questionable conduct or seeking advice about appropriate ethical behavior.

Any employee who in good faith raises an issue regarding a possible violation of law or Company policy will not be subject to retaliation and their confidentiality will be protected to the extent possible, consistent with law and corporate policy and the requirements necessary to conduct an effective investigation. Any supervisory personnel who retaliates against an employee as a result of such employee's report of an alleged violation of law or Company policy shall be subject to disciplinary action, including termination, and may risk criminal sanctions as a result of such actions."

Essential ingredients of an effective internal reporting system

Having clearly established a policy providing for employees to report concerns about potential violations of company policy, including the enterprise's anti-corruption policy, an enterprise needs to establish a clear road map indicating what employees should do when they have a concern. This will encourage employees to report promptly and in a way with which they feel comfortable. The road map should contain the following provisions:

1. *Employees need a number of available reporting channels within the business unit where they can take a concern* (for example, to a supervisor, company legal counsel or to the next higher level of management). This is important because the concern may involve a fellow worker within the same business component or possibly the employee's own manager. In this regard, an enterprise, in addition to establishing a help-line, would be well advised to appoint at least one company ombudsperson, outside and possibly also within each major business unit, who is committed to dealing fairly and objectively with all concerns reported to them.

2. *Employees should be encouraged to use the reporting procedure with which they are most comfortable.* Often reporting to someone within their own business unit can be most effective in arriving at the prompt resolution of an issue. Also, reporting channels should reflect the languages spoken in the different countries of operation.

3. *Prompt reporting of a concern about a possible violation of the company's "no-bribery policy"* and other anti-corruption policies is crucial. Delays are likely to allow a problem to grow. Often the potential problem can be averted or the damage minimized if the issue is raised early. Companies are therefore increasingly adopting an affirmative duty to report.

4. *An employee should be encouraged to report openly but should be able to report anonymously.* However, there are circumstances in which the company must disclose the concern and the findings of its subsequent investigation to appropriate management personnel or government authorities. It is not possible, therefore, for an enterprise to guarantee confidentiality in all circumstances.

5. *As emphasized earlier, company policy must clearly prohibit any form of retribution or retaliation against an employee who reports information about a policy concern in good faith.* This is a critical element of a successful whistleblower policy, as employees will not report concerns (particularly those relating to those in more senior positions) when they fear their position in the company will be compromised. This does not, however, exclude a company from taking appropriate disciplinary action if an employee abuses the policy by making false accusations against another employee. In most companies, whistleblowing policies will not be limited to bribery and will extend to other policy areas, such as anti-trust, environmental compliance and improper accounting practices.

6. *If the problem reported on recurs or if the employee feels that corrective action has not been taken within a reasonable time, he or she should be encouraged to raise the matter with one of the other contacts listed in the company guidelines.* Clearly, if the situation seems to be recurring or has not been resolved, the employee should raise it again.

7. *A company needs to differentiate between various problems raised by whistleblowers and establish a process for each.* This involves classifying the concern to determine what needs to be done next, assigning appropriate personnel to investigate, determining appropriate corrective actions (clarifying the issues, providing education/training or improving procedures, etc.) and, where warranted, taking disciplinary action appropriate to the breach. The latter may range from a warning to suspension or outright dismissal.

8. *In order for the process to be fair and objective, all whistleblower reports should be diligently acknowledged, recorded and screened, and the enterprise should also provide feedback about the outcome of the investigation to the employee who originally reported the concern as well as to the person whose behaviour was reported.*

9. *Finally, the enterprise should at all times comply with all legal requirements relating to the establishment of whistleblowing procedures, as well as those related to providing notice to relevant governmental authorities.*

In short, early reporting, identification and resolution of potential issues are critical to the success of the process.

The Ombudsperson system

In his recent book, Ben Heineman Jr, General Electric's Chief Legal Officer for nearly 20 years, currently a Senior Fellow at Harvard University, commented on the ombudsperson system as follows:

"Virtually every oral and written integrity communication to employees, starting with the fundamental integrity guide, should stress the importance of reporting concerns and spotlight the ombuds system. The ombudsperson:

- Refers matters raising integrity concerns to financial, legal and HR staffs for investigation
- Tracks all such matters to ensure prompt close-out
- keeps employees up-to-date on the status of the concern

The word *concern* is more appropriate than possible violation or charge because it encourages people to report broadly on ethical and reputational questions as well as formal policy issues – and it is better to have more, rather than fewer, reports.

An effective [Ombuds] system has these elements:

- Employees should be strongly encouraged to report concerns immediately, through corporate or business ombudspersons or functional staff, using integrity help lines, letters, phone or e-mail.
- Employees have a duty to report concerns and not to retaliate. The ombuds system only works if (1) employees have an obligation to report concerns, and (2) failure to do so leads to discipline, including termination in cases where very serious matters (e.g., improper payments, accounting fraud) are left unreported. The corollary is that retaliation is an equally serious offense, with termination as the likely result.
- Finance and legal staffs must fully, fairly and promptly investigate all concerns, without fear or favor. If allegations relate to people at the top of the company, the CFO or the GC may recommend that outside investigators be retained.
- The ombuds system's important cases and statistical summaries should be regularly reported to the CEO and the board." Employees can report anonymously if they so choose.
- Employees have a duty to report concerns and not to retaliate. The ombuds system only works if (1) employees have an obligation to report concerns, and (2) failure to do so leads to discipline, including termination in cases where very serious matters (e.g., improper payments, accounting fraud) are left unreported. The corollary is that retaliation is an equally serious offense, with termination as the likely result.

- Finance and legal staffs must fully, fairly and promptly investigate all concerns, without fear or favor. If allegations relate to people at the top of the company, the CFO or the GC may recommend that outside investigators be retained.
- The ombuds system's important cases and statistical summaries should be regularly reported to the CEO and the board."

From High Performance with High Integrity, *reprinted with the permission of Harvard Business Press (2008).*

Summary of the ICC Recommendations on whistleblowing

It is very much in the interest of an enterprise that wishes to prevent bribery and other forms of corruption to establish, as an integral part of its integrity programme, a whistleblowing system, commensurate with their size and resources, under which employees (and, to the extent possible, any of the enterprise's agents, suppliers and customers) will feel comfortable reporting concerns without fear of retribution. Such an approach will enhance the company's chances to become aware of, and to appropriately deal with, a concern before an illegal act has been committed rather than after the fact, when the damage has already been done. If reporting is delayed, the company's reputation can be seriously harmed and the company can face a serious risk of prosecution. Having an effective internal whistleblower process is highly preferable to facing external whistleblowing, which can be more detrimental to the company and its employees.

Therefore companies should:

- Establish an internal disclosure programme ("whistleblowing")which encourages or requires employees to identify concerns within the company about what is or could be a possible violation of the company's anti-corruption policy;
- Not limit the reporting obligation to information relating to actual breaches of the policy, but extend the obligation to concerns or suspicions relating to actions which might lead to illegal acts in order that they can be prevented;
- Encourage employees to report concerns promptly, again so that the company can stop the illegal activity before it occurs;
- Establish effective mechanisms, such as hot-lines and ombudspersons, that can deal confidentially with employee reports and with which an employee will feel comfortable;
- Guarantee that there will be no retaliation or repercussions regarding issues raised or information provided in good faith;
- Encourage reports to be made openly but allow them to be made anonymously (since a company would be foolish not to pay attention to anonymous reports) and make best efforts to honour an employee's desire for confidentiality;
- Establish a process within the enterprise for effectively dealing with concerns that are raised;
- Take appropriate steps to respond to problems that are identified - including education, modifying processes and disciplinary action when required - and maintain statistical records that identify trouble spots;
- Provide periodic reports and summaries to the board and comply with laws relating to external reporting to relevant authorities;
- Ensure that, whenever possible, the reporting employee receives appropriate feedback.

Michael Davies is a member of the ICC Commission on Anti-Corruption. He is also the author of Chapter 4 in this handbook.

Acknowledgements to Unicorn and TUAC for making available their Initial and Comparative Review on Whistleblowing and Corruption, August 2001, and to Ben W. Heineman Jr. for allowing us to include excerpts from his book High Performance with High Integrity published by Harvard Business Press (2008).

Chapter 8

Compliance by Small and Medium-Sized Enterprises (SMEs)

By Phyllis A. Erikson and François Georges

Introduction

Small and medium-sized enterprises defy precise definition; descriptions vary widely, especially as to size. Perhaps it is best to describe them for this chapter as those companies that lack institutionally separate structures and staff to develop and maintain all of the elements of a formal compliance programme.

However, for purposes of anti-corruption, national laws, international conventions and the ICC rules do not differentiate between the duties of large companies and small and medium-sized companies. Although there may be some recognition that SMEs' programmes can be effective, though less elaborate, because of the smaller size of the company, the basic requirement remains that every company's anti-corruption compliance programme must be designed to prevent, detect and correct problems.

This chapter seeks to point out some of the advantages SMEs have, as well as some of the difficulties they may face, in complying with anti-corruption laws and regulations. It is not intended as a roadmap for creating a comprehensive compliance programme. Rather, it is meant to demonstrate how, in a practical way, SMEs, with limited resources, can develop effective anti-corruption compliance programmes that could prevent problems having costly, disruptive and even ruinous consequences.

There are many sources of information for anti-corruption compliance; in fact, most relevant subjects are covered by the chapters in this book. There are also websites, both private and governmental, books, periodicals, organizations and consultants, too many sources, one might argue, for the beleaguered SME, already feeling overburdened by the incessant flow of new regulations and requirements. ("When", they might ask, "do we run our business?") Unfortunately, regulators and enforcers are generally unsympathetic to such complaints, especially in the face of violations.

RELEVANT PROVISIONS OF THE ICC RULES AND THE OECD CONVENTION

Part I of ICC Rules states: "*All enterprises* should conform to the relevant laws and regulations of the countries in which they are established and in which they operate, and should observe both the letter and the spirit of these Rules of Conduct" (emphasis added). The OECD Convention, in Article I, makes it unlawful for "*any person*" to offer, promise or give pecuniary or other advantage ... to a foreign public official" (emphasis added).

The challenge

How do SMEs observe national laws implementing international conventions, which prohibit domestic and foreign bribery of public officials as well as private-to-private corruption?

Corporate culture

Corporate culture is the most important variable in the success of an anti-bribery compliance programme. On the positive side, small companies have the advantage of cohesiveness compared to large companies, which have more disparate and far-flung operations.

Experts have highlighted that one of the most important elements in successful anti-corruption programmes is the tone set at the top. Many SMEs are still run by the owner or the owner's family, and their employees are generally more likely to identify personally with the code of ethics of a smaller company and its leadership, including when these "codes" have not been formalized in a document. The CEO ("the tone at the top") should make it clear to employees that bribery, extortion and other forms of corruption are prohibited, and they should implement effective procedures to prevent such risks.

Resources

SMEs do not have large staffs of specialists to assign to full-blown anti-bribery programmes. However, the necessity to develop an effective scaled-down programme should ensure that the programme is more closely tailored to the SME's specific circumstances, including identified risks, such as the use of agents. The programme should, therefore, be both relevant and efficient for smaller companies.

Procedures and processes

Unlike large companies, SMEs do not have extensive systems for complying with the whole panoply of local and international rules and regulations governing all aspects of their operations, nor do they generally have systems for communicating, training and monitoring. Because they are smaller, they can operate more informally. However, they do have the advantage of less management turnover; the staff know whom to call, which facilitates compliance with confidential reporting requirements. An SME's general approach should be to encourage discussion of sensitive matters, regardless of whether a formal whistleblowing process is in place. However, care needs to be taken to maintain some written records to be able to defend the SME in case of later investigations.

Virtually all SMEs have routines and controls to deal with other compliance issues, such as accounting, employment law and environmental rules. Consequently, there should already be a framework on which to build anti-corruption compliance. Because that framework is less elaborate and less bureaucratic, it should be easier to adapt for anti-corruption compliance.

Disadvantages

In spite of some advantages, there is no question that SMEs face difficulties in attempting to comply with national laws implementing international conventions. A smaller number of employees means less flexibility in assigning responsibilities to accommodate a compliance programme's developing demands: conducting training and performing monitoring and follow-up activities. It also means that the documentation of instructions, decisions and actions is often less elaborate than that in a larger company. Any lack of documentation, even in a simple form, represents a significant risk should there be later involvement by investigators.

In addition, many SMEs are publicly traded and listed and therefore must comply with applicable securities regulations and audit requirements. These activities are frequently outsourced to legal and accounting firms, so that extensive procedures and processes are not "embedded" in the SME's infrastructure.

Moreover, because few SMEs are highly visible, they may not have had the awreness-raising experiences that their well-known larger counterparts have had that would help them avoid "getting into trouble". Therefore, they may not have developed the vigilant and informed culture that would motivate them to prevent problems. Suggestions for overcoming inertia and any resistance on the part of upper management may be found in Section II of the Transparency International USA "Toolkit for SME's", at http://transparency-usa.org.

Finally, SMEs may be more inclined to use agents to effect sales and address administrative and logistical matters, because volume in a given country or region may not warrant the costs of basing company employees in that area. Reliance on agents presents more risks for SMEs, because agents are more difficult to train and control (see Chapter 4). Furthermore, agents are more likely to be focused on simply getting the next order and not on longer-term company concerns. This makes screening of agents and monitoring any facilitation payments more important and also more burdensome.

Checklist for selecting an agent

In choosing an agent, the SME should:

- Appraise the integrity and reputation of prospective agents and their partners, in particular through contact with diplomatic representatives from their govenments and others, such as ICC national committees, TI national chapters or business federations;
- Perform a due diligence investigation on prospective agents, which can be done free of charge by internet search;
- Include provisions in contracts whereby the agent agrees explicitly not to pay bribes;
- Ensure that any payment made to any agent represents no more than an appropriate remuneration for legitimate services rendered by the agent and is paid directly to the bank account of the agent, not in cash;
- Determine the customary commission for similar sales in the country where the agent is working.
- Verify the effective presence of the agent in the country in which its services are rendered.

Meeting the challenge

SMEs can ill afford any problem in this area. While an anti-corruption enforcement action may be a temporary, albeit expensive and traumatic experience for a large enterprise, it could easily threaten the very survival of an SME. In addition, lack of an effective programme, or any misstep in this area, could cause an SME to lose its best customers by being "blacklisted".

SMEs must meet the challenge. Clearly, the international climate has changed. The World Bank blacklist of companies predominantly contains SMEs. The OECD monitoring of enforcement has raised awareness and is encouraging more vigorous enforcement. In the past, OECD suggested that the US government was not sufficiently raising the awareness of SMEs, notwithstanding a table of cases showing prosecution of a substantial number of them. OECD reviews can be expected to continue to make sure that enforcement authorities are aware that problems in this area are not limited to large companies. Furthermore, because of increasing globalization, an increasing number of SMEs are entering unfamiliar markets.

These companies may not have local business experience and are more likely to get into difficulties. Consequently, prosecutors may find it easier to focus on them.

Suggested actions

In view of the changing business environment for SMEs, following are some suggestions upper management should consider when confronting issues of bribery and other forms of corruption:

1. **Look for opportunities to sensitize employees to the need for a programme to combat bribery by initiating some of the following steps:**

   - Allocate time on management meeting agendas to raise and discuss the sub ject;
   - Determine the most likely areas of exposure, by country and by function,within the enterprise (e.g., marketing and sales);
   - Circulate news clippings about enforcement actions and relevant law changes in countries of business activity;
   - If expansion into other countries is contemplated, include a corruption survey in the country risk assessment process;
   - Circulate the Transparency International Corruption Perception Index and Bribe Payers Index, highlighting relevant countries' rankings;
   - Enlist legal, finance, human resources and risk management as natural allies, pointing out the benefits related to each;
   - Gather information from operating departments for their views on the risks and the success or failure of other programmes.

2. **Assess current compliance systems and procedures, be they financial, environmental or other. In doing so:**

   - Make sure a provision on anti-bribery regulation is in the company's internalional code of conduct or compliance policies;
   - Make sure the company's accounting practices can accommodate financial requirements, such as those of the national laws implementing international conventions against foreign bribery;

- Use environmental and safety monitoring and auditing to provide a template for analogous anti-bribery procedures;
- Trace the company's "order-to-cash" (sometimes called "order-to-remittance") process; the staff tracking this are frequently those that can most effectively monitor compliance with an anti-corruption policy;
- If the company is ISO certified, use some employees who are familiar with analyzing and documenting procedures and who can be helpful for training.

3. **Create policies and training materials, including the following:**

- Check materials used by enterprises of similar size and nature;
- Draft a simple summary policy suited to the enterprise's size and activities;
- Prepare several Frequently Asked Questions and common "close-call" factual examples, especially concerning business gifts and entertainment;
- Summarize enforcement actions, emphasizing the impact on companies and their management. Some of the consequences include jail sentences, fines, blacklisting and extensive (and expensive) compliance programmes imposed by the government when violations are discovered;
- Consider translating these materials into the local languages used b by employees in different locations; this has been found to be highly effective, not only in enlisting cooperation, but in building good intra-company relationships;
- Include information for reporting concerns internally as well as a "hot-line" so that potential problems can be caught and resolved early. External hot-line providers are cost-effective and frequently assist with printing materials and developing internal procedures.

4. **Sketch out the outline of the programme:**

- Enlist a trusted, high-level person to act as compliance or ethics officer and publicize this appointment throughout the company;
- Have a simple procedure to log complaints and reports of concern, including follow-up to the originator indicating resolution of the problem or the action taken;
- Ensure that Human Resources conducts routine background (agency) checks on all applicants for employment, where legally permitted.

5. **Implement by obtaining the governing body's (e.g., Board of Directors') authorization to:**

- "Implant" monitoring and auditing of compliance onto existing financial or environmental audit procedures;

- "Cascade" the policy and training materials, starting with CEO's/President's/Managing Director's staff, and then conduct "train the trainers" for all managers, so the material is disseminated throughout the organization, preferably in presentations by managers to their staff in relevant functions;
- Encourage open access to lawyers and compliance personnel to encourage reporting;
- Rigorously enforce whistleblower protection; news of retaliation against whistleblowers travels fast in an SME;
- Where feasible, use the senior staff as a compliance review committee to oversee the programme and ensure consistent discipline throughout the organization;
- Conduct training periodically, keep sessions short and target the most sensitive functions; use inexpensive, commercially available training materials in various media.

6. **When mergers, acquisitions and joint ventures are involved:**

- Include enquiry of commercial practices in due diligence;
- If unacceptable practices are found, determine the difficulty of eliminating them and investigate any impact on revenue, as well as on the acquisition, merger or joint venture project itself or its pricing.

More detailed guidance on creating and tailoring an anti-corruption compliance programme can be found on major international websites such as those of the UN Global Compact, the World Bank, the OECD, as well as on ICC national committee websites such as that of he Austrian National Committee. Managers can also consult NGO websites, such as that for Transparency International (especially the French and US national chapters).

Conclusion

Size the programme realistically, to one that can be implemented and maintained. A "paper" programme (one with the right words on paper, but not communicated or enforced) can be used by prosecutors as evidence that the company knew the standard, but did not meet it when it failed to follow its own policies. A well-designed and enforced programme is an SME's best protection against liability. Either it will prevent serious problems or, in case of a "rogue" employee or agent, will provide an effective defence for the company which has taken all reasonable precautions.

Phyllis A. Erikson, is retired Vice President, General Counsel and Secretary of J.M. Huber Corporation.
François Georges, who formerly headed Electricité de France's (EDF) compliance, is Chairman of ICC France's Commission on Anti-Corruption.

Part III
Problem Areas

Chapter 9

Money Laundering

By David Lyman, assisted for this edition by Carlos Natera

RELEVANT PROVISIONS OF THE ICC RULES AND THE OECD AND UN CONVENTIONS

The 2005 Revised ICC Rules of Conduct to Combat Extortion and Bribery in International Business Transactions as yet have no specific provisions on money laundering. However, the provisions on financial recording and auditing in Article 8 of the Rules (dealt with elsewhere in this manual) - which insist on proper and fair recording of financial transactions, prohibit "off-the-books" accounts and require independent systems of auditing - can all be viewed as preventive measures Against Money Laundering ("AML"). Article 9 deals with compliance, sanctions and public disclosure of corporate codes of conduct.

The 1997 OECD Convention does contain an article on money laundering, Article 7, which reads: "Each party which has made bribery of its own public official a predicate offence for the purpose of the application of its money laundering legislation shall do so on the same terms for the bribery of a foreign public official, without regard to the place where the bribery occurred."

The 2003 UN Convention Against Corruption (UNCAC) specifically addresses money laundering issues. These include model preventive policies, such as the establishment of anti-corruption bodies and the criminalization of the concealment and laundering of the proceeds of corruption. Offences committed in support of corruption, including money laundering and obstructing justice, are also dealt with. In addition, countries are required to undertake measures which will support the tracing, freezing, seizure and confiscation of the proceeds of corruption regardless of where the corruption occurred.

Why this chapter?

Other chapters of this manual deal with extortion and bribery and the curtailment of corruption in public-private and private-private transactions. This chapter addresses how the ill-gotten moneys therefrom are disposed of if not spent promptly. By common usage and statutory definition, such "money laundering" is a crime. Consequently, an examination of money laundering extends beyond corruption, extortion and bribery into a plethora of illicit activities, such as illegal trade in narcotics, arms and weapons and people trafficking, terrorism, fake passport/travel documents, intellectual property counterfeiting, trade in human organs and illegal trade in wild animals and endangered species, as well as art crimes, toxic waste, prostitution, financial frauds, tax evasion, insider securities trading, computer fraud schemes and other serious offences, domestic and transnational. The focus of this chapter, however, will be on the narrow use of money laundering, i.e., to cover up instances of public-private corruption, with some attention being given to other criminal and business-related transactions. Terrorist financing is also addressed because of its impact on the world today.

This chapter defines "money laundering", looks at the techniques thereof and dwells on the international conventions and rules dealing with AML, finishing with some recommendations for the reader to reduce the occurrence of money laundering.

The Issues

Governance

Should companies in the conduct of their business care about money laundering? Yes. Money laundering is a crime. AML counter-measures and compliance are essential elements of good corporate governance and corporate social responsibility (CSR). Any business, whether a financial institution, professional service, industrial enterprise, charitable non-governmental organization (NGO) or other entity, caught in the web of money laundering could have its reputation irreparably damaged. Even its well-intentioned directors, management and staff could be the subjects of private and public investigations out of which indictments and criminal and civil prosecutions could arise. At best, it would be a public relations nightmare. As the corporate scandals from 2001 to the present have demonstrated, it only takes one unethical person with the discretion to make decisions to jeopardize an entire organization. A reputation for integrity takes many years to build and only a few moments to damage or destroy.

To avoid losses and possible prosecution, virtually all businesses would be wise to be alert to money laundering methods and tactics. For their own protection, businesses should implement AML defenses and counter-measures and install, implement and monitor various other forms of prevention, detection and protection, as detailed later in this chapter.

Anti-money laundering measures – a new dimension

Money laundering, the illegal use of banking and other financial channels to hide the origin of the money and identity of the criminal owner of the money, has been with us for decades. Traditionally associated with tax evasion and the Mafia, it was, until the late 1980s, an often neglected problem. It became a matter of growing global concern, however, as the narcotics trade blossomed, organized crime networks disposed of the proceeds of their illegal activities and terrorist cells and networks sought new sources of funding.

In the aftermath of the terrorist attacks of 11 September 2001, AML efforts have been allocated much greater attention and support by governments and legislative bodies. Moreover, the public, largely because of its fear of more terrorism, is becoming better educated about money laundering. Recently, the Financial Action Task Force (FATF) has focused on methods to prevent the financing of WMD – Weapons of Mass Destruction.

Terrorists employ the same money laundering techniques and mechanisms as organized crime, corrupt officials in governments and businesses and others engaged in illegal activities that generate significant amounts of illicit money. Denying access to the financial systems to those who rely upon money laundering is the major objective of AML.

Money laundering defined

In its simplest non-legal terms, money laundering is "the processing of criminal proceeds (profits or other benefits) in order to disguise their illegal origin" (the Financial Action Task Force [FATF]). Note that the illegal act of money laundering occurs only after a defined predicate criminal offence has been committed to generate the criminal proceeds, which in turn need to be laundered to convert them into "legitimate capital". This transformation process has become a thriving business, albeit quite illegal in most, but not yet all, countries.

If the money being moved did not come from an illegal activity, then its handling and processing are not considered to be money laundering. Thus, preparatory measures only, such as pre-positioning funds to be used for, say, bribing a foreign government official, are not necessarily illegal in the money laundering context.

Cash is heavy

Actual cash currency in large amounts is heavy. For that reason, it must generally be placed into the financial system as early as possible to move it back into circulation. Contrary to movie and television lore, USD 1 million in cash will not fit into a briefcase. For example, USD 1 million in USD 100 bills weighs 22 pounds (10 kilos); USD 10 million in USD 20 bills weighs 1,100 pounds (500 kilos); the same amount in USD 100 bills still weighs 220 pounds (100 kilos); and USD 100 million in USD 100 bills weighs 2,200 pounds (1000 kilos, i.e., 1 metric ton)!

The washing cycle

"There are three distinct stages to the money laundering cycle. The first is *immersion or displacement or physical disposal*, which means consolidation and placement. A drug dealer who amasses USD 5 million in cash is faced with the herculean task of putting perhaps as many as one million pieces of paper into the banking system. Unlike the counterfeiter, who needs to get his forged notes into circulation, the laundryman takes his money out of circulation by relying on bank accounts, postal orders, traveler's cheques and other negotiable instruments to funnel the cash into the banking system.

Continuing the metaphor, the second step – known as *layering* – might also be called *heavy soaping*. This is where the laundryman disassociates his gains from their illicit source. By moving his money between as many accounts as he can – in and out of dummy companies that he has set up around the world for just this purpose – and relying on bank secrecy and attorney-client privilege to hide his own identity, he deliberately creates a complex web of financial transactions, keeping in mind at every step that his main task here is to obliterate any sort of audit trail.

The final stage is in the *spin dry* – sometimes described as *repatriation and integration*. This is the point where the washed funds are brought back into circulation, now in the form of clean, and often taxable, income."

Excerpted from "The Laundrymen" by Jeffrey Robinson. Reprinted by permission of Simon & Schuster Inc., London, UK

The washing Cycle

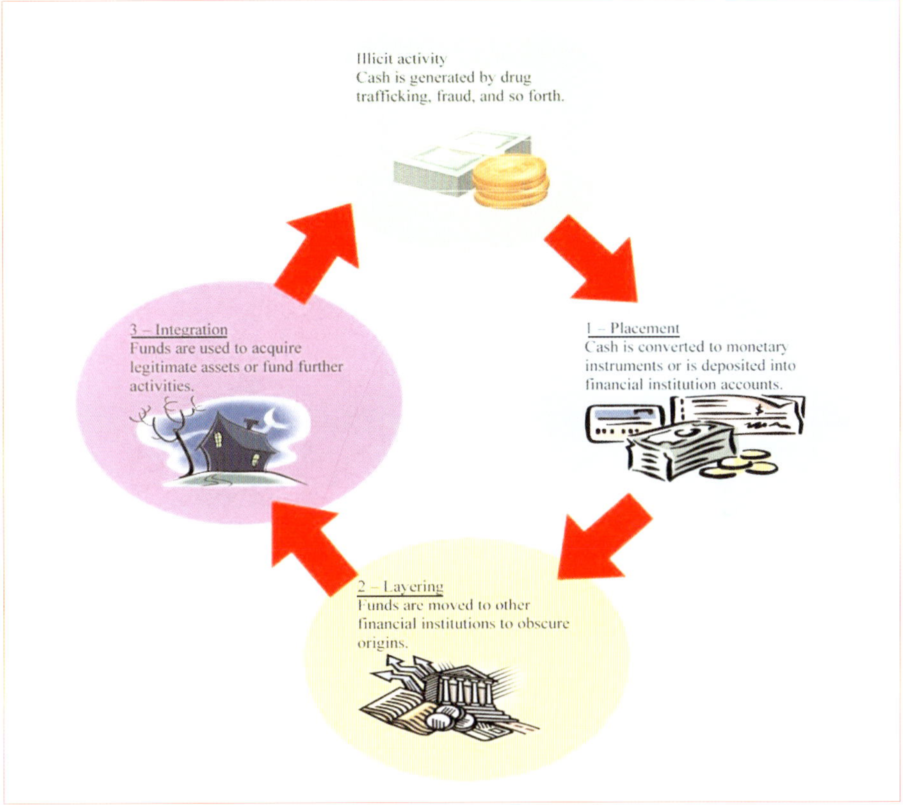

Sources of illegal proceeds

In their modern context, AML precepts and laws were originally only aimed at preventing the disposal of the proceeds of the trade in narcotics, including psychotropic substances. Though hiding money has probably been around since currency was invented, the US, through its Bank Secrecy Act in 1970, was the first country in the world to criminalize money laundering, albeit only as it then related to the illegal drug trade.

The US and other countries soon realized that the ill-gotten proceeds of extortion, bribery and fraud also needed international cooperation legislation to inhibit money laundering, to track and recover the illegal money and to prosecute offenders. With the onset of globalization, the lifting of exchange controls, instantaneous electronic money transfers, internet banking, the growth in the last decade or so of organized crime and the public disclosure of corporate and political scandals, public-private and private-private corruption and other serious crimes involving money laundering practices have, unfortunately, been blossoming.

How pervasive is money laundering?

Money laundering is said to be the world's third largest business in terms of value. And it is growing. But these are just educated guesses. No one really knows how big it is. Both the experts and competent authorities have avoided estimating the scope of the practice except to conclude it is large, pervasive and growing. Annual Reports of FATF say: "It must be said that overall it is absolutely impossible to produce a reliable estimate of the amount of money laundered and therefore the FATF does not publish any figures in this regard." The IMF estimates that money laundering amounts to 2.5 per cent of the world's GDP, but this is simply a broad estimate.

The overall turnover in organized crime had a value of USD 800 billion in 2001 and increased to USD 1,500 billion in 2005. These figures are very preliminary and have a large margin for error, but they give a clear indication, of the importance of one aspect/source of money laundering and the turnover of organized crime.

In 2008, the OECD estimated that trade in counterfeit goods amounted to 9-10 per cent of world trade, up from about 3 per cent in 1990. In 2008, the World Health Organization (WHO) reported that counterfeit drugs represent in EUROS 45 billion or about USD 70 billion in sales, which equals almost 10 per cent of the world's pharmaceutical markets. The proceeds of trading derived from intellectual property violations, such as counterfeiting, must also pass through money laundering systems.

In addition, a recent business report from Australia found that international trade in all types of counterfeit goods was growing at an alarming rate and, according to the International Chamber of Commerce, is worth USD 650 billion.

According to the World Customs Organization (WCO), a group of 170 Customs administrations that collectively administer 98 per cent of international trade, counterfeiting and piracy account for about 10 per cent of global commerce. The US Department of Commerce reports that seizures of fake and counterfeit goods at US borders have doubled since 2001. The US Customs and Border Protection agency made 14,500 seizures in 2006, 80 per cent more than in 2005.

Thus, according to Interpol, the WCO and ICC, estimates are that roughly 9–10 per cent of world trade every year is in counterfeit goods. *In other words, one of every ten items purchased is fake.*

Fraud

For the purposes of this manual, another important AML issue is corporate fraud, which often leads to money laundering. Businesses are subject to fraud through simple and complex deceptions by both insiders – managers, employees, agents, et al – and outsiders. Being a victim of fraud is embarrassing and expensive, while recoveries are limited. On a wider scale, in the information age, fraud can be perpetrated through credit cards, smart cards, stored value cards, e-money, e-commerce, internet scams, identity theft, loss of customer data, etc. Technology helps the good and the evil alike.

The element of fraud involved in the deliberate falsification of company accounts by insiders, whether employees or senior management, is a principal concern of corporate governance. These frauds can be the subject of civil or criminal proceedings depending on the individual country. If this falsification is compounded by an effort to launder the funds illegally received, the legal implications can be very serious indeed. Beginning in 2001 and 2002, a number of massive corporate frauds were uncovered and caused the collapse of major corporations then and since.

Conventional arms vs. terrorism

Terrorism occupies the world's attention today. This section looks at terrorist financing and the acquisition of WMD, which are aided by money laundering. The techniques used to raise, move, use and launder money are essentially the same as those used to conceal the sources of, and uses for, terrorist financing. Funds used to support terrorism may originate from legitimate sources, criminal activities or both. Legitimate sources may include donations of gifts of cash or other assets to organizations, such as foundations or charities which, in turn, are used to support terrorist activities or terrorist organizations. This difference requires special laws to deal with terrorist financing. If derived from illegal sources, these funds may already be covered by a country's AML regime, depending upon the scope of predicate offences for money laundering.

There are some distinctions between conventional criminal activities and terrorism with respect to money laundering and AML measures. The following comparisons are illustrative:

Conventional crimes

Conventional Crimes	Terrorism
• Dirty money to clean money • Destination of funds needs to be disguised • Needs assistance of the financial sectors • Deals in *large* sums • Money cycles from a criminal act back to the criminal owner • Complex laundering processes • Tracing is *to find the money* • Tracing is to find the criminal	• Clean(or dirty) money for illegal acts • Destination of funds needs to be disguised • Needs assistance of the financial sectors • Often deals in *small* sums • Money goes one way, i.e, is withdrawn and spent • Simple transfers • Tracing is *to find those who furnish the money* which can also originate from legitimate sources • Tracking often useless, as money is withdrawn and used quickly

By way of illustrating the above differences, the following is extracted from the FATF Report on Terrorist Financing of 29 February 2008:

The direct cost of terrorist attacks and conflict

"The precursor materials necessary to stage specific attacks are highly diverse and include, for example, vehicles, improvised bomb-making components, maps, surveillance material, etc. These direct costs of terrorist attacks are often very low relative to the damage they can yield, as illustrated by the following estimates:

The direct cost of terrorist attacks and conflict

Attack	Date	Estimated cost
London transport system	7 July 2005	GBP 8 000
Madrid Train bombings	11 March 2004	USD 10 000
Istanbul truck bomb attacks	15 & 20 November 2003	USD 40 000
Jakarta JW Marriott Hotel Bombing	5 August 2003	USD 30 000
Bali bombing	12 October 2002	USD 50 000
Twins Tower, World Trade Center bombing	11 September 2001	USD 400 000 – 500 000
USS Cole attack	12 October 2000	USD 10 000
East AfricaN embassy bombings	7 August 1998	USD 50 000

To these direct costs must be added funds needed for salaries, subsistence, family support, communications, training, travel, logistics, propaganda, other organizational costs and funding shared with kindred cells or networks."

Money laundering techniques

The experts have noted little difference in the ways that terrorists and other criminals use the financial and other systems to launder money. The methods identified include cash smuggling by couriers or bulk cash shipments; structured transactions, both into and from bank accounts; purchases of money instruments in various forms and movements of funds via the non-bank or underground systems, the internet and other electronic methods.

The most common methods

The vast majority of criminal money laundering still follows the well-worn trails created by the tax evasion industry. Many offshore banking and tax haven centres still offer corporate and commercial secret facilities, and so far the tax planning industry has been sufficiently lucrative to ensure that a whole sector of commercial business activity is not going to disappear overnight. At the same time, global business continues to make use, both legitimate and questionable, of the structures and complex corporate holdings to protect commercial secrecy and discourage financial transparency. Lawyers, accountants and other "gate keepers" have close relationships with the world's major businesses and financial institutions.

The techniques used in money laundering can be broken down into funds channeled through three principal conduits: (a) banking, (b) non-bank institutions and (c) non-financial businesses. Summarized, but not all-inclusive, these channels and their most common laundering techniques are as follows:

Banking

- Large deposits and transfers;
- False name accounts;
- Accounts of friends, relatives and cronies;
- Smurfing (electronic structured transactions of electronic cash);
- Shell and front companies, usually offshore, for layering transactions;
- Lawyers, accountants, consultants, trustees, fiduciaries;
- Private investment corporations (PICs);
- Collection accounts; special name accounts; correspondent and concentration accounts;
- Acquisition of compliant banks;
- "Payable through accounts";
- "Loan back arrangements";
- Swaps and options;
- Telegraphic transfers (TT) (SWIFT);
- Bank drafts, money orders, cashier's cheques;
- Cash deposits and withdrawals;
- Smuggling currency in bulk across borders;
- Travelers' cheques;
- Internet banking and electronic purse accounts; and
- Internet shell banks.

Non-bank financial institutions

- Illicit foreign exchange arbitrage;
- Bureaux de change, exchange offices, casas de cambio;
- Money remittance services (giro houses);
- Underground or parallel banking; "Black Market Peso Exchange"; "hawala"; "hundi"; "fei qian"; chit and chop shops which handle both legal and illegal foreign exchange transactions in India, South and East Asia, the Middle East and Africa;
- Single premium insurance products; and
- Postal services: money orders, packages (for smuggling cash).

One problem for law enforcement efforts to find, freeze and confiscate funds earmarked for terrorists is that some of these funds, particularly in small to mid-sized amounts, are moved through "underground or parallel banking channels", i.e., alternative and unregulated remittance systems. These are virtually untraceable.

Parallel banking, money and trade networks had their origins in China 4,000 years ago. They are used extensively by workers to send money home to small villages in their home countries often without using formal banks. "Hawala" or "Hawallah" (meaning "in trust" in Hindi) and in Chinese – "fei-ch-ien" (meaning "flying money") is an ancient system mainly used in China, South and Southeast Asia and the Middle East for transferring money or value across borders without any physical movement of money or paper transactions, thereby escaping the attention of financial regulators. It is swift and efficient. The system is thought to be one of the key channels for terrorist financing which often does not require large amounts of money. Hence parallel banking is now on everyone's radar screen.

Hawala

How hawala works

"Say a Pakistani immigrant living in Baltimore [Maryland, US] wants to send USD 5,000 home to his parents. He contacts a local hawaladar, as dealers are called, known to him through cultural or ethnic ties, and gives him or her USD 5,000 plus a small fee for the latter's efforts. The dealer then phones another hawaladar in Karachi. The Karachi dealer delivers USD 5,000 worth of Palestani rupees to the man's parents. End of story.

Sort of. the Karachi dealer is not now out USD 5,000? Yes, but only temporarily. As stated earlier, the key to hawala is trust: the Karachi dealer knows that the USD 5,000 will be returned to him – his outlay will be remitted – in the future, when he initiates a similar deal.

Hawala dealers give money out and take money in, not necessarily from the same client, so that in the end, their books balance … what appears to be invisible accounting, isn't.

Written accounts of transactions, if they are done at all, are done in code on scraps of paper that are destroyed when the transaction is over. The code may be a combination of serial numbers taken from currency notes and known only to the hawaladar and the recipient."

Excerpted from US Customs Today, published by the US Customs Service, April 2002

The hawala system can handle large transactions of millions of dollars as well.

In 2003, the IMF sponsored the first international conference on Informal Funds Transfer Systems. A result of that conference is the Abu Dhabi Declaration on Hawala. The IMF's Occasional Paper 222, "Informal Funds Transfer Systems", provides an analysis of the informal hawala system. It encourages a two-pronged approach toward regulation: (1) In countries where an informal hawala system exists alongside a well-functioning conventional banking sector, it is recommended that hawala dealers be registered and keep adequate records in line with the FATF recommendations; (2) simultaneously, the regulatory response should address weaknesses that may exist in the formal sector.

Policymakers should address economic and structural weaknesses that encourage transactions outside the formal financial systems, as well as the weaknesses in the formal financial sector itself. Regulators need to possess the appropriate supervisory capacity to enforce the regulations and there need to be incentives to comply with the regulations.

The report also cautions that the application of international standards needs to pay due regard to specific domestic circumstances and legal systems. The broader response of well-conceived economic policies and financial reforms, a well-developed and efficient payments system and effective regulatory and supervisory frameworks are required.

Non-financial businesses or professions

- Professional facilitators, e.g., lawyers, accountants, financial advisors, Notaries, secretarial companies, trustees and other fiduciaries;
- Systems based on trust and loyalty (see "hawala" above);
- Real businesses: false invoicing, commingling of legal and illegal money, loan back arrangements, layering of transactions through offshore shell companies and false import/export declarations;
- Commercial trade transactions through Free Trade Zones;
- Casinos, bookmaking, internet casinos/gambling/underground lotteries;
- Real estate companies;
- Purchase and cross-border delivery of precious metals and gems;
- Use of warrants in the metals market;
- False insurance claims – ghost ships;
- New electronic/internet payment methods (NPM) such as prepaid cards, stored value cards (electronic purse), mobile phone payments, internet payment services and digital precious metals/digital currency; and
- Trade-based money laundering.

FATF, in a study on money laundering typologies, highlighted "gate keepers", such as lawyers and accountants, as the common element in complex money laundering schemes. Money launderers often target struggling professional practices that are in financial difficulties, since the latter may find it hard to turn away lucrative business, high-risk or not. FATF reports that lawyers are primarily used to establish corporate entities through which money can be laundered by their clients or to provide bank accounts (client accounts).

To hide illegitimate sources, charities and NGOs can be established to receive donations that stem from criminal activities and to fund terrorist activities. Some solicitors arrange to hold funds in their clients' accounts or in an off-shore trust, making the identification of the true beneficiary impossible. Other services offered by lawyers include advising on complex financial transactions and investment schemes. The law firms in question are not expected to become involved, but rather to serve as a shield of legitimacy to give third parties confidence.

Non-profit organizations

The world should take notice of what the US has done with respect to its non-profit sector. Independent Sector, a major private national organization that promotes the non-profit sector, explored ways to apply elements of the American Sarbanes-Oxley law to non-profits (NPOs).

The Sarbanes-Oxley Act and implications for non-profit organizations provides some practical recommendations on promoting effective oversight of NPOs: "(1) understand fully all laws regarding compensation and benefits to directors and executives and establish a conflict of interest policy and a regular and rigorous means of enforcing it; (2) establish an independent and competent audit committee, with specific responsibilities for auditors; (3) ensure certified financial statements with Board review and approval; (4) use proper disclosure forms if required by the national government; (5) develop, adopt and disclose a formal process to deal with complaints and prevent retaliation; and (6) have a written, mandatory document retention and periodic destruction policy which includes guidelines for electronic files and voicemail."

FATF Interpretive Note to Special Recommendation VIII, "Non-Profit Organizations" explains the objectives of the Recommendation and offers specific measures that countries should put into place to ensure that their non-profit sectors are not misused for terrorist or illegal or illicit financing purposes.

Money laundering and the internet

It is a common belief that the internet provides new and undetectable methods of money laundering ("cyber laundering"). However, the internet is nothing more than a messaging system. To move money, banks move information by several different kinds of messaging systems.

Identifying customers is the primary problem arising from internet usage. Though emails leave audit trails, there are ways to circumvent such traces. Characteristics of internet banking (easy access, depersonalized contact between customer and financial institutions and the speed of electronic transactions) make customer identification and the monitoring of transactions difficult for the authorities.

In a recent report, FATF found that in the context of internet banking –

- Proof of signature authority for accounts is not always available;
- Lack of human intervention makes the detection of suspicious activities more difficult;
- Large number of accounts per manager makes monitoring ineffective;
- Determination of jurisdiction for licensing purposes is difficult;

- Regulatory supervision and law enforcement are made complex because of difficulty in determining where on-line-transactions took place.

FATF has also identified what they call NPM – New Payment Methods. These consist of prepaid cards, electronic passes, mobile payments, internet payment services and digital precious metals. These are explored in a FATF Report of October 2006. New techniques continue to evolve.

To reduce online money laundering, the FATF recommends that Internet Service Providers (ISPs):

- Maintain reliable subscriber registers;
- Establish log files with traffic data relating internet protocol number to subcribers and to telephone numbers used in making connections;
- Maintain information for up to a year;
- Make information available to law enforcement agencies.

The important personnel issues to consider are privacy and confidentiality. One of the internet's advantages is that it is a largely unregulated medium, allowing free access to, and exchange of, information. The conflict between freedom of access and the demands to track suspicious transactions has yet to be resolved.

Worldwide initiatives on cyber laundering include the Draft Council of Europe Convention on Cybercrime, and that promulgated by the Electronic Banking Group of the Basel Committee. ICC Commercial Crime Services (CCS) has also done important work in this field.

Deterrence and countermeasures: company responsibilities

Several means of deterrence have garnered broad support. Companies concerned with good corporate governance should work AML practices into their own normal accounting and financial control systems. To assure adherence, such initiatives should be backed up by commitments from the Board of Directors as to monitoring compliance and imposing sanctions for failure to do so;

- The first step is to access your own risk profile and vulnerability to money laundering. Check your internal control systems, policies and operations;
- Establish internal AML policies and procedures and put senior people in charge of compliance and staff training;
- The fundamental theme common to most of the counter measures is the old maxim, *Know Your Customer (KYC)*" and its corollary *Know the Counter Partners*. Identify and verify them through third party due diligence. Maintain files on them. Know who you are dealing with at both ends of a transaction. Report on suspicious persons such as Politically Exposed Persons (PEP) and those with criminal records or associations;

- *Know Your Business (KYB)*" is another vital concept. Protect your integrity and reputation. Know how, when and where to recognize unusual transactions;
- *Know Your Administration.* Accurate and complete record-keeping and reporting compliance is crucial to protect your own business and ensure the functioning of an anti-money laundering system. Create audit trails. Audit to test and track your own AML compliance systems;
- Recognize suspicious transactions and transaction sizes and report them to internal compliance officers and the competent authorities in accordance with anti-money laundering regulations, laws and policies. Check the suspicious indicators lists for guidelines;
- Educate, train, monitor and periodically test employees to create and maintain their awareness of the dangers money laundering poses to them as individuals and to the financial well-being and reputation of their companies;
- Develop and impose sanctions for lapses, negligence and wanton disregard of approved AML practices.

Legislation

The next two sections deal with national and regional legislation, international conventions, the OECD, the UN and private sector organizations' individual and collective efforts to be collaborative in addressing and countering money laundering.

While AML laws have been or are being adopted in over 120 countries, no country yet requires its financial institutions to detect money laundering. Realistically, the most they can do is to require that "suspicious transactions" (hard to define) be reported, subject to a plethora of regulations and policies. Despite the pressing need, which is slowly being recognized by nation states, the effectiveness of anti-money laundering laws has been mixed, i.e., better than having no laws at all, but falling far short of the ideal of strict, fair and universal enforcement with well-knit international cooperation within and between governments, regulatory and supervisory authorities, law enforcement agencies, the judiciary and the private sector. As usual, vigorous enforcement is limited to too few countries.

FIUs

A major part of a country's AML regime is its Financial Intelligence Unit (FIU). The Egmont Group of FIUs, formed in 1995, is the international standard setter for FIUs, and has adopted the current definition of an FIU: "A central, national agency responsible for receiving (and as permitted) requesting, analyzing and disseminating to competent authorities, disclosures of financial information: concerning suspected proceeds of crime and potential financing of terrorism, or required by national legislation or regulation, in order to combat money laundering and terrorist financing."

As of June 2008, 108 member countries of the Egmont Group had established FIUs. The Egmont Group's definition of an FIU is entirely consistent with FATF's Forty Recommendations.

The UN

The UN has published a Legislative Guide for the United Nations Convention Against Transnational Organized Crime and the Protocols thereto. The guide spells out the "basic requirements of the Convention and the Protocols thereto, as well as the issues that each State party must address". It also furnishes a "range of options and examples that national drafters may wish to consider as they try to improvement the Convention and its Protocols".

The United Nations' International Convention for the Suppression of the Financing of Terrorism (1999) has attracted recent attention. The Convention only came into force on 10 April 2002 after years of being ignored. As of this writing, it had 132 signatories, with 42 parties having ratified the Convention. Since the Convention had not come into force by 11 September 2001, the UN Security Council – calling on all nations to sign, ratify and implement all relevant conventions criminalizing terrorism – on 28 September 2001 adopted Resolution 1373, which provides the primary legal basis for requiring member states of the UN to take concrete steps to suppress terrorist funding (a resolution by the Security Council taken in response to a threat to international peace and security is legally binding).

The UN Convention Against Corruption (UNCAC), adopted on 31 October 2003 (see Chapter 2), tries to cover all activities related to deterring, preventing, detecting, evidence gathering, cross-border cooperation, prosecuting those concerned and recovering the ill-gotten gains of corruption. The Convention, which entered into force two years later on 14 December 2005, contains provisions which address money laundering. As of this writing only 117 countries had ratified or accepted the Convention and passed domestic laws to implement it. Monitoring and enforcement of these laws remain uncertain.

Among other provisions, the 2001 UN Security Council Resolution 1373 stipulates that countries must cooperate in criminal investigations and other proceedings, as required by the earlier 1988 United Nations Vienna Convention against Illicit Traffic in Narcotics Drugs and Psychotropic Substances.

EU initiatives

At a regional level, several organizations have adopted conventions or other agreements to combat terrorism, including regulations concerning money laundering and/or designated laws that solely tackle money laundering. For example, the European Union in November 2001 widened the scope of the original EU money laundering directive in its Second EU Money Laundering Directive (Directive 2001/97/EC) amending Council Directive 91/308/EEC. The Directive required EU member states to update their national legislation by June 2003. It criminalizes laundering the proceeds of all serious crimes; extends its applicability to a series of non-financial professionals who are believed to offer or provide vital services for criminals (e.g., casinos, bureaux de change, auctioneers, lawyers, notaries, estate agents, fund transporters and dealers in high cost goods); extends the "KYC" record-keeping and suspicious transaction reporting requirement to external accountants and auditors, notaries, lawyers and others.

Other legislative initiatives

Other legislative developments include the following:

- 1990 Council of Europe Convention on Laundering, Search, Seizure and Confiscation of the Proceeds of Crime;
- 1992 Resolution of International Organization of Securities Commission (IOSCCO);
- 1998 BIS – Basel Committee on Banking Supervision – Prevention of criminal use of the banking system for the purpose of money laundering;
- 1999 The Communique of the G8 Finance Ministers in Moscow calling for "gatekeepers" – attorneys, accountants, auditors – to be required to report suspicious transactions of their clients to national authorities "The Gatekeeper Initiative";
- 2001 Egmont Group of Financial Intelligence Units – Statement of Purpose;
- 2004-2006 Basel II Framework adopted by the BIS.

A number of individual countries enacted new legislation on money laundering or extended laws that were already in place. Some did so under pressure by the FATF, others in a voluntary attempt to intensify the fight against terrorist financing.

Examples are:

- China: The Peoples Bank of China (Central Bank) AML Regulations effective 1 March , 2003;
- Thailand: The Anti Money Laundering Act of B.E. 2542 (1999). Created the legal authority for the legal Anti-Money Laundering Office.
- UK: Proceeds of Crime Bill 2002 and Financial Services and Markets Act 2000; Anti-Terrorism Act, Crime and Security 2001;
- US: International Money Laundering Abatement and Anti-Terrorism Act of 2001 (USA Patriot Act) signed into law on 26 October 2001. This landmark legislation (see box) contains provisions enhancing US domestic security, improving surveillance procedures, cutting off sources of terrorist finance, protecting US borders and providing for the victims of terrorism;
- Russia established a Committee of Financial Monitoring in November 2001 that will operate as the country's financial intelligence unit (FIU);

- Israel issued regulations concerning the identification and reporting of suspicious transactions and record-keeping for stock exchange members, port folio managers, insurance companies and provident funds in November 2001;
- Philippines: Anti-Money Laundering Act of 2001;
- EU: Directive 2005/60/EC on the prevention of the use of the financial system for the purpose of money laundering and terrorist financing, implementation by 15 December, 2007.

USA Patriot Act passed by the US Congress, 25 October 2001 (excerpts)

SEC. 314. COOPERATIVE EFFORTS TO DETER MONEY LAUNDERING.

(a) COOPERATION AMONG FINANCIAL INSTITUTIONS, REGULATORY AUTHORITIES, AND LAW ENFORCEMENT AUTHORITIES

(1) REGULATIONS

The Secretary shall, within 120 days after the date of enactment of this Act, adopt regulations to encourage further cooperation among financial institutions, their regulatory authorities, and law enforcement authorities, with the specific purpose of encouraging regulatory authorities and law enforcement authorities to share with financial institutions information regarding individuals, entities, and organizations engaged in or reasonably suspected based on credible evidence of engaging in terrorist acts or money laundering activities.

(2) COOPERATION AND INFORMATION SHARING PROCEDURES

The regulations adopted under paragraph (1) may include or create procedures for cooperation and information sharing focusing on(A) matters specifically related to the finances of terrorist groups, the means by which terrorist groups transfer funds around the world and within the United States, including through the use of charitable organizations, nonprofit organizations, and nongovernmental organizations, and the extent to which financial institutions in the United States are unwittingly involved in such finances and the extent to which such institutions are at risk as a result;

(B) The relationship, particularly the financial relationship, between international narcotics traffickers and foreign terrorist organizations, the extent to which their memberships overlap and engage in joint activities, and the extent to which they cooperate with each other in raising andtransferring funds for their respective purposes; and

(C) Means of facilitating the identification of accounts and transactions involving terrorist groups and facilitating the exchange of information concerning such accounts and transactions between financial institutions and law enforcement organizations.

Other worldwide initiatives

Apart from the OECD and UN Conventions and the new laws mentioned above, there have been other international efforts to counter money laundering. AML laws, policies and practices are gaining broad acceptance among nation states and regional and international organizations.

FATF

In 1989, the G-7 countries created the Financial Action Task Force, the "FATF", mentioned previously, an independent intergovernmental agency consisting of 29 (now 34 plus 2 observers and 175 jurisdictions in the FATF network) countries (including the major economies) and two regional organizations. FATF's purpose is to examine and report on measures to combat money laundering, to monitor implementations of counter money laundering measures, to track and review money laundering activities in combating the financing of terrorism and otherwise promote FATF activities and advise members and non-member countries. This global watchdog has its headquarters located within the OECD in Paris, France, though it is not part of the OECD.

In 1990, FATF issued its now famous Forty Recommendations which"provided a comprehensive blueprint for action against money laundering, covering the criminal justice system and law enforcement, the financial system and its regulations; and international cooperation". Amended in 1996 and then again in 2003 to reflect changes in money laundering trends and potential future threats, the Forty Plus Nine Special Recommendations (of 2001) are the most comprehensive set of AML directives yet created for governments, legislatures, law enforcement, financial institutions and businesses in general. They are under review again for updating in light of FATF's expanded responsibilities.

FATF conducts an annual review to identify Non-Cooperative Countries or Territories (NCCT) – a "name and shame" campaign – aimed at countries and territories that do not comply with the FATF's 25 AML criteria. It also monitors compliance with its Forty Plus Nine Recommendations. FATF reported that as of 13 October 2006 there were no NCCT countries or territories. All jurisdictions have finally complied.

The FATF also monitors compliance with its Forty Plus Nine Special Recommendations through its Mutual Evaluation Process. This has represented a central pillar of the work of FATF over the last ten years and is aimed at assessing the effectiveness of the anti-money laundering systems in FATF member jurisdictions. These evaluations are based on the Forty Recommendations 2003 and the Nine Special Recommendations 2001 and use the Anti-Money Laundering/Combating Terrorist Financing (AML/CFT) Methodology 2004.

Rounds of mutual evaluations for its members are ongoing. The scope of these evaluations is to assess whether the necessary laws, regulations or other measures required under the new standards are in force and effect, that there has been a full and proper implementation of all necessary measures and that the system in place is effective.

In 2001, FATF's mission was expanded to include combating terrorist financing. Eight Special Recommendations (SRs) implementing this new objective were concurrently adopted. All countries were called upon to ratify and implement the UN Convention on Suppression of Financing of Terrorism, SC Resolution 1373 and numerous related measures. The Ninth FAFT SR was adopted and addresses cross-border cash movements by terrorists and criminals.

Wolfsberg Group of Banks

Other international self-regulatory organizations, for example, the Basel Committee on Banking Supervision and the Wolfsberg Group of Banks, now numbering twelve, have focused on extending standards for international financial regulations to cover transparency issues.

The Wolfsberg Anti-Money Laundering Principles for Private Banking were published, in cooperation with Transparency International, in October 2000 and revised in May 2002. In 2007, the Wolfsberg Group issued its "Statement against Corruption", again in close association with Transparency International and the Basel Institute on Governance. This Statement identifies some of the measures financial institutions may consider in order to prevent corruption in their own operations and protect themselves against the misuse of their operations in relation to corruption.

OECD

An indirect initiative started in 1998 is the OECD's List of Uncooperative Tax Haven naming countries or territories that have not committed to the principles of transparency and effective exchange of information. Another OECD initiative concerns the misuse of corporate entities for money laundering, bribery and corruption – a new OECD publication, *Behind the Corporate Veil: Using Corporate Entities for Illicit Purposes* – urges governments to combat such misuse by ensuring the availability of information about ownership and control of corporate entities.

IMF/World Bank

Since 2000, the International Monetary Fund and the World Bank have joined the world of AML and counter terrorist funding. They focus on threats and vulnerabilities within their mandates.

Private sector

In general, unfortunately, industry-led initiatives (especially on a domestic level) seem to be lacking, but some organizations are beginning to catch up with responsible governance practices. ICC, Transparency International, the World Economic Forum's Partnering Against Corruption Initiative and the UN Global Compact are jointly addressing this issue of promulgating common standards against corruption and money laundering.

International and regional bodies

A variety of international and regional bodies have issued or adopted similar guidelines and initiatives, in whole or in part. The United Nations, in cooperation with leading anti-money laundering organizations, has established the International Money Laundering Information Network (IMoLIN). This is an internet-based database that includes legislation and regulation throughout the world (AMLID), as well as an electronic library and a calendar of events in the anti-money laundering/countering the financing of terrorism fields. Several other specialized agencies are important in the fight against corruption and money laundering: the International Organization of Securities Commissions, the European Union (EU), the Council of Europe, Gulf Cooperation Council, Organization of American States (OAS), South Pacific Forum, Council for Security Cooperation in the Asia-Pacific (CSCAP), INTERPOL, ASEANPOL, World Customs Organisation (WCO), Bank for International Banking Security Association and the Banking Federation of the European Union.

CARIN

One of the newest (established in 2004) groups to join the fight against criminal profits is the Camden Asset Recovery Inter-Agency Network (CARIN). Originally an initiative within the European Union, CARIN is now connected to EUROPOL and is an informal international network for tracing, freezing, seizing and confiscating the proceeds from criminal activities. The network will assist in setting up national points of contact or help with the preparation of legislation regarding the recovery of assets. It also serves as a medium for the exchange of best practices with its database which will be accessible to police officers and prosecutors from all over the world.

Summary of Major International Developments since 1999

FATF

- Annual Review to Identify Non-Cooperative Countries or Territories;
- Annual Report on Money Laundering Typologies;
- Review of Forty Recommendations;
- Eight Special Recommendations and Self-Assessment Exercises;
- Guidance for Financial Institutions in Detecting Terrorist Financing.

Basel Committee on Banking Supervision

- Custom Due Diligence Guidelines for Banks in October 2001.

Wolfsberg Group

- Adoption of the Wolfsberg Principles – a set of global anti-money laundering; guidelines for international private banks – October 2000, revised May 2002;
- Wolfsberg Statement on the Suppression of Financing Terrorism, including a review of the Wolfsberg Principles.

Guidelines and recommendations for setting KYC standards

A number of international and domestic KYC guidelines and recommendations have been designed for particular industries (e.g., banking). Guidelines and regulations are normally not legally binding but can become effective, either by voluntary adherence to such agreements/contractual obligations and/or adoption into domestic law. Most of the current guidelines concern financial institutions:

- FATF's Forty Plus Nine Special Recommendations;
- Customer Due Diligence for Banks" by Basel Committee on Banking Supervision;
- Bank of International Settlement Rules (BIS Rules);
- Wolfsberg Principles (Global Anti-Money Laundering Guidelines for Private Banking that have been adopted by 12 major international banks);
- International Association of Insurance Supervisor Rules;
- National laws and regulations, e.g., in the UK, Joint Money Laundering Steering Group Guidance Notes (JMLSG Guidelines) that provide guidance for different professions.

Sources of information

The FATF annual reports and reports on types of money laundering are some of the best sources of information on the subject. See the FATF website at www.oecd.org/fatf/reports.html. FATF's Forty Plus Nine Special Recommendations can also be downloaded from this site.

In 2006, the World Bank and the International Monetary Fund published their second edition of the *Reference Guide to Anti-Money Laundering and Combating the Financing of Terrorism*. It includes items including international standards setters, impacts on development, regional bodies and relevant groups, legal system requirements, preventive measures, international cooperation and the Bank's and IMF's respective roles. See their websites at www.worldbank.org and www.imf.org respectively, and in their site search engines type in the phrase "money laundering".

Another source of current information on money laundering is "Money Laundering Alert" by Alert Global Media, a subscription service which is available at www.moneylaundering.com. Its list of "suspicious activities" is instructive.

For more detailed descriptions of money laundering techniques and how they work, case studies can be found in the *Money Laundering Guide* published in mid-1998, as amended, by the Commercial Crime Bureau of ICC, located in Barking, England, UK. See a more recent book from the Commercial Crime Bureau, *Preventing Financial Instrument Fraud: The Money Launderer's Tool*, published in 2002 and also available from www.iccbooks.com.

By far the most comprehensive website for information and sources on "Money Laundering – how it is done, and what is being done about it; A guide to sources" is found at www.projects.ex.ac.uk/RDavies/arian/scandals/launder.html.

See also "Billy's Money Laundering Information Web Site" at www.laundryman.u-net.com. Another interesting site is the US Government's Financial Crimes Enforcement Network at www.ustreas.gov/fincen.

As to a list of and reports on a myriad of financial scandals, visit www.projects.ex.ac.uk/RDavies/arian/scandals/

For readers who want more information, refer to lists of internet links on the Web. The authors typed in "money laundering" on www.google.com and got 5,870,000 results. For British-oriented material, see the money laundering compliance website at www.countermoneylaundering.com and www.compliance.co.uk. Also, periodically check the web site of Transparency International, the coalition against corruption in international business at http://www.transparency.org. See also www.globalkyc, which gives practical advice to companies; www.vortexcentrum.com dealing with AML on a global basis; and www.imolin.org for UN AML programmes. To help reduce money laundering risks, check out the database of World-Check at www.world-check.com

Finally, there is a variety of magazine and professional periodicals on the subject. A particularly useful one is Foreign Policy, www.foreignpolicy.com.

Summary of the ICC Recommendations on Money Laundering

Money laundering is big business, i.e., thought to be 2/5 per cent of global GDP. Should a business inadvertently, directly or indirectly, become a victim of or a participant in any serious crime, the chances are high that its money will disappear through one or more money laundering ploys. Finding money and recovering it will be time-consuming and expensive, and, for some, embarrassing. Probably less than 10 per cent of the victims, corporate and individual, even make the effort to recover lost funds. Little of the lost money is actually recovered.

Yet it is not just corporate reputations that are at risk when money laundering occurs. Officers, directors and other individuals involved can face prison terms, substantial fines and confiscations. The costs of reputation repair and recovery are enormous, far outweighing the costs of precaution.

Self-policing by business is crucial to attack this scourge of international commerce.

Therefore companies should:

- Carry out a company-wide assessment of their vulnerability to money laundering;
- Establish internal anti-money laundering procedures to prevent and to punish instances of money laundering;
- Train staff to recognize the "red flags" of suspicious transactions;
- Ensure that all such suspicious transactions are reported to internal compliance officers;
- Keep current on AML techniques,policies,procedures,developments, legal cases and trials, new legislation and regulations of all concerned agencies and instrumentalities;
- Establish a compliance officer with responsibility for AML reporting directly to the Board of a company and its Chief Executive Officer;
- Keep complete records;
- Protect the company by putting in place the "Know Your" concepts detailed in this chapter.

David Lyman is Chairman and Chief Values Officer of Tilleke & Gibbins International Ltd, Advocates & Solicitors, Bangkok, Thailand. He was assisted in the preparation of this 2008 revision by Carlos Natera, who was a legal consultant at Tilleke & Gibbins International Ltd Thailand.

Chapter 10

Political and Charitable Contributions and Sponsorships

By Jean-Pierre Méan

RELEVANT PROVISIONS OF ICC RULES AND THE OECD CONVENTION

Article 1 of the 2005 edition of ICC Rules of Conduct on Combating Extortion and Bribery provides that enterprises should prohibit bribery and extortion, and defines bribery to include:

> " ... the offering, promising, giving or accepting of any undue pecuniary or other advantage to or by: a political party, party official or candidate in order to obtain or retain a business or other improper advantage, e.g., in connection with regulatory permits, taxation, customs, judicial and legislative proceedings".

Article 4 of the Rules deals with political and charitable contributions and sponsorships and provides:

a) Enterprises should only make contributions to political parties, party officials and candidates in accordance with applicable laws, and all requirements for public disclosure should be fully complied with. The amount and timing of political contributions should be reviewed to ensure that they are not used as a subterfuge for bribery.

b) Enterprises should take measures within their power to ensure that their charitable contributions and sponsorships are not used as a subterfuge for bribery. Charitable contributions and sponsorships should be transparent and in accordance with applicable law.

c) Enterprises should establish reasonable controls and procedures to ensure that improper political and charitable contributions are not made. Special care should be exercised in reviewing contributions to organizations in which prominent political figures, or their relatives, friends and business associates are involved.

Accordingly, ICC Rules of Conduct permit political and charitable contributions and sponsorships if they are made transparently and in accordance with the law, and are not used to obtain an improper advantage. Where the latter is the case, contributions to a political party or a charity or sponsorships constitute a bribe in the same way as any undue advantages granted to a public official, and should therefore be prohibited.

By contrast, the OECD Convention is limited to the bribery of foreign public officials and does not address the issue of political contributions. Item 10 of the Commentaries on the Convention recognizes that " ... there is a commonly shared concern and intent to address this phenomenon through further work". However, at this point, contributions to political parties or politicians who do not hold any legislative, administrative or judicial office are not covered by the Convention.

The issues

Political parties and democracy

Political parties are a crucial elements of a democratic system and are also a key factor in protecting the liberties of expression and association. When individuals have the right to express themselves freely and publicly, they will articulate different opinions, and those sharing the same ideas will naturally join forces to work toward their common goals. The expression and consideration of various currents of thought will permit the development of pluralistic structures in the political arena similar to what competition is to the economy. This will serve to reinforce the legitimacy of the decision-making process by screening issues through a wide spectrum of diverging opinions.

Attempts to establish democracy without political parties, such as in the early days of the American Republic, have failed. On the other hand, there cannot be true political parties in non-democratic systems but, at the most, factions representing tribal, ethnic or religious divisions with no plan for the future beyond their own interest. The "single parties" of authoritarian regimes do not permit the emergence of a differentiated public opinion but, on the contrary, diffuse the official "party line" and prevent any deviation from orthodox thinking.

Political parties are a bridge between state institutions and civil society (a role for which they are often challenged by NGOs). They develop a programme for state action, take positions on issues arising in the legislative process and make those positions known to the public. They also identify candidates for office and help them make their ideas known. Thus, political parties make an essential contribution to democracy by facilitating the participation of the largest number in the political process.

Essential financial resources

Political parties need financial resources in order to fulfill their role. Although a large number of volunteers will turn out to help in an election campaign, every party needs permanent staff for professionalism and continuity. The major area of spending, however, is for advertising, media time and printing in order to disseminate the party's ideas and programme and to mobilize voters.

The 2008 US Presidential election was arguably the most expensive political campaign in history. Its spending topped USD 500 million for each candidate. This was more than 15 times the amount spent in 1976 and more than one-and-a-half times the amount spent in 2004.

Although the costs of a US presidential election dwarf the costs of similar campaigns in other countries, there is a consensus that the costs of politics is exploding everywhere, with the most important cost item being electoral advertising in the media.

Power and funding needs

Political parties do not exercise power directly, but they are in the antechamber of power. They organize and designate the members of the legislature and, to a certain extent, the executive and judiciary. They commonly use their position as political power brokers in order to procure financial resources or for purely partisan goals. This may be the object of an explicit commitment to large contributors, but even if it is not, when the election has been won, party officials are likely to accommodate these backers in the hope that the flow of money will continue.

Contributions to political parties can help build up a network of contacts and secure access to the highest levels of government, which is not questionable as such. However, the interaction of private interests with those of party officials can also occur in such hazardous areas as the awarding of public works contracts, the granting of permits and licences, the drafting of new laws, the granting of titles or the nomination to positions in the civil service or to ambassadorial postings.

Where the regulatory framework is weak or lacks independence, political parties have been highly creative in harnessing resources often in questionable ways. In order to build up their war chests, political parties in power have used subterfuges, such as adding fictitious or non-working employees to the payroll of a state or local agency or levying a quasi-tax on construction companies that are awarded public works contracts. In all of these cases, the public interest is derailed by reciprocating financial support with illicit favours. It is not surprising that, at a time when the costs of the political process is increasing exponentially, widely publicized scandals in many countries have highlighted the dark side of party financing. These scandals and the lack of transparency in party financing have stirred up considerable mistrust of the political process.

Party financing

Several attempts have been made to curb abuses in the financing of political parties by addressing the various sources of funding. The questions which arise in this context include the following:

- Is it necessary or appropriate to limit the use of the candidates' own funds?
- Should parties be financed from public funds or is this a threat to their independence? If public funds are made available, should there be a threshold for access and on what basis should they be distributed, such as the number of seats in parliament or a percentage of votes received in prior elections?
- Should public funds be made available to parties indirectly by granting allowances to parliamentarians and parliamentary groups?
- Should the activity of political parties be subsidized in kind, such as by keeping voters' registries and making media time, the postal service, meeting places, offices and poster space available free of charge?
- Is it appropriate to encourage donors to contribute to political parties by tax credits and matching private with public funds?
- Should there be contribution limits for individual donors and limits (or even a ban) on donations by corporations or labour?
- Should anonymous donations or donations by foreigners be barred?
- Should there be disclosure and reporting rules in order to ensure the transparency of political parties? financing? Will these disclosure provisions deter excessive corporate or individual donations?
- Is there the risk of an escalating funds race if no limitations are imposed?

So far no single system has come up with the ultimate solution to party financing in spite of a wide spectrum of different approaches, some leaning towards more public funding, others towards limitations on private contributions and detailed reporting. There probably is no perfect solution, and the optimum compromise is some combination of these approaches.

Some legislative approaches to party financing

A brief survey of national approaches to party financing shows that the methods vary widely from country to country, going from total regulatory freedom to practical exclusion of private financing. Legislation on party financing is also relatively new and therefore changing quickly to close detected loopholes or adapt to new circumstances.

In a minority of countries, the financing of political parties is left entirely to the private initiative. This is the case in **Sweden**, where the issue has been raised and the decision taken to abstain from legislating. This is also the case in **Switzerland** where the issue has never been confronted head-on, and the financing of political parties is an area of great opacity. So far, this lack of transparency has not been perceived to interfere unduly with the democratic process, because of the relatively low level of funds invested in the political process. However, this is changing, and there is a growing unease about the increasing resources engaged in the promotion of party ideas and positions or the choice of electoral candidates.

By contrast, in **Belgium** the financing of political parties is made almost exclusively through public funds. Individuals may only make nominal contributions, and corporations are entirely barred from making any contributions. All parties represented in parliament are entitled to a public grant consisting of a fixed amount applicable to all parties and a variable amount proportional to the number of votes validly cast for a party in the elections to both chambers of parliament.

In **France**, the lack of control over party financing led to the use of subterfuges such as the use of phony "bureaux d'études" (consulting firms) or nationalized companies (most notably Crédit Lyonnais) to channel funds to political parties. The public exposure of these shams caused much public outcry and, in 1988, a first Act was passed to create some transparency in the finances of political parties. Several other Acts followed and political parties now have access to public funds proportionately to the votes obtained in the first round of the last legislative election and to the number of elected parliamentarians. Donations by legal entities are forbidden (except for donations by other political parties), and donations by individuals are subject to an annual ceiling (euro 4600 for donations to candidates and euro 700 for donations to political parties). Campaign expenses must be submitted to a special commission (the Commission Nationale des Comptes de Campagne et des Financements Politiques – CNCCFP) and are reimbursed if they do not exceed set limits. However, expenses incurred by third parties without the express consent of a candidate do not have to be reported and thus escape any control.

In **Germany**, a series of scandals culminated in 1999 with the discovery of a whole system of party financing by illegal donations put into place under the aegis of ex-Chancellor Helmut Kohl for his party, the CDU. Chancellor Kohl steadfastly refused to disclose the names of the donors and, as a consequence, his party had to pay a penalty of DM 47.5 million (some euro 24 million). In response to this and other scandals, efforts were then made to improve the transparency of party financing. Under the current version of the law, parties must file an annual report of their income and expenses, a balance sheet of their assets and liabilities and a list of all contributions received exceeding a certain threshold (contributions exceeding another (higher) threshold must be reported immediately). The annual reports are verified by auditors. The bulk of the resources of political parties comes from public funding and members dues; between 5 and 20 per cent comes from donations, with the Socialist party (SDP) being at the lower and the small parties at the higher end of the range. The German system has brought more transparency into party finances, but this transparency comes after the fact and, although the information is available, it is doubtful that it reaches the wide public.

In the **United Kingdom,** party financing is governed by the Political Parties, Elections and Referendums Act 2000 (as amended by the Electoral Administration Act 2006) which, as in France and Germany, was enacted following public criticism of the funding of political parties. It establishes an Electoral Commission to overview party financing and receive annual statements of accounts, as well as reports on campaign expenses and donations. Anonymous and foreign donations are prohibited. There is no limit on individual donations, but details of donations exceeding GBP 5000 (for donations received centrally) or GBP 1000 (for donations received locally) must be provided to the Electoral Commission. However, public knowledge of donations has not muted critics who keep questioning the motives of donors that contribute large sums. Questions were also raised regarding the provision of commercial loans which, it was alleged, may have been a way to dress up donations in order to avoid the disclosure prescribed by the law. In 2006, reports that individuals nominated for peerages had made such loans caused considerable embarrassment to the goverment.

The United States has the most comprehensive system, with a mix of disclosure and caps on contributions and spending. The principal legislation is the Federal Election Campaign Act (FECA), administered and enforced by an agency, the Federal Election Commission (FEC). However, the latter's lack of efficiency has drawn criticism. It is said to lack resources and its structure (six members, three from each party) has often caused its decisions to be blocked by deadlock. It has also investigated only a small number of alleged violations and has imposed rather mild penalties.

The FECA provides for limits on spending and donations from individuals or political action committees, as well as aggregate limits on all donations. It also bars unions and corporations from making donations in support of a candidate, although they may make contributions through Political Action Committees (PACs).

Until recently, corporations and unions, as well as individuals, could also make unlimited contributions of "soft money", i.e., funds spent on electioneering materials (badges, bumper stickers, yard signs, leaflets, voter registration). In 1995–6, soft money collected by both parties' national organizations exceeded USD 250 million. It was therefore decided in 2002 to ban the contribution of soft money in federal campaigns by the Bipartisan Campaign Reform Act (BCRA). The BCRA also restricted "issue advocacy", i.e., spending on materials supporting certain policies or issues (often the same as those advocated by one candidate), without expressly recommending the election or defeat of a candidate.

Another issue addressed by the BCRA in an effort to establish a level playing field is the use of their own money by wealthy candidates. The Supreme Court had decided that any limitation on candidates' using their own wealth was a violation of the first amendment. The BCRA then introduced a "millionaire opponent" provision, which raised the ceilings on individual contributions for the opponents of House and Senate candidates spending large amounts of their own money. Although the BCRA has been challenged on several counts in court, most of its provisions have been upheld.

International conventions

International instruments remain vague with respect to political donations. The United Nations Convention against Corruption provides in its article 7 (3) that: "Each State Party shall also consider taking appropriate legislative and administrative measures, consistent with the objectives of this Convention and in accordance with the fundamental principles of its domestic law, to enhance transparency in the funding of candidatures for elected public office and, where applicable, the funding of political parties". This is a discretionary article; parties shall consider taking legislative and administrative measures (emphasis added).

The Council of Europe Criminal Convention on Corruption provides in its Article 12 under the heading "Trading in influence" that signatories shall criminalize " ... the promising, giving or offering, directly or indirectly, of any undue advantage to anyone who asserts or confirms that he or she is able to exert an improper influence over the decision-making of [public officials or members of public assemblies] in consideration thereof, (...) as well as the request, receipt or the acceptance of the offer or the promise of such an advantage, in consideration of that influence ... ". The Committee of Ministers of the Council of Europe has also issued a Recommendation Rec (2003) to member states on common rules against corruption in the funding of political parties and electoral campaigns. Member states are encouraged to provide for disclosure of political donations and to possibly introduce limits on the value of such donations, and should also regulate or prohibit donations from foreign donors. Best practices in the area of party financing are further detailed in Financing political parties and election campaigns – guidelines published by the Council of Europe.

The OECD Convention on Combating Bribery of Foreign Public Officials in International Business Transactions does not cover political contributions. This has raised concern and led a TI-sponsored group of 28 individuals to issue, on 14 October 2000, a document known as the La Pietra Recommendations, in which they recommend to extend the scope of the Convention to bribe payments to foreign political parties and their officials; action taken in this respect could include a prohibition of trading in influence. Signatories of the Convention should also require appropriate disclosure of political contributions and expenditures and should prohibit corporations based in their own countries from making political contributions in violation of the laws of other countries.

Comprehensive information on party financing worldwide can be found on the site of the Institute for Democracy and electoral assistance (IDEA) at: http://www.idea.int/parties/finance/db/index.cfm.

Companies and political contribution

Companies must consider several angles when addressing political contributions to political parties or candidates for public office.

First, companies must comply which the law applicable to the contributions which They contemplate. This implies knowing the law of the country in which the contribution is made and also considering the law of the country from which the contribution will be made, as both may be relevant to the permissibility of political contributions and their tax deductibility.

Companies should also consider the possible reputational risk linked with the support of political parties or candidates to an election. Because of many scandals in the past, the public tends to view political contributions as an attempt by the corporate sector to influence the political decision-making process in their interest. As a consequence, they are viewed with distrust. For this reason, there are companies that have a policy of abstaining completely from making any political contributions at all.

There may, however, be good *bona fide* reasons for companies to support the democratic political process. Companies who decide to make financial contributions are well-advised to carefully reflect on how to proceed, as there are numerous pitfalls on the way. Should they support only one party or candidate at the risk of being on the losing side of an election or should they support two or more parties and candidates? In the latter case, should they spread their support equally or according to a neutral key (such as representation in parliament), or should they mark their preference for one party or candidate by making a higher contribution than to the other(s)?

Companies making political contributions should avoid the appearance of any link between their contribution and a possible decision in their favour. This could be the case if their contribution to one party or candidate is so disproportionate compared with the contributions of others that it makes the party or candidate overly dependent on them, or if they bring substantial support to a local candidate in an area particularly relevant to the activities of the company. The appearance of a link could also arise from the closeness of the contribution to the award of a government contract to the company or to a favorable decision in a matter of interest to the company. Political contributions should therefore be timed so as to avoid the appearance of such a link.

Several countries have disclosure rules for political contributions. In countries where this is the case, companies should, of course, comply with these rules. Where such rules do not exist, companies may be well-advised to consider disclosing their political contributions in any case. There is a definite trend for transparency of parties' financing, and the Transparency International Business Principles for Countering Bribery do, in fact, advocate the disclosure of all political contributions. The benefit of transparency is to diffuse any subsequent accusation of conniving to manipulate the democratic process. The disclosure can be made in the company's annual report or in its corporate social responsibility or corporate citizenship report. It can also be disclosed on the internet site or in any other way to make the information accessible to the public.

Because of the sensitivity of political contributions, companies should have a clear policy on whether they are allowed and, if so, to what extent and in which form. They should also provide for an approval process at high level at least for political contributions exceeding a pre-established threshold, and for a monitoring process in order to ensure compliance with the letter and the spirit of the policy.

Model Code of Conduct for Corporate Political Spending

The Center for Political Accountability has issued the following 11-point model code to provide guidance to companies on political spending :

1) Political spending shall reflect the company's interests and not those of it individual officers or directors.
2) The company will disclose publicly all expenditures of corporate funds on political activities. The disclosure will include regular reports on the company's website.
3) The company will disclose dues and other payments made to trade associations and other tax-exempt organizations that are or that it anticipates will be used for political expenditures. The disclosures shall describe the political activities undertaken. In the case of trade association payments, the disclosures will involve some element of pro-rating of the company's payments that are or will be used for political purposes.

4) Company disclosure of political expenditures shall include direct and indirect political contributions (including in-kind contributions) to candidates, political parties or political organizations; independent expenditures; electioneering communications on behalf of a federal, state or local candidate; and the use of company time and resources for political activity.

5) The board of directors or a committee of the board shall monitor the company's political spending, receive regular reports from corporate officers responsible for the spending, supervise policies and proce- dures regulating the spending, and review the purpose and benefits of the expenditures.

6) All corporate political expenditures must receive prior written approval from the General Counsel or Legal Department, and the company shall identify all senior management officials responsible for approving corporate political expenditures.

7) In general, the company will follow a preferred policy of making its political expenditures directly rather than through third party groups. In the event that the company is unable to exercise direct control, the company will monitor the use of its dues or payments to other organizations for political purposes to assure consistency with the company's stated policies, practices, values and long-term interests.

8) No contribution will be given in anticipation of, in recognition of, or in return for an official act.

9) Employees will not be reimbursed directly or through compensation increases for personal political contributions or expenses.

10) The company will not pressure or coerce employees to make any personal political expenditures or take any retaliatory action against employees who do not.

11) The company shall report annually on its website on its adherence to its code for corporate political spending.

Source : *Open windows: How Codes of Conduct Regulate Corporate Political Spending* and *A Model Code to Protect Company Interest.*

Companies and charitable contributors and sponsorships

Charitable contributions and sponsorships are commendable ways for corporations to further, and be associated with, cultural, educational, welfare or other non-profit making activities. They deserve to be encouraged. However, the rationale for a cautionary approach toward political contributions also applies to charitable contributions and sponsorships as they can be used to disguise an improper advantage. This is obviously the case when these contributions are diverted from the purpose for which they have been made and are used for private gain. That risk is greatest when charitable organizations are controlled by politicians or their relatives. It is also the case when a public official or a politician benefits indirectly from the charitable contribution or the sponsorship.

A contribution to a foundation fighting heart and circulatory disease and used essentially to finance the heart operation of a close relative of a public official is thus, in fact, a bribe and a donation to a local community to build a school at a time when the local government is standing for re-election can be as effective as a political contribution in supporting the incumbent administration. It is therefore essential to check the integrity of those involved and the use of the funds made available for charitable goals and sponsorships in order to make sure that they are used unequivocally in the public interest for the intended purpose.

Before making a charitable contribution or engaging into a sponsorship, a due diligence review should be conducted on the organization requesting the contribution or the sponsorship to make sure that it enjoys an untarnished reputation, does not have a hidden agenda and has the financial and personnel resources required to reach its goal. The charitable contribution should be made against a receipt, and the sponsorship should take the form of a sponsoring agreement specifying the use of the funds in detail and providing for the opportunity to check whether the funds are, in fact, used as intended. Larger amounts should be disbursed in several installments after checking that each installement has been properly used.

Fully disclosing charitable contributions and sponsorships is an efficient way to avoid subsequent accusations of manipulation. As for political contributions, the disclosure can be made in the annual report or on the internet site.

The TI Business Principles for Countering Bribery

The Business Principles for Countering Bribery issued under the aegis of Transparency International and Social Accountability International address political contributions and charitable contributions and sponsorships as follows:

Political Contribution

- The enterprise, its employees or agents should not make direct or indirect contributions to political parties, organisations or individuals engaged in politics, as a way of obtaining advantage in business transactions.
- The enterprise should publicly disclose all its political contributions.

Charitable Contributions and Sponsorships

- The enterprise should ensure that charitable contributions and sponsorships are not being used as a subterfuge for bribery.
- The enterprise should publicly disclose all its charitable contributions and sponsorships for approving corporate political expenditures

Summary of the ICC recommendations on political and charitable contributions and sponsorships

Although political contributions are allowed in most countries, there is an evolution towards more regulation. In reaction to scandals widely covered by the media, which have brought political contributions in disrepute, many countries have tried to impose limits on contributions or spending or the disclosure of either or both of them. International conventions are lagging behind these developments, but the regulatory framework is changing rapidly.

It is therefore important for companies to comply strictly with the letter and the spirit of all applicable laws and to establish internal procedures and safeguards in order to avoid possible adverse exposure in the media with the consequent negative reputational impact.

With respect to charitable contributions and sponsorships, the emphasis must be on monitoring the use of funds in order to avoid their misuse or misappropriation.

Therefore companies should:

- Establish a review process at high level before political or charitable contributions or sponsorships exceeding a certain threshold are made;
- Identify all political and charitable contributions and sponsorships made throughout the company;
- Inform themselves of all legal provisions applicable to political and charitable contributions and sponsorships and comply with them;
- Abstain from making political and charitable contributions and sponsorships in order to obtain or retain business;
- Avoid political contributions which could be misinterpreted preted as a way to influence the democratic decision-making process;
- Check that charitable contributions and sponsorships are used for their intended purpose and are in the public interest;
- Disclose their political and charitable contribution.

Jean-Pierre Méan has been General Counsel and Chief Compliance Officer for SGS SA, the world leading verification, inspection and certification company from 1996 until 2008.

Chapter 11

Private-to-Private Bribery

By François Vincke

RELEVANT PROVISIONS IN THE ICC RULES AND IN INTERNATIONAL INSTRUMENTS

ICC Rules of Conduct of 2005 encompass all forms of bribery, both public and private and, in Article 1, the Rules specifically refer to private-to-private corruption:

> "Enterprises should prohibit bribery and extortion at all times and in any form, whether direct or indirect, including through agents and other intermediaries:
>
> a) Bribery is the offering, promising, giving or accepting of any undue pecuniary or other advantage to or by:
>
> [...]a director, officer, employee or agent of a private enterprise in order to obtain or retain a business or other improper advantage[...]
>
> c) Enterprises should not (i) kick back any portion of a contract payment to government officials or to employees of the other contracting party, or (ii) utilize intermediaries such as agents, subcontractors, consultants or other third parties, to channel payments to government officials, or to employees of the other contracting party, their relatives, friends or business associates."

Article 21 of UNCAC contains a discretionary provision on "Bribery in the private sector":

> "Each State Party shall consider adopting such legislative and other measures as may be necessary to establish as criminal offences, when committed intentionally in the course of economic, financial or commercial activities:
>
> a) The promise, offering or giving, directly or indirectly, of an undue advantage to any person who directs or works, in any capacity, for a private sector entity, for the person himself or herself or for another person, in order that he or she, in breach of his or her duties, act or refrain from acting;
>
> b) The solicitation or acceptance, directly or indirectly, of an undue advantage by any person who directs or works, in any capacity, for a private sector entity, for the person himself or herself or for another person, in order that he or she, in breach of his or her duties, act or refrain from acting."

Article 22 of the UNCAC Convention is another discretionary provision, which covers the embezzlement of property in the private sector.

Article 7 of the Council of Europe Criminal Law Convention on Corruption criminalizes "active bribery in the private sector" in the following terms:

> "Each Party shall adopt such legislative and other measures as may be necessary to establish as criminal offences under its domestic law, when committed intentionally, in the course of business activity, the promising, offering or giving, directly or indirectly, of any undue advantage to any persons who direct or work for, in any capacity, private sector entities, for themselves or for anyone else, for them to act, or refrain from acting, in breach of their duties."

Article 8 of the same Convention covers "passive corruption in the private sector":

> "Each Party shall adopt such legislative and other measures as may be necessary to establish as criminal offences under its domestic law, when committed intentionally, in the course of business activity, the request or receipt, directly or indirectly, by any persons who direct or work for, in any capacity, private sector entities, of any undue advantage or the promise thereof for themselves or for anyone else, or the acceptance of an offer or a promise of such an advantage, to act or refrain from acting in breach of their duties."

Article 2 of the Framework Decision of the Council of the European Union of 22 July 2003 requires the member states of the European Union to criminalize both active and passive corruption in the private sector. The deadline for transposition of the Decision's provisions into national law was 22 July 2005.

"Member States shall take the necessary measures to ensure that the following intentional conduct constitutes a criminal offence, when carried out in the course of business activities:

a) Promising, offering or giving, directly or through an intermediary, to a person who in any capacity directs or works for a private-sector entity an undue advantage of any kind, for that person or for a third party, in order that that person should perform or refrain from performing any act, in breach of that person's duties;

b) Directly or through an intermediary, requesting or receiving an undue advantage of any kind, or accepting the promise of such an advantage, for oneself or for a third party, while in any capacity directing or working for a private-sector entity, in order to perform or refrain from performing any act, in breach of one's duties."

Article 1 of the same Framework Decision defines "breach of duty" in the following way:

"'Breach of duty' shall be understood in accordance with national law. The concept of breach of duty in national law should cover as a minimum any disloyal behaviour constituting a breach of a statutory duty, or, as the case may be, a breach of professional regulations or instructions, which apply within the business of a person who in any capacity directs or works for a private sector entity."

The African Union Convention on Preventing and Combating Corruption of 11 July 2003 also contains a provision concerning establishing active and passive private sector corruption as an offence.

The Introduction to the ICC Rules makes it clear that bribery is an offence against open competition. "The International Chamber of Commerce (ICC) has always been at the forefront of the drive for integrity in business life, because only a corruption-free system makes it possible for all participants to compete on a level playing field." The Introduction also stresses the importance of fighting private-to-private corruption: "ICC has [...] insisted on the need to confront private-to-private corruption (corruption between private entities), as this form of bribery also distorts competition and can no longer be ignored in light of increasing moves to privatization as well as the blurring of lines between the private sector and the public sector."

The OECD Convention is specifically aimed at the bribery of foreign public officials and does not deal with private bribery. However, private corruption is a subject of OECD concern. The OECD has placed the matter on its program of future work and has entrusted the ICC Commission on Anti-Corruption with the important task of making concrete proposals in this field. As a result, ICC, with the help of the Max Planck Institute of Freiburg, Germany, has performed considerable work to obtain a better understanding of private sector bribery and to compare the various regimes in a number of countries, with a view to defining the best possible options to combat private-to-private bribery.

Private corruption is the subject of sanctions in many jurisdictions, be they criminal, civil or administrative. Nevertheless, as the study discloses, prosecutors rarely start investigations or initiate prosecutions against private sector bribery, probably preferring to direct all of their energy against the bribery of public officials. ICC has, in recent years, made specific proposals to the OECD with a view to including provisions prohibiting private sector corruption in its instruments.

The Issues

Introduction

Not surprisingly, a chapter on private-to-private corruption does not come at the beginning of a handbook on international corporate integrity. Indeed, this form of bribery is not the first that comes to mind when one discusses corporate integrity. Corruption is first seen as an illegal effort to influence civil servants, political authorities or political parties – to "buy" a favourable decision from persons holding a public office or having political influence. This practice is almost universally condemned: it is considered to be intolerable that those entrusted with public responsibilities in the community would "sell" their independent judgment for money or some other consideration.

Private corruption, on the other hand, is directed to private individuals entrusted with the furtherance of *private interests*. This form of corruption, though considered illegitimate, does not generally meet with the same censure in the public eye as the corruption of public officials.

Why is this the case? Perhaps it is because the public views the decision-making power of public authorities and private companies in different ways. Judge Noonan puts it this way: "It is beyond debate that officials of the government are relied upon to act for the public interest, not their own enrichment. When they take bribes they divide their loyalty ... The [...] resultant conflict of interest is always a dilution of loyalty, always a betrayal of trust ... [This] trust comes with the office. A person is no mere power holder but an officer of government because he is invested with this trust" (John T. Noonan, Jr., *Bribes, The Intellectual History of a Moral Idea*, University of California Press, 1984, p.704).

Generally speaking, the expectations of society vis-à-vis corporate employees, managers and executives is different. These individuals are not seen to be entrusted with the responsibility "to act selflessly for the public good". They are supposed to act for the good of their corporations - and that good might be, but does not always have to be, identical with the common good - and in accordance with the instructions of their superiors. When managers and employees perform their corporate tasks, the common view is that they are pursuing the enrichment of their corporations and thereby contributing to the promotion of their own careers. They are allowed, and even encouraged, to pursue both these aims, as long as they avoid any conflict of interests between corporate and individual aims.

Corporate responsibility and the golden parachute

"It's no secret that CEOs have been raking in millions of dollars in salaries, stock options, retirement benefits, and perks like country club memberships and private jet use at a rate that far outpaces the growth of rank-and-file workers' wages. What's more, even when their companies don't perform well or when the top dog gets the boot, the CEO still gets out with a golden parachute worth millions in severance pay, retirement benefits, stock options, and other benefits.

Ordinary people have been crushed by the deepening housing crisis … 2,203,295: Number of foreclosures reported in 2007 … 12 months: Number of consecutive months of declining house prices, as of December 2007.

…While CEOs of the companies that led us down this path have been let go with golden parachutes.

Countrywide's founder and CEO Angelo R. Mozilo

$704 million: Countrywide Financial Corp. net loss in 2007. 11,000: Number of workers Countrywide laid off between July, 2007, and January 29, 2008.
$37.5 million: Approximate value of cash severance payments, consulting fees, and perquisites (including private airplane use) that Angelo Mozilo, founder and CEO of Countrywide, gave up after Countrywide's merger with Bank of America.
$23.8 million: Estimated value of Mozilo's company retirement plan in December 2006, the last year for which data are available. Mozilo did not forego these benefits.

Merrill Lynch's former Chairman and CEO E. Stanley O'Neal (ret. Oct. 30, 2007)

$161.5 million: Value of securities and retirement benefits that Stanley O'Neal walked away with from Merrill Lynch when he retired. O'Neal did not receive a traditional severance payment.
$7.8 billion: Merrill Lynch net loss for all of 2007.

Citigroup's former Chairman and CEO Charles Prince (ret. Nov. 4, 2007)

$17.4 billion: Citigroup write-downs on subprime related direct exposures in 2007. $9.83 billion: Citigroup's 2007 fourth-quarter loss. $40 million: Approximate value of Prince's retirement package, shares, and options in Citi stock upon his retirement in November, 2007."

(Center for American Progress, 27 February 2008)

Still, the actions of corporate personnel, while not directed against the public interest, are not always identical with it. Their loyalty, therefore, is essentially a corporate loyalty. But one has to consider that this corporate loyalty will comprise obligations towards a large number of people – not only the management, staff and workforce of the company, but also, shareholders, who may be dependent on the corporation for their retirement income.

Retirees and the 2008 financial crisis

An article in the 23 September 2008 edition of the New York Times pointed up the severe consequences for American retirees from the autumn 2008 financial crisis in which major banks and insurance companies failed because of risky investments. In part, the article read:

"Older Americans with investments are among the hardest hit by the turmoil in the financial markets and have the least opportunity to recover. … 'There's a terrified older population out there,' said Alicia H. Munnell, director of the Center for Retirement Research at Boston College. 'If you're 45 and the market goes down, it bothers you, but it comes back. But if you're retired or about to retire, you might have to sell your assets before they have a chance to recover … .'
For older people, there is no upside to the distress. 'They've got to adjust their expectations of retirement,' said Martin Baily, a senior fellow at the Brookings Institution. 'The market will recover, but you won't.'"

Directors, executives and employees have to act in accordance with their professional duties, while companies have to be sensitive to the implications of corporate social responsibility. A corporation must take into account the legitimate expectations from an increasingly large number of other parties on societal, ethical and environmental issues. The corporate community has to become aware that a failure within the corporate system often will have ripple effects beyond the company.

During the years 2007 and 2008, one has witnessed how risky corporate practices can have catastrophic consequences for the world economy. Prestigious financial and insurance institutions had to be rescued, many banks saw their liquidity position weakened or went bankrupt, huge amounts of shareholders money disappeared, employment was slashed, credit became rare and the general economy slowed down. Certain commentators expressed doubt about the capacity of private enterprise to organize itself properly. Irresponsible lending practices of many financial organizations during the property boom (the "subprime" scandal) linked to the use of sophisticated derivatives, such as CDOs, showed how deeply corporate mismanagement can affect people's prosperity and society's well being. The failure by corporate executives and managers to perform their professional duties diligently, the taking of badly evaluated risks out of sheer greed, the lack of transparency about such risks and the absence of adequate overview and control systems have caused considerable damage to the world community.

Conflicts of interest in the financial sector

The accounting and financial scandals, which, in the 1990s, battered corporate America and the rest of the world, not only had the effect of stimulating new oversight legislation in the United States and elsewhere – and new stock exchange rules to prevent conflicts of interests from occurring again – they also revealed how corporate trust can be betrayed by private individuals.

In the matter of initial public offerings (IPOs), the limits of corporate trust were difficult to define and easy to transgress. Certain top executives clearly gave a narrow interpretation to their duties to their corporation and the general public.

Specifically, many investment bankers managing IPOs provided lucrative rights to buy IPO shares to top executives of companies whose business the bankers wanted to obtain or retain. This resulted in an immediate profit for these executives when they resold the stock, because the offering price was set below the market price, which typically rose sharply after the offering date. This practice had several questionable consequences. The executives who received the profits usually did not report the favours they received to their own board of directors. Therefore, the board was in no position to scrutinize whether future business relationships with the investment bankers were influenced by these favours. It has also been argued that the investment bankers abused their duty to their IPO clients, to maximize the proceeds from the offering, by the favours provided to the bankers' other clients. In addition, these transactions were not reported to other investors in the IPO.

In these and other instances of private corruption, the recipient accepts the advantage granted to him by a person from outside the company, without informing the corporate bodies or persons (the board of directors, the supervisory board, the executive committee or the immediate supervisor). In doing so, the recipient does not act for the common corporate good – and certainly not in the public interest. This is a clear conflict of interest.

Another conflict of interest was uncovered when it was revealed that stock analysts affiliated with some investment banks were pressured by managers to produce favourable research on companies with which the banks did substantial business. In some cases, analysts published reports inflating a company's prospects, while within the bank they were downgrading their published recommendations. Shareholders and the general public were deceived, market values suffered and confidence in the financial system was undermined.

Different phenomena, same condemnation?

Corrupt practices within and between enterprises are unacceptable. In an impressive number of jurisdictions (such as Austria, Denmark, France, Germany, the Netherlands, Switzerland, the United Kingdom and most states of the United States), private corruption has already been condemned, and laws of a civil or criminal nature provide for appropriate sanctions, but, as noted above, enforcement cases are still relatively rare. In other jurisdictions, however, private corruption is a matter to be resolved between the employer and employee or between enterprises. In these latter jurisdictions, no legal intervention is available to cover private-to-private corruption and no judicial action can be brought to bear against it, except that employers can bring breach of trust actions against dishonest employees.

The FBI and corporate fraud

In a speech on 17 April 2008, Federal Bureau of Investigation ("FBI") Director Robert S. Mueller, III, warned white collar criminals that agents are busy at work. Citing an alarming increase in fraud (up by "more than 80 per cent since 2003"), Mueller provided some interesting facts to attendees of the American Bar Association, Litigation Section Annual Conference.

- The FBI has nearly 2,000 agents working on almost 17,000 white collar cases, "from public corruption and financial fraud to health care and mortgage fraud".
- The FBI has successfully prosecuted more than "490 corporate and securities fraud convictions in 2007" with more than 30 insider trading indictments affecting employees of at least four major banks.
- The FBI is investigating in excess of 1,300 mortgage fraud incidents and has identified "19 corporate fraud matters related to the subprime lending crisis".
- The FBI has its sights on "accounting fraud, insider trading, and deceptive sales practices".

Urging reform to protect shareholders and other relevant parties, Mr Mueller cited the need for independant (and arguably competent and objective) auditors, outside counsel and independent directors.

With the advent of deregulation, privatization and liberalization, large parts of what used to be the public sector have now been devolved to private enterprise. The lines between a state controlled economy and private enterprise have become blurred. Nationalized enterprises, such as public utilities, are now quoted on the stock exchange; public services companies, such as postal services, are subject to market economy rules; free competition has become the general rule and state monopolies are being dismantled. The distinction between public and private economy has become either purely artificial or only ideological. ICC approves of this evolution, as it corresponds to ICC's support for a more open and free world economy.

The transition to an economic system based on market values – rather than one based on state ownership – had been demanded by the world business community. But, as events in 2008 have demonstrated, a free market still requires a framework of workable regulatory rules. Morever, this development does not mean that large sectors of the economy, which were formerly subject to criminal laws on corruption, should now, as private enterprises, benefit from immunity.

Inversion of the roles

There is probably no better definition of private-to-private corruption than the one given by the late French philosopher Alain Etchegoyen, (*"Le corrupteur et le corrompu"*, Paris, 1995). Etchegoyen takes the example of a vendor of goods who wants to sell his products to a corporation and uses bribery as "a selling argument". He offers his products for sale to a purchasing manager, but by introducing corruption into what would otherwise be an arms' length transaction, he indicates his willingness to "buy" the decision of the purchaser of the goods. The latter is supposed to only consider buying the products offered, but in fact he offers his decision-making power to the corruptor.

In effect, the buyer becomes a seller and the seller a buyer. The organizational structure of the company is distorted, since the decision-making power is diverted from within the company to an outsider. The corrupted executive or manager abdicates his powers and abandons his freedom of judgment in return for money (or some other consideration). There is a significant risk that purchases will be made at overstated prices (in order to recover the bribes) and under unfavourable conditions, and that the products sold will not be of the optimal, or even the required, quality.

Some examples

- In July 2006, public prosecutors began an enquiry in Frankfurt and Munich involving a large auto parts manufacturer, having its headquarters in France and listed on the Paris Stock Exchange. In 1998, a scheme was allegedly conceived by the French company to pay bribes to executives of a number of large car manufacturers operating in Germany to help win business. The chairman and CEO of the French corporation was suspected of having known about these corrupt payments since 2001. He resigned his position a few days after the probe was made known in the media and admitted knowledge of the payments, though he declared that he had not been directly involved in making them.
- In April 2008, the media revealed that the largest Belgian supermarket chain (quoted on Brussels Euronext) had lodged a complaint with the Brussels public prosecutor against one of its executives in charge of real estate projects. There were suspicions that this person had rigged tender bids and accepted bribes from building contractors. He was fired by the company, his house was searched, money was seized, he was arrested and spent time in jail. The company then completely reorganized its control system.
- In November 2007, the Dutch Public Prosecutor's office revealed that it had carried out searches in 54 offices and homes in Holland, Switzerland and Belgium and had arrested 15 persons. On the day of the searches, no less than 600 public officials cooperated in the operation. The suspected persons were active in real estate management for three Dutch pension funds and had set up large building projects or sold parts of their employer's real estate at advantageous prices in exchange for considerable amounts of money. The Prosecutor's office reckoned that tens of millions euros were involved. Real estate, bank accounts and valuable items were seized.

In all of these cases, open, fair and transparent competition among potential parties was rendered impossible. Candidates with better offers or lower prices were outmanoeuvred by others using non-transparent methods. The efforts and resources spent to establish complex and costly bidding documents were wasted. The trust of *bona fide* bidders in an open bidding system was betrayed. The flow of money resulting from the giving and receiving of private bribes was not accounted for, nor was it recorded in the company accounts.

The same occurs when an employee or an executive, in exchange for money, reveals corporate secrets or shares confidential documents. This also results in an inversion of roles and gives the briber an illegitimate position of power in the company. If the data are related to a bidding procedure, the procedure is rigged.

Why disclosure and transparency matter ?

- Empirical evidence indicates that high standards of transparency and disclosure can have a material impact on the cost of capital.
- Reliable and timely information increases confidence among decision-makers within the organization and enables them to make good business decisions directly affecting growth and profitability.
- Information also affects decision makers outside the entity – shareholders, investors and lenders – who must decide where and at what risk to place their money.
- The information a company provides should show decision-makers and outside interests whether and to what extent corporations meet legal requirements.
- Disclosure helps public understanding of a company's activities, policies and performance with regard to environmental and ethical standards, as well as its relationship with the communities where the company operates.
- Disclosure and transparency, as well as proper auditing, serve as a deterrent to fraud and corruption, allowing firms to compete on the basis of their bestofferings and to differentiate themselves from firms who do not practice good governance.
- Research has demonstrated that disclosure and transparency also enhance stock market liquidity.

From the ICC Corporate Governance Guide. *The full text is on the ICC website www.iccwbo.org/cg.htm*

Corporate governance

The exchange of roles, transfer of functions, diversion of powers to an illegitimate outsider – all run counter to the most elementary teachings of sound corporate governance. The corporate governance theories, which are of American and British origin, have, in the last decade, contributed to new thinking about the conduct of corporate affairs. In particular, they have helped re-define the respective powers within a corporation; re-determine the roles of the shareholders, directors and executives; and impose higher standards of accountability.

Each part of the corporate system is supposed to act to achieve the corporation's interest, and to optimize the shareholder value. *The abuse of powers, misuse of corporate funds or assets, creation of conflicts of interests or confusion of roles are all inimical to a proper division of powers in the corporation, and contradict the basic rule that the shareholders' interests must be served first.* Shareholders have the right to a fair return, in addition to full and fair information through transparent accounts. No distribution of profits or transfer of value should be allowed that has not been approved by the shareholders or their duly appointed agents.

Accordingly, private-to-private corruption cannot be tolerated in corporations, because money, assets or value which belong to or are destined for the shareholders are diverted from their legitimate destination, while the power vested in an executive or manager is illegitimately transferred to persons who have no accountability to the corporation.

In addition, given the size of major corporations, the economic damage which can be caused by breaches of trust in the private sector can be just as serious as breaches of trust in the public sector.

The Solutions

The role of corporate codes

Employees, managers and executives should not act against the instructions of their principals or superiors and, above all, their board of directors. But how can they be expected to know, with a reasonable degree of certainty, what the board expects from them? Have they received clear, sufficient and understandable guidelines? When they are in doubt, do they receive the necessary practical guidance? Can they approach someone who, in confidence, will give them explicit advice?

To pose these questions is to prove the need for a well-written corporate code of conduct and a well-established system of compliance (see Chapter Five on Responsibilities of Enterprises). These codes are important tools in the battle against private, as well as public, corruption.

In fact, public corruption is quite well defined in national laws and international treaties. Private corruption, on the other hand – although just as destructive of corporate culture – is not so easily defined. Yet tolerating bribery in dealings with private customers has the same corrosive effect on the moral climate of the bribe-paying company as does the bribery of public officials. In both situations, bribe payments have to be kept secret, and accounting subterfuges, such as misleading book entries, are required. Senior management, corporate lawyers and auditors will be kept in the dark.

If an executive is asked what the difference is between public and private corruption, he may not know the answer. For him, corruption, in whatever form, is a kind of economic fraud that undermines market rules, can destroy the profitability of his enterprise and expose him to severe embarrassment. The subtle nuances between the public service status or the commercial position of the recipient of the bribe will not change his appreciation of the situation a great deal.

Consequently, those responsible for the corporation need to define clear guidelines in widely disseminated codes of conduct, which forbid any form of corruption. These codes not only help avoid misunderstandings, they can also provide assistance and support to all members of the corporate community. ICC recommends that companies draw up their own codes, consistent with the ICC Rules and tailored to the particular circumstances of their business. Companies should also develop clear policies, guidelines and training programs for implementing and enforcing the provisions.

In codes of conduct, private corruption should be explicitly and openly addressed. A code should define private-to-private corruption and clearly forbid it, preferably by using examples, so that no manager or employee can later claim being unaware of the risks incurred by certain behaviour. Special attention should be given to gifts and entertainment provided to private sector guests or visitors and the precise conditions imposed on them.

In this regard, a corporate code should define the limits for gifts that can be offered and received (see Chapter Three on Prohibiting Bribery and Extortion: Narrowing the problem areas). It should also precisely define (in a dollar, euro or other currency amount) what value a gift can have and address the question of whether such gifts can have value in terms of promoting business relations or whether they should be forbidden altogether, even if they have a very small or nominal value. Also relevant in this context is the question of entertainment. Should entertainment be limited to accepted business practices in the country or region concerned, or must it be declined in all circumstances? Should entertainment be accepted only if it can be reciprocated, or is it unacceptable only if it reaches such proportions that it can influence the receiver's judgment?

Generally, a good test is for employees to ask themselves whether the gifts or entertainment are of a nature that, if disclosed, would be an embarrassment for the receiver or the donor. Indeed, *an effective corporate policy would require that all such favours (above a modest amount, to be defined) be disclosed within the corporation.*

Codes: the importance of implementation

"Because corporate guidelines are voluntarily applied, critics often dismiss them as lacking teeth. But what matters is the way they are applied within individual companies. Corporate rules can carry just the same authority for the employees of a company as national laws do for the citizens of a country. *The key is management commitment*" [emphasis added].

Excerpted from an article by Maria Livanos Cattaui, Former Secretary General of ICC, in the magazine World Markets.

The implications for competition

In combating private-to-private corruption, corporations can make an important contribution to open competition. Rigorous and consistent policies against corruption among enterprises are crucial in this regard. The elimination of advantages granted by one corporation to the executive of another company will restore confidence in the "truth of the market" and ensure that companies transact business on the merits of their goods and services. No bribe should have to be recouped through inflated invoicing, and no sacrifice in quality should be based on unfair bidding procedures. If the free flow of goods and services is based on sound competitive practices, this will contribute to the well-being of corporations and the community as a whole. The establishment of clear rules in corporate codes by boards of directors – and their effective implementation – will demonstrate to the members of the enterprise and to the outside world that these policies are fundamental to the company as well.

Non-profit organizations

Non-profit organizations have the same responsibilities as for-profit companies. In fact, questions of private-to-private corruption in these organizations have been widely publicized. Public interest was first captured some years ago by illicit payments within sports' organizations, which attracted broad media and public attention.

In the 1990s, the corruption scandal surrounding the International Olympic Committee (IOC), and the payment of bribes to a number of sports figures generated a strong international reaction. Some cities that were candidates for organizing the Olympics provided various advantages (e.g., scholarships and expensive travel arrangements) to certain IOC members in order to "buy" favourable votes for holding the Olympics in their cities.

The reaction against these disclosures was forceful, because expectations surrounding the Olympic ideal were very high: the Olympic spirit and the holding of an international sporting event symbolizing international friendship were, in the public mind, associated with the highest standards of behaviour.

Corruption brought an element of disruption destructive of common values. The events in the sporting world vividly demonstrated that corruption is a pervasive phenomenon and that no culture, country or organization (public, private, for profit or non-profit) is exempt from corrupt practices.

Non-profit bribery: the Abramoff scandal

In a special report on 25 June 2006, The Washington Post reported that documents in the Jack Abramoff investigation shed light on how the lobbyist secretly routed his clients' funds through tax-exempt organizations with the acquiescence of those in charge. The federal probe brought a string of bribery-related charges and plea deals. Abramoff, a once-powerful lobbyist, was sentenced to five years and ten months in prison on 29 March 2006 after pleading guilty to fraud, tax evasion and conspiracy to bribe public officials in a deal that required him to provide evidence about members of Congress.

Dozens of e-mails revealed that Abramoff and his team considered tax-exempt groups a ready resource in their efforts to influence Congress. In one instance, Abramoff's team wanted to send two lawmakers on a trip to the Mississippi Choctaw reservation in 2001, but one congressman's office had concerns about accepting such a trip from a gaming tribe, so suggested that a non-profit organization, the National Center for Public Policy Research, sponsor the trip. Abramoff apparently viewed the non-profit as a convenient pass-through. Evidence revealed the Center was aware of the scheme.

At the time, the then IRS Commissioner Mark W. Everson said, "One of the most disturbing elements of this whole sordid story is the blatant misuse of charities in a scheme to peddle political influence." Tax experts said it is impermissible for a tax-exempt organization to act as a pass-through for money destined for private business purposes.

One lesson to be drawn is that non-profit organizations, no less than their corporate counterparts, should have their own codes of conduct and strict compliance programs to implement them. In this instance and others, the non-profit sector could well profit from successful examples provided by their colleagues in business.

Summary of the ICC Recommendations on private-to-private bribery

The economic and social climate in which corporations operate is constantly changing. Private sector rules, such as the ICC Rules on Extortion and Bribery, and international instruments, such as those emanating from the OECD, the Council of Europe and the European Union, have placed new emphasis on corporate responsibility in the modern age.

The evils of private bribery, long overlooked in international discussions, are now being seen in a new light. Clearly, private bribery has consequences that can be as destructive as those wrought by public corruption. The abdication of responsibility in a corporation, the willingness to place decisions in the hands of outsiders, the consequences of acts not in the interest of shareholders or the community, anddistortions of price and competition caused by private bribery all must be forcefully addressed.

Therefore, companies should:

- Develop or strengthen corporate codes of conduct to explicitly forbid acts of private, as well as public, corruption;
- Adhere to governance rules and regulations forbidding conflicts of interests by corporate managers and employees, as well as personal enrichment at the expense of the corporation and the public;
- Provide concrete examples in corporate codes of acts of private corruption which the company finds unacceptable;
- Place particular emphasis on problems raised by gifts or entertainment and provide guidelines as to their limits. Disclosure of all such activitiesis highly recommended; and
- Set up a system of compliance within the company so that people who commit unacceptable acts are subject to warnings and, in the case of gross violations, dismissal.

François Vincke is member of the Brussels Bar and Chair of the ICC Commission on Anti-Corruption. He is the author of Chapter 5 in this handbook.

Chapter 12

Preventing Extortion

By Maximilian Burger-Scheidlin and Thomas Pletscher

ICC RULES, THE OECD AND THE UN CONVENTION AGAINST CORRUPTION

ICC Rules specifically include a prohibition against extortion. Article 1, entitled "Prohibition of Bribery and Extortion", states: "Enterprises should prohibit bribery and extortion at all times and in any form, whether direct or indirect, including through agents and other intermediaries."

The OECD Convention focuses primarily on criminalizing the supply side of bribery. Bribery of foreign public officials is prohibited (punishable under the laws of the home country). However, the Convention does not adequately address the problems arising when companies are confronted with direct or indirect solicitation/extortion of bribes.

The UN Convention (UNCAC) goes further and, in addition, formally criminalizes the demand side (solicitation/extortion) and private-to-private bribery.

- Article 15 refers to "Bribery of *National* Public Officials". Here it is mandatory that national governments criminalize bribery as well as solicitation.
- Article 16 refers to "Bribery of *Foreign* Public Officials and makes it mandatory for national governments to criminalize bribery; it is discretionary to criminalize solicitation.

UNCAC has – as yet – no efficient monitoring process.

In any case, extortion cannot be used to justify or defend bribery. This would encourage the complicity of both sides in corruption and undermine all efforts to eliminate it. OECD Commentary No 7 provides that "the alleged necessity to obtain or retain business is not a defence" against bribery.

In reality, companies still operate in an environment in which bribery – though forbidden – is still prevalent in practice. In many countries the perception is that unless a company bribes its way through the administration, it will never be able to win orders and implement planned contracts, projects and investments.

Extortion – the deafening silence

by Maria Livanos Cattaui, former Secretary General of ICC

"Perhaps some observers have the impression that companies seeking contracts abroad willingly open their pockets and distribute largesse to a range of corrupt foreign officials. However, what happens in the bulk of cases is that companies are either told – or are strongly led to believe – that unless payoffs are forthcoming, no business will be coming their way. Blatant and discrete extortion is a fact of life, and it is a stain on international commerce."

Introduction

Corruption/extortion causes competitive disadvantages for honest businesses, unpredictability for investments (especially in new markets) and adds to the costs of doing business.

Businesses have actively supported international efforts to fight bribery. However, a company's decision to stop bribing is only the first step. It does not change the environment if a company does business where extortion is still prevalent. In fact, even when companies do not allow their executives and employees to bribe, businessmen are often confronted with demands to make payments in order to secure business, obtain a permit or receive official documentation. These demands can come in the form of either blatant or discrete extortion,

In general, large companies having an established market position and companies known for having a strict no-bribery policy are confronted less frequently with extortion or other forms of solicitation (except in large projects where political influence prevails). The companies that suffer most are smaller-scale companies entering new markets. Their smaller structures, fewer resources and recent appearance in the international market make them more vulnerable than larger and more experienced corporations.

Through the adoption of appropriate strategies, companies, both large and small, can reduce the risk of being faced with solicitation or extortion. SMEs especially need the concrete support of their home governments.

Extortion: some real-life examples

- A small manufacturer of specialized chemicals has sold its product for the last seven years to a giant textile mill in an emerging country. Their new purchasing manager indicates that its competitor had offered substantial gifts and wonders if the company can match these.
- A company bids in a public tender to build a power plant in a difficult country. Before it bids, it researches local suppliers for the needed construction materials and includes their prices (with a small margin) in its calculations. The company wins the tender, starts construction and then finds that there is virtually no cement available and that there are no import licences issued.
- Having made an in-depth study of costs, availability of qualified staff, local suppliers etc., a company decides to set up its factory in Country X. When construction comes to an end, it asks the local telephone company for 30 outside lines. One evening one of the telephone company's staff visits and asks if the company needs these lines in three days, three months or two years...
- A company has a manufacturing subsidiary in an emerging country. One day an employee of the local power supply company informs the company of impending power cuts. The power company indicates that these might be avoided with a little extra help;
- A company has finished construction of a plant to produce chemicals. All that remains is to recuperate the 15 per cent retention bond after a successful start-up. A messenger informs the company that it would be advantageous to pay 8 per cent to Mr X to ensure that the start-up runs smoothly and, following this, the protocol confirming the successful start-up will be signed;
- A businessman from a country rich in first-class raw materials offers a company interesting quantities of them substantially below world market prices. However, the company is asked to pay substantial funds to a Geneva account to assure a second delivery.

How bribing can lead to extortion

The problem is that once a company starts bribing, it will always be asked for more. It will not only have to pay to obtain contracts or licences or to start up factories, etc., but once local administrators, subcontractors and others in the business and social surroundings find out that the company pays bribes, scores of other people will find (or invent) an excuse to "kindly" ask for "favours". New artificial barriers will be erected, so that someone can show up to solve the problem. In short, if a company starts bribing at the outset, it will be subject to extortion throughout the years of the project's operation.

A company should also be prepared for some nasty experiences if it pays one solicitor of bribes but rejects another. It is easy for a disgruntled party to throw metal parts into machines, flatten tyres, put sugar into the tank of a car or delay the delivery of supplies.

Time and again, a "rejected" solicitor of a bribe will produce evidence – whether true or false – that a company has bribed an official or a private business person of the host country and show this evidence to this company with the intention of blackmailing it (by threatening to inform the press, the public prosecutor, the tax office, for example). Often companies will give in and pay and pay again. This also opens opportunities for blackmail, requests for protection money and longer-term industrial espionage.

Solicitation: the consequences

When faced with solicitation, companies can find themselves facing different predicaments:

- Solicitation can be made indirectly and implicitly, often via middle men. Companies are often told, or strongly led to believe, that with out payment of bribes, their planned business transaction will not be accepted.
- Often insufficient evidence is available to prove a case of solicitation. Therefore, companies may be reluctant to report incidences of solicitation for fear of facing defamation lawsuits.
- Extortion is not considered to be a defence against bribery under the relevant international conventions. Therefore, companies that give in to demands for bribes face the threat of criminal prosecution.

When demands for bribes are made in the early stage of business transactions, companies typically try to safeguard their business interests. If they turn to their home government for help, they face a dilemma – they have to guard against reprisals, such as the disqualification of the concerned company from the bidding process. On the other hand, if companies have already made large investments in a project, this renders it more difficult for them to resist extortion at a late stage of the venture.

A definition of extortion

"Extortion is unlawful exaction of money or property through intimidation or undue exercise of authority. It may include threats of physical harm, criminal prosecution, or public exposure. Some forms of threat, especially those made in writing, are occasionally singled out for separate statutory treatment as blackmail."

Britannica Concise Encyclopedia

Other difficulties in dealing with solicitation

- In many countries it is difficult to obtain quick and reliable information about the true costs of obtaining tender documents, licences, etc. Ideally, such information should be provided by the relevant authorities, ministries, etc.)
- Solicitation is often hard to identify when it is part of an on-going business relationship. A company may be in such a relationship for some time and not be aware that certain payments made in exchange for services rendered may be for the benefit of a public official and constitute a bribe.
- Invoices from agents may include items for "commissions" or "fees" which can be legitimate payments for services rendered – or may, in some instances, be disguised bribe payments. Accounting procedures aimed at greater transparency often do not detect instances of solicitation, because companies may not always know whether the fees paid are legitimate government requirements (e.g., fees to obtain documentation during a bidding process) or payments demanded by officials to improperly influence the outcome of a decision (e.g., fees in exchange for being short-listed or selected in a bidding process). Companies need to be sufficiently diligent to distinguish legitimate payment from the creation of slush funds.
- Even in countries where there is generally little enforcement of anti-corruption laws, the police and judiciary can be extremely efficient – "if they want to get you".

Public and private extortion – case studies

- A government official asks for bribes as a condition for granting permits to conduct business. Payments are to be made in cash or by purchasing paintings at excessive prices. In addition, he offers his services to identify potential business partners – for a fee;

- In a public procurement process, bidders have to pay a "reasonable fee" to obtain copies of necessary documentation. Later, they are asked to pay a substantial amount to be put on the short list and an even greater amount to win the bid;
- A manager of a supplier asks for a bribe to provide urgently needed materials;
- Employees organize a network to obtain kickbacks from their company's suppliers. The purchase prices are increased accordingly;
- An employee of a big corporation extorts suppliersto pay money into his account and provide travel vouchers for his family;to form another company (with himself as a major shareholder); to give him thousands of shares of a major supplier of his own employer;
- A company needs formal authorization to obtain export credit insurance for a project close to realization. As this authorization is not dealt with, a middleman offers his services "to solve the problem" for USD 1 million – payable offshore;
- A company suggests that granting an unsecured loan at favourable terms to a member of an influential family will ensure the unhindered acquisition of a substantial part of an infrastructure company;
- A machinery company pays low salaries, but provides generous incentives for individual performance. The sales manager has been reproached for poor performance. With a new contract in an emerging market, the frustrated manager pays a large bribe and secures a nice kickback for himself. A competitor learns about this and blackmails the director, who – over the next three years – divulges almost all of the company's secrets, including technical drawings.

What companies can do on their own

Even in notoriously corrupt societies, there are businessmen doing good business without having ever paid bribes. They have declared from the beginning that their corporate policies and principles forbid them to bribe, and they have kept their word. At the beginning, they were possibly viewed with some curiosity or suspicion by the potential solicitors of bribes, but their position was (mostly) respected. These businessmen promised impeccable quality, timely delivery (unless hindered by bribe solicitors), good, long-term after sales service, spare parts supply, etc. Everyone in the market knew that they were keeping their word, and their refusals to pay bribes were accepted.

Companies can lessen their exposure to solicitation by their own efforts. The following measures can substantially reduce the likelihood of solicitation from government officials and others:

Before starting to negotiate in a foreign country

Companies should –

- Do their homework in depth – draw up an in-house ethics or anti-corruption code. The CEO should make public statements to announce the new anti-corruption strategy to the media. Staff and salesmen should be trained in anti-corruption policies and techniques;
- Communicate to their staff that management knows that without bribes it will take more time to finalize sales and projects, but that the additional time will be largely offset by reduced costs (no bribes) and fewer problems during the life-span of the project. Furthermore, management should be prepared to lose some orders rather than pay bribes;
- Have staff on the company team who know both the country it is targeting, as well as its national customs, the legal and market situation and the local language;
- Educate employees and agents (as well as sub-contractors) in the host country, so that they know the laws and company rules. It will be necessary to translate their anti-corruption code into the local language and to insert anti-corruption clauses into employment and agent contracts; it might be necessary to re-formulate the code, so that the company's local staff interprets it in the same way as headquarters;
- Pay adequate salaries, especially in delicate sectors. Pay bonuses for the performance of whole teams, rather than individuals. In sectors where the result can only be seen in several years time (extractive industries, plant construction, finance), pay extra bonuses some years down the line to make sure that the responsible team takes the long-term view, rather than just have an interest in a first signature and short-term implementation;
- Research – in depth – the background of agents, consultants etc. with whom the company wants to work;
- Research future business partner(s) in depth, i.e., what is their company history, their personal reputation, the most influential managers in their company, their weak points;
- Research the government officials who might be relevant to their project. Are there officials higher up the ladder who are known to be "clean"? or, on the contrary – known to be "on the take";

- Research the legal situation, i.e., are there anti-corruption laws? Can one sue under these laws? Is there a functioning appeal mechanism to a higher court? Is there a law covering public tender? What is the legal timeframe for bidding? Is there an appeal process and authority against decisions of the tender board? (see Chapter 14 on Public Procurement);
- Draw conclusions – if the result is not encouraging, and there are no apparent ways around corruption, consider abandoning the project.

After starting to negotiate in a foreign country

Companies should –

- Communicate a clear "no bribe" policy. In its first negotiation abroad,the company should make it clear that it has a strict policy not to pay bribes or any form of "facilitation payment". The company may also wish to add that it offers excellent after sales service and that it will inform authorities of the host country about a bribe solicitation;
- Never let a solicitation (extortion) go unanswered. A company manager or staffer should not give the impression that he will think about the situation and/or refer it to top managers at headquarters;
- Inform the party with whom the company is negotiating that under their contracts the company is obliged to report any solicitation/extortion attempt to its headquarters and that it will report it to all relevant authorities;
- Communicate, that in case of solicitation, the solicitor will be sued for violation of local law in the local courts;
- Keep detailed records of all solicitation/extortion attempts with dates, etc., and later estimate the loss of time and increased costs due to them. When the CEO visits a high-level official in the host country, have him present this list and explain how much extra costs his staff have incurred due to extortion attempts;
- Insert anti-corruption clauses into all of its letters of intent, contracts, etc.;
- Provide assistance to subsidiaries in host countries. A company should establish procedures to assist employees with guidance from the head office and from staff whose internal responsibilities include dealing with these issues;
- Consider regular job rotations for staff in delicate sectors and countries;

- Establish intra-company help lines in a department that inspires trust (so that staff can discuss delicate situations without the fear of immediate consequences;
- Not cover up mishaps. When they occur, they should be discussed and lessons should be drawn from them;
- Make use of anti-corruption agencies, help lines or ombudsmen where they exist in the host country. These sources can be a first assistance point for advice in cases of doubt;
- Continuously check adherence to the company's anti-corruption rules;
- Try to reach an "integrity pact" with other bidders;
- Seek out organizations – such as national committees of the International Chamber of Commerce, Transparency International and local business organizations – to provide help and advice and to coordinate anti-corruption measures with the host country government.

International Investment projects

In many countries it is assumed, that unless a company bribes its way through the administration, it will never be able to implement his proposed investment. However, with the right preparation, an investor can better the situation and strongly reduce the likelihood of solicitation from government officials and others involved in the implementation of its investment.

As mentioned previously, it is important to be clear from the start, that the company has a strict policy not to pay bribes or any other form of "facilitation money". It will also help to have staff on the company's team who know the country the company is targeting for its investment and who speak the local language(s); to find (local) allies, who have an interest in the investment.

After the company specialists have made their in-depth research on the target country and region for the investment, as well as on the legal situation and the local actors, the company, at its first meeting may wish to inform its partners about its long-term strategy and show the advantages to their region (increased taxes, training, education, etc.). If necessary, it can inform its partners of the alternative options it has in other countries for the investment.

Local officials will find it difficult to solicit bribes, if they know that the company is not in a hurry, that all of the information on the project may be published, including transaction payments and that the local community will benefit from the project in terms of jobs, training and improvements in the living standards of local people.

In addition to talking to the relevant officials and politicians, companies should quickly seek help from the local community where they plan to invest. They should visit the local major, the local press, the local priest and all opinion leaders in the community and be prepared to help local inhabitants with their difficulties, to create jobs, to educate job applicants, but never simply to dispense money unless the villagers contribute their share, their physical work. etc. It must remain "their project".

Local politicians and officials will find it difficult to solicit/extort bribes or reject a project, if they know that the villagers want the project and that the project is good for the region.

Governments and international organizations

Governments, international organizations and various associations can help reduce the likelihood of extortion. When confronted with demands for bribes, companies need a contact person or department to which they can report these cases, find guidance and obtain support for possible action. Confidentiality and discretion must be assured. A contact independent from the prosecution authorities will enhance the business community's confidence in the reporting system.

Contacts should be established in embassies or consulates abroad. Companies seeking to determine whether a specific transaction could violate anti-bribery laws will find it useful to obtain a prior opinion from a competent body as to the legality of the transaction along the lines of mechanisms set up under the US Foreign Corrupt Practices Act (FCPA).

While the United States – the country with the longest experience of criminalizing bribery of foreign public officials – has established a notification mechanism in cases of solicitation and while other countries (e.g., Bulgaria, Hungary) have laws stating that extortion constitutes a defence, most current governmental actions focus only on the supply side, i.e., the offering of bribes.

At a minimum, governments should establish help lines so that their companies know where to turn in the event they are confronted with extortion. This procedure has worked reasonably well in the United States, and other countries can learn from it. Once help lines are set up, the OECD, as noted earlier, should establish networks to facilitate multilateral intervention.

Before doing business in a delicate environment, companies would do well to establish contact with the commercial counsellor in the home country embassy and explain their project. With regard to large projects, it will also be helpful to inform the ambassador to ask for guidance and the assurance of back-up. These officials may know higher officials in the bureaucracy concerned with the company's project. In some cases, they may communicate with these officials, endorse the company's anti-corruption stand and make it clear that they will keep a watchful eye on the project.

In the case of large, well-connected companies, embassy officials may engage in discussions with the host country's government to set up procedures and support and to explain their anti-corruption policy. If satisfactory solutions cannot be found, companies should carefully consider whether to do business in that country.

Streamlining regulation

Many instances of solicitation occur in areas of economic activity subject to complex, overlapping and non-transparent regulations. Government efforts to modernize and simplify regulations will be useful. Appeal mechanisms in bidding processes further reduce the risk of decisions being influenced by bribe/extortion payments. National governments should also work in tandem with international organizations to promote principles of good governance.

Raising awareness

The OECD and the signatory countries of UNCAC should do more to raise awareness of the OECD and UNCAC Conventions. An extensive educational process has to be implemented to accomplish that end. Business should be supported in its no-bribe policy by a clear message, directed to trading and investment partners, that the OECD and UNCAC Conventions require governments to criminalize the bribery of foreign public officials; consequently, solicitation will/should be in vain. When discussing the issue of bribery and other forms of corruption, the supply side and the demand side should be addressed publicly to make it clear that neither paying nor demanding bribes will be tolerated.

Furthermore, governments should be made aware that one reason for solicitation is the low salaries of government officials. Streamlining the tax system and raising salaries is a more efficient way to allocate resources and to improve the economy.

International cooperation

The follow-up mechanisms of the international conventions should encompass actions to counter explicit or implicit demands for bribes in close cooperation with business. Collecting data may be difficult, since formal proof will seldom be available and business secrets have to be safeguarded. Therefore, it will be necessary to establish reporting bodies as "filters" that can provide the necessary information in an anonymous and aggregated form. In order to avoid conflicts of interest, these reporting bodies should be separate from entities or individuals having competence in judicial or penal prosecution.

The World Bank, ICF and other multinational donor agencies have established increasingly efficient anti-corruption programmes and departments. They screen projects and establish blacklists of violators.

Therefore companies should:

- Prepare for their new business by doing their homework in depth;
- Demonstrate a quiet, relaxed, but clear strength in their negotiations;
- Never be in a hurry; never have rigidly fixed dates unless necessary. Many emerging countries do not have the concept of "time is money";
- Seek reliable information about the legitimacy of business arrangements from official sources not engaged in penal prosecution;
- Reduce exposure to solicitation by making clear from the start to counterparts that the company has a strict "no-bribe" policy;
- Establish procedures to provide employees with guidance when they are faced with blatant or discrete demands for bribes;
- Depending on local circumstances, inform local business partners that – as a basic policy – the company will respond to requests for extortion by reporting them to higher-level governmental officials or suing in local courts for violation of the local anti-corruption laws;
- Seek agreements with other bidders on contracts to ensure that competitors also resist instances of extortion or other forms of solicitation ("integrity pacts");
- Clearly signal that they may scrap their project(s) if their local counterparts demand facilitation payments (and be prepared to do so) – and openly let counterparts know of options the company has in other countries;
- Resist paying bribes in all circumstances, not only because it is illegal, morally wrong and a distortion of trade, but also because it can lead to extortion and "requests" for further payments.

Maximilian Burger-Scheidlin is Executive Director, ICC Austria and a member of the ICC Commission on Anti-Corruption.

Thomas Pletscher is Secretary General of ICC Switzerland and Vice-Chair of the ICC Commission on Anti-Corruption.

Chapter 13

Overcoming Corruption in Customs

By Sandy Merber and John Raven

Introduction

Customs integrity has acquired a recent, quite new importance in the wake of two converging strategic forces – an extensive set of proposals for the reform of many important border crossing procedures in continuing discussions on a possible Trade Facilitation Agreement in the World Trade Organisation (WTO), and the emphasis on border controls in global anti-terrorist security policies.

While serious and pervasive customs and associated commercial dishonesty is usually a reflection of a much wider cultural environment, customs officers are subject to exceptional temptation because they exercise strong legal, often discretionary powers in respect of two major financial functions – the collection of import duties and taxes and the control of declared export prices as a basis for repatriation of foreign currency receipts.

In many developing countries, customs collections on imports account for a very high proportion of the national revenue. Exports are a key source of scarce hard currency and double invoicing, with the profitable difference accruing to the trader in secure external accounts, is a widespread practice. Customs officers are uniquely placed to control and derive irregular personal benefits from both these cash flows. Traders and agents in corrupt cultures are subject to corresponding pressures to accede to customs illicit demands, or to themselves initiate illegal overtures.

These malpractices, regrettable enough in the context of a national economy, are now a notable international concern. They pose an increasingly potent threat to the reliable, rapid delivery of raw materials, components, sub-assemblies and products essential for modern globalized trading. They also distort and constrain its naturally free-flowing investment in production and processing facilities in many developing countries. There is, therefore, an urgent and obvious need for effective mechanisms to encourage, receive, record, report on and redress serious complaints of corruption.

All Customs services have extensive legal powers to instigate criminal proceedings against fraudulent traders and also the less formal, but sometimes even more formidable, resources of operational disciplines and penalties, causing commercially unacceptable systematic delays and uncertainties to consignments. As a result, there is little need to enhance Customs power to take action against errant declarants. The real need, rather, is for reliable means of securing a proper response to commercial complaints of Customs wrongdoing.

The revised World Customs Organisation (WCO) Kyoto Convention obliges signatories to arrange that aggrieved traders should have the right to pursue such complaints to an independent tribunal outside the Customs service. This may be very effective in dealing with some exceptional Customs irregularity in a normally law abiding environment, but is of little use in countries where official and judicial corruption is pervasive.

In such circumstances, where recourse to any national tribunal alone could be imprudent, the recent precedent set by Guatemala Customs could be instructive. In their very comprehensive modernization programme Guatemala Customs, with World Bank backing, established an "ombudsman" facility whereby the Guatemalan anti-corruption agency is working jointly with the national chapter of Transparency International.

Requirements

Behavioural reform has two evident requirements: first, some means of attracting and focusing essential political and commercial attention and will and second, a set of practical measures to heighten honesty in day-to-day trading operations.

Political interest and action can be stimulated and directed by some globally recognized means of lodging details of instances of Customs malpractice, for accumulation and regular publication and comment in a form avoiding any possibility of attribution to particular complainants. More could be done if managements of global commercial enterprises could publicize keen interest in such national Customs integrity ratings as a focal factor in their investment and production planning.

Overall reform, even when international political and business support has been enlisted, will be a prolonged and painstaking process. It will call for and draw strength from progressive extension of adherence to the Kyoto Convention, eventual implementation of a WTO Facilitation Agreement and patient pursuit of capacity building and technical assistance programmes in the hands of the WTO, World Bank and WCO.

The analysis of operational difficulties will be a key practical accompaniment to action to improve any particular national rating in a global Customs integrity index. That analysis will have to be followed by a concerted Customs/trade move to ensure that the most notorious and frequently exploited procedural hot-spots are progressively eliminated or insulated from possible extortion or collusion.

This chapter offers a summary view of the main problems likely to be met and the most likely means of solving them.

Categories

Analysis of main features of corruption at the Customs/trade interface will be greatly assisted by the account and analysis of three case studies – Pakistan, Bolivia and the Philippines – provided by Irene Hors in OECD Technical Paper 175 "Fighting Corruption in Customs" (2001).

- Her rough categorization of illegal practices in terms of varying trade/Customs relationships identifies three principal scenarios.
- The practice, not entirely confined to, but especially widespread in, developing countries, of accompanying almost every Customs formality with what are perversely termed "facilitation payments", usually routinely accepted charges than intentional and conscious acts of corruption.
- Corruption in the context of "normal" commercial operations, for example, customs connivance with business in the acceptance of deliberate errors for valuation or classification of import consignments, or for declarations of export value.
- Finally, some blatantly corrupt activities, which pose very serious problems for public safety and security. These concern outright criminal acts, just as likely to focus on arms or money laundering for terrorism as on more familiar illicit drug dealing or counterfeiting.

Characteristics and remedies

Facilitation payments

Characteristics

"Facilitation payments" generally are defined as small, customary payments to low-level officials for the performance of non-discretionary tasks to which the applicant is entitled under law. Such payments are almost always illegal under local law, but hardly ever the subject of enforcement. And while some of the laws forbidding the bribery of foreign officials exempt "facilitation payments" (e.g., the United States, Canada and Sweden), this exemption does not exist in similar laws of other significant jurisdictions (e.g., the United Kingdom, France and Brazil). The sting of the apparently harmless "facilitation payment" lies in Customs' ability to use their always extensive regulatory powers to apply a wide range of punitive measures to anyone refusing to offer customary "tea money".

Such pressures can be disproportionately draconian. If a certain international maritime container service or one of its major customers stands up against this apparently innocuous "facilitation" practice, Customs can submit every future container movement to all the inevitable and contingent handicaps of deliberately unsympathetic physical inspection.

Such practical blackmail, if applied routinely to express and other air cargo carriers, could deprive the commercial community in some developing countries of essential communications and trading facilities.

There is no trade benefit in supporting this system, which is almost exclusively a Customs imposition. If underlying Customs pressures were removed, traders and carriers would be delighted to see the practice disappear overnight.

Many respectable and law-abiding traders, weighing the relatively modest financial effects and widespread prevalence of "facilitation payments" against the brutal operational consequences of refusal, and perhaps conscious of the explicit exception in the anti-bribery laws of their home countries, feel obliged to allow their agents or brokers to absorb costs and responsibilities in tacitly agreed, inflated commissions, fees and charges.

However, increasing enforcement of laws prohibiting the bribery of foreign officials, coupled with inherent limitations of the "facilitation payments" safe harbour, have compelled a growing number of multinational traders and others to severely limit or eliminate entirely the use of such payments by both their employees and agents.

There are no reliable criteria to establish when a payment may be considered to be "small" and therefore meet the first criterion of a true facilitation payment, particularly where the repetitive payment of "small" amounts may aggregate over time to substantial sums. Furthermore, Customs classification and valuation often require the exercise of judgment about which reasonable people may differ, and even compliant, responsible traders sometimes make inadvertent errors in Customs documentation. Thus it is difficult to be certain that a retrospective examination of any particular payment may not be characterized as a payment to exercise discretion or overlook an error. A misstep in either of these areas may turn a "facilitation payment" into a full-fledged bribe, with significant consequences for the reputation and financial well-being of the trader. In this environment, the perpetuation of the routine expectation of "facilitation payments" creates increasingly intolerable tensions for honest traders.

In the numerous countries, where petty corruption is still endemic and Customs officials are systematically underpaid, even the very useful suggestions for assessment and selection of agents provided in Chapter 4 may prove unworkable. Agents will need, as a condition of commercial survival, to get their principals the best routine arrangements with Customs, by keeping disbursements within the usually well-understood schedule of irregular charges. Trader principals are subject to parallel, supporting competitive pressures. Where companies are forced to meet Customs demands through under-the-counter arrangements with agents, they are bound to incur significant additional costs in the form of inflated fees and commissions.

Remedial action

Apart from their many vicious consequences for traders, "facilitation payments" have, for many years, entangled and frustrated trade facilitation itself in the true sense of simpler and more reliable trading.

For example, numerous Customs administrations have imposed and sustained completely ineffective systems of so-called comprehensive physical inspection of import consignments, incompatible with modern trade and transport timings and practices, solely because essential exceptions can be readily and profitably negotiated. The commercial pressures that could otherwise have forced governments to push Customs into basing inspection on selective risk-assessment are diverted and damped down by the potent combination of inadequate salaries and the "facilitation payment" alternative.

An entirely new situation may be created by current, intensifying pressures for global anti-terrorist security policies in which honest, effective border management, including, especially the close control of containerized traffic, is a basic requirement.

ICC is taking every opportunity to bring legitimate security concerns behind a broad, synergetic security/facilitation agenda, in which the elimination of "facilitation payments" should merit early priority. It would be salutary to dispel and counter the assumption underlying the OECD Commentary that these routine payments are too pervasive and deep-rooted to reduce or eliminate.

In fact, there are many ways, making for efficiency as well as integrity, in which opportunities for such payments can be limited and the disciplinary and regulatory background, against which they are easy to extort, can be improved.

The most common procedural opportunities for exactions are well known and relatively easy to overcome. Cash payment of duties can be switched to bank transfers, deposits and guarantees. Manual handling of paper documents can be replaced by electronic messaging. In surviving documentary systems, the need for signatures, favourite perches for petty peculation, can be minimized and processing arrangements can be altered so that personal contacts between traders/agents and Customs officers are limited to a one-time deposit of all documents needed for release of the goods.

Paper documents and information technology

Paper documents offer special opportunities for irregular payments. Conversely, automation aids rectitude. Well-designed automation ought to get rid of most paper forms, but such dinosaurs as "supporting documents" carried with the goods and presented only at import still haunt even the most advanced Customs computer systems. Customs normally retain the option to require these. While honest administrations with good automated services will usually reduce manual exceptions to a minimum, other services fighting a rear-guard action against computerized reform may find them a highly convenient opportunity for continuing extortion.

Customs should be obliged to give advance, binding rulings on classification and valuation. Complainants who cannot obtain satisfaction for a disputed decision within the Customs hierarchy should be given the opportunity to appeal to a neutral authority outside the Customs service.

Many individual Customs are moving towards such improvements, some in accordance with agreements with the IMF or World Bank, others in response to government recognition that an efficient and honest Customs service is essential to good external trade performance and to attract and retain increasingly selective foreign investment.

The WCO has revised the basic Kyoto Convention to simplify basic Customs procedures and identify all the specific remedial efficiency/integrity measures already mentioned, as well as many others, designed, individually and collectively, to raise service morale as well as functional capability. ICC representatives have played a full part in the Kyoto revision process and are giving strong support to the Convention's much wider adoption.

Revised Kyoto International Convention on the simplification and Harmonization of Customs Procedures

Chapter 7

Application Of Information Technology

7.1. Standard

The Customs shall apply information technology to support Customs operations, where it is cost-effective and efficient for the Customs and for the trade. The Customs shall specify the conditions for its application.

7.2. Standard

When introducing computer applications, the Customs shall use relevant internationally accepted standards.

7.3. Standard

The introduction of information technology shall be carried out in consultation with all relevant parties directly affected, to the greatest extent possible.

7.4. Standard

New or revised national legislation shall provide for:

- Electronic commerce methods as an alternative to paper-based documentary requirements;
- Electronic as well as paper-based authentication methods;
- The right of the Customs to retain information for their own use and, as appropriate, to exchange such information with other Customs administrations and all other legally approved parties by means of electronic commerce techniques.

Finally, while it is difficult for individual companies to resist or restrict "facilitation payments", some traders have been able to make substantial progress. Perhaps the most effective strategy is to adopt a firm policy against making "facilitation" payments, followed up by a number of supportive measures:

- Clear communication of the policy forbidding "facilitation payments" to the trader's employees and agents, and providing clear guidance and training in how to handle demands for such payments;

- Clear communication of the policy to the Customs Administration, both at a supervisory level and through consistent conduct when payments are demanded;
- Contingency plans to accept a degradation of service while the resolve to avoid payments is being demonstrated;
- Enlistment of assistance from local allies such as customers and other poten tially sympathetic groups, as well as the relevant diplomatic community; and
- Persistence.

Experience, over time, has shown that many companies following such strategies have been able to avoid "facilitation" payments or substantially reduce demands for them. Large enterprises also should take every opportunity to stress the importance of efficient and honest Customs service to inward investment decisions, particularly in developing countries.

Bribery in commercial operations

Characteristics

Here the balance of responsibility often lies with the trader. Customs officers may occasionally make it evident that they are open to irregular payments to accept or condone false statements or declarations. They may, much more frequently, raise issues of value or classification or call for a quite unnecessary physical inspection, knowing that the trader, carrier or agent will well understand that the difficulty can be overcome by a cash adjustment. The majority of fraudulent practices, however, originate with the trader who calculates that the bribe he offers is small in relation to the benefit he expects to obtain in relief from taxation or undeclared foreign currency receipts and all associated competitive advantages.

Under-valuation is the most usual offence and causes the greatest difficulty for revenue authorities and so governments. The IMF too, as lender and adviser, fights strongly against consequent erosion of national tax bases and has devoted much attention and considerable research to quantifying and reducing associated revenue losses.

The WCO is well aware of the importance of this issue for the majority of its members. It has chosen valuation as a priority and focus in its wider strategy for capacity building.The ICC also has strong interest in securing improvements in trade behaviour in valuation and other especially sensitive procedures where Customs, in many countries, have most cause to suspect and criticize the business sector. Constant disputes and suspicions are a major obstacle to the introduction of automation, risk-assessment and associated simplified procedures for the honest and compliant trader.

Sustained, all too often justified, mutual mistrust in daily contacts at the Customs/trade operational interface, in the many countries where import duties and taxes still loom large in national revenues, has obvious corrosive consequences for the entire government/business relationship. While the root of "facilitation payments" lies in low-level extortion, commercial fraud usually stems from deliberate, often substantial, bribery, in which the initiative lies with the trader, his agent or the carrier.

Under the heading of relative honesty, or mitigated dishonesty, one can cite the normal trader faced with a notoriously inefficient, poorly paid Customs officer, already exacting and receiving "facilitation payments", who may or may not wish to inspect, and so delay and possibly expose to extra damage and pilferage, overdue, perfectly legal, containerized consignments, presented on the basis of absolutely correct declarations as to value, provenance and the nature of the goods themselves. This trader may be understood, if not forgiven, if he offers an extra payment to ensure that he can by-pass a patently ineffective, because superficial, Customs inspection of a consignment he knows to be innocent.

Criminal actions

The situation is sadly different for a trader seeking to use illicit means to achieve obviously illicit ends. A common example would be bribing a Customs officer to accept a false invoice value, overstated for purposes of acquiring and hiding hard currency earnings on export consignments or understated for the purpose of evading full import duties and taxes. Another would be payment to secure agreement to misdeclaration of the classification of a consignment in order to reduce assessment for tax or duty.

Some of these practices, already criminal in themselves, can open the door to offences reaching far beyond commercial fraud. The Customs officer who accepts a bribe to refrain from inspecting what he believes is an innocent container may, for all he knows, be opening his border to illicit drug dealers or arms smugglers. The severe disciplinary or penal consequences of such misbehaviour, which sometimes prevail, even in services where "facilitation payments" are commonplace, is another reason why, in fraudulent irregularities, Customs officers are more often guilty of accepting bribes than proposing them.

It is worth noting, however, that this category of dishonesty is most likely to flourish in social and economic cultures where commercial and administrative standards are equally low. Prudent, if dishonestly inclined businessmen are unlikely to risk making an illegal proposition to Customs unless they have a reasonable chance of finding a willing partner.

Moreover, it is inevitable that a Customs force which turns a blind eye to, or even favours, unofficial payments for routine services will be much more open to fraudulent practices than an administration where no such arrangements are permitted. It is easier to conceal discords against an already noisy background.

Remedial action

While this is a category of Customs dishonesty in which the main responsibility and opportunity for detection and repression lies with administrations themselves, all relevant trade bodies, including ICC, have obligations parallel with those of individual Customs services and the World Customs Organisation.

Here also trade and Customs can and should march side-by-side in a range of precautionary and protective strategies and measures. The continued activity of what are often global criminals, using the same transport and other operational services as legitimate traders, constitutes a patent threat to good governance and, by stimulating regulatory complexities and controls, imposes unwelcome and costly constraints at many key points in international commerce.

ICC has a special interest in fighting commercial fraud, because this is where Customs in many countries have most cause to suspect and criticize the business sector and question its ethical qualities and standards.

It is important to note that, while Customs services, in any country are strictly national, the trading community usually contains a growing proportion of external, internationally active, traders, carriers and other service industries, using very high quality automated operational systems and practising the highest professional standards of financial probity. Cooperation between the WCO and ICC, drawing on such commercial resources and influence, to improve valuation standards and outcomes could be a key element in a much wider reform and modernization policy.

There are many developing countries in which global enterprises, many of which are ICC members, together with supportive local companies from relevant national ICC Committees, could form a core of honest traders with substantial unblemished valuation records. Customs, once reassured by an established, resulting high-level of compliance and reliability in valuation experience, could be encouraged to rely on modern risk-assessment systems and follow the EU Commission lead in giving special status to Authorised Economic Operators, entitled to a range of trade-facilitation improvements, such as cargo release on the basis of advance control data and reliance for duty payments on post entry audit, that can only operate in a context of mutual confidence.

Continued interest in and support for the existing ICC Code of Conduct, against the background of a much wider development of corporate ethics, should help convince Customs that most participants in international trade are well aware of their responsibilities and observe the highest standards of business behaviour.

While the most favourable and frequent opportunities for commercial fraud occur in countries with a generally undisciplined culture and operate through Customs/trade connivance, there are also cases in which a trader seeks to suborn an otherwise perfectly honest official in a normally honest administration. In such circumstances it is in everyone's interest that the Customs officer should report this approach and that full legal penalties should be exacted and publicized.

Customs fraud control policy

Australian Customs Notice – 2002/29 – Sunday, 30th June 2002

"Fraud is not restricted to monetary or material benefits. In the Customs Fraud Control Policy fraud is defined, very broadly, as:

'Inducing a course of action by deceit or other dishonest conduct, involving acts or omissions or the making of false statements, orally or in writing, with the object of obtaining money or other benefit from, or of evading a liability to, the Commonwealth.'

The definition of fraud was made even broader in the updated Commonwealth Fraud Control Guidelines approved by Cabinet in May 2002. Fraud is now defined as:

'Dishonestly obtaining a benefit by deception or other means.'

The benefit involved can be either tangible or intangible.

Examples of fraud include.

- Evasion of payments (e.g., Customs duty);
- Obtaining benefits by deceit (e.g., false claims for import credit scheme, tariff concession orders and tourist refund scheme, and unlawful movement of goods through airports/ports);
- Abuse of Customs facilities (e.g., unlawful use of laptop computers, vehicles, telephones, credit or fuel cards);
- Making, using or possessing forged or falsified documents;
- Bribery, corruption or abuse of office (e.g., unlawful disclosure of information or hacking into, or interfering with a Customs computer system);
- Theft of Customs' property;
- Causing a loss, or avoiding or creating a liability by deception (e.g., charging Customs for non-delivery or incomplete delivery of services); and
- Providing false or misleading information, or failing to provide information where there is an obligation to do so."

Organized crime and terrorism

This category of criminal offences is in no way related to business operations. It is the meeting place of corrupt, or corrupted, Customs officers and smugglers, money launderers and terrorists.

Here again, new and very powerful security forces could produce some important innovations and improvements. In promoting the Secure Supply Chain concept, aiming at watertight control mechanisms, and invoking a rapid spread of Customs-to-Customs mutual assistance agreements, governments in major trading nations are seeking voluntary arrangements for commercial origin-destination cooperation going well beyond bare legal obligations.

The ICC is leading an active and constructive business response to these requirements which may well provide new opportunities for building more effective barriers to criminal extortion and bribery in all aspects of international trade transactions.

A rough initial view of Customs integrity "performance" can be provided by reference to the ICC Integrity Toolkit (www.iccwbo.org/policy/customs).

This brings together those items in the more comprehensive ICC Customs Guidelines that are particularly relevant to honest administration.

They include recruitment, salary levels, complaint and appeal provisions, consultation, automation, risk assessment and elimination of cash payments. These are accompanied, in the Toolkit, by Explanatory Notes listing the importance of these factors to governments, business and Customs themselves.

ICC Integrity Toolkit: an overview

"Experience has shown that there are certain features of Customs management and operation that are particularly important in encouraging and sustaining integrity. The Toolkit identifies these through the choice of relevant Guidelines and their associated Explanatory Notes that add useful detail and outline the benefits, often linking integrity to efficiency, that adoption of the Guidelines can bring to governments, business and Customs themselves.

The Guidelines grouped under the general heading of "Workforce and structure" are clearly relevant to integrity. Guideline 3 (Customs Workforce) sets some basic requirements in salary levels, recruitment, promotion and career management. Guideline 4 (Customs Integrity) instances the need for an internal security unit to supervise staff standards, known and readily accessible to the trade community. Guideline 5 (Customs Employee Identification) helps ensure public confidence in Customs by stipulating reliable means of identification.

A further set of Guidelines focus on procedural elements that reduce special openings and opportunities for malpractice, bearing in mind that dishonest traders normally seek and reward Customs to obtain their collusion in fraudulent arrangements."

(From www.iccwbo.org/policy/customs)

Any Customs service that meets all these requirements is very unlikely to have a serious integrity problem either in respect of its own staff or from any external pressures towards dishonesty.

The WCO has produced a much more detailed Self-assessment Guide, (www.wcoomd.org), for member administrations. This contains useful check-lists under such pertinent heads as quality of regulation, transparency, automation, staff rotation, accountability, audit and internal investigation, morale and organizational culture, recruitment and selection, code of conduct, professional development, remuneration and relations with the trade. While this guide is intended primarily for Customs services, it is also a most useful basis for external efforts to assess Customs integrity standards and to identify the most relevant points at which to exercise influence and focus appropriate assistance and support.

Therefore, companies should:

- Avoid making facilitation payments;
- Pay Customs duties with bank transfers, deposits and/or guarantees instead of using cash payments;
- Support the revised Kyoto Convention on Customs simplification and harmonization;
- Apply strict measures to ensure that company personnel do not bribe Customs officials to secure any improper advantage;
- Cooperate fully with Customs authorities to improve security procedures that will prevent criminals from engaging in illicit drug dealing or laundering the receipts from organized crime.

Sandy Merber is Chairman of the ICC Commission on Customs and Trade Regulations.

John Raven is Adviser to the ICC Commission on Customs and Trade Regulations.

CHAPTER 14

Moving Anti-Corruption to the Next Level

By Fritz Heimann and Mark Pieth

Since the mid-1990s, anti-corruption has made impressive progress. It has been transformed from a subject that was kept in the closet to a high place on the agenda of multinational companies, international organizations, national governments and non-governmental organizations. However, the goal of greatest importance to the international business community – a corruption-free, level playing field for trade and investment – has not yet been achieved. This chapter will review the current status of the principal anti-corruption programs and consider the obstacles that must be overcome to move the anti-corruption agenda to the next level. Our key message is that greater cooperation among the key players is needed so that the ongoing programs can reinforce each other to achieve the common objective.

Combating corruption is like mountain climbing; making progress becomes more difficult the further you go. With international conventions, getting foreign ministers to sign is the easiest step. Obtaining ratification from legislatures is somewhat harder. Achieving implementation and enforcement by national bureaucracies is difficult. Follow-up monitoring to ensure that lagging governments meet their commitments is the most controversial step.

Corporate integrity programs face a similar progression. Publishing statements of ethical principles is easy. Formulating detailed integrity programs is harder. Implementing these programs so they become part of the corporate culture is much more difficult. Accepting the need for external verification remains very controversial.

There are several reasons why making progress combating corruption becomes harder. Announcing anti-corruption policies is popular. However, moving from words to deeds requires allocation of money, experienced people and real commitment from top executives. It will also arouse opposition from those who benefit from corruption. Such opposition is strongly entrenched and intensifies when anti-corruption programs move from political gestures to real enforcement.

Another difficulty is that making discernible progress in reducing corruption will take time. It has taken ten years from the adoption of the OECD Convention to reach the point where there is substantial enforcement by half the parties. The UN Convention is much more complex, and considerable time will be needed to produce tangible results. Strong long-term commitment to anti-corruption programs is essential. Maintaining this commitment presents a difficult challenge, because public and political priorities change over time. Sustained advocacy by many parties will be required.

To overcome the obstacles confronting the anti-corruption agenda will require, not only persistence in pursuing the ongoing programs, but also marshalling much greater cooperation by key stakeholders. Such cooperation can build on the strong inter-relationships among different anti-corruption initiatives. For example, enforcement of anti-bribery laws and adoption of corporate integrity programs play an inter-dependent and mutually reinforcing role. Widespread adoption of corporate compliance programmes usually does not occur until there is active enforcement of anti-bribery laws.

However, law enforcement alone has difficulty changing business behaviour. Adoption of integrity programs by leading companies helps establish the moral framework that facilitates law enforcement. In addition, corporate programs also have a considerable multiplier effect on law enforcement: for every government prosecutor investigating foreign bribery, there will be scores of corporate lawyers and auditors enforcing corporate integrity standards. Similar inter-relationships among anti-corruption initiatives will be discussed below.

Closer cooperation among all the stakeholders will make it easier to overcome resistance to anti-corruption programs and to demonstrate discernible results. This will raise public and political support to the level at which continuing progress will become irreversible.

OECD Convention

The adoption of the OECD Convention in 1997 and the enactment of laws prohibiting bribery of foreign public officials by all 37 signatories of the Convention have been widely regarded as breakthroughs in the fight against international corruption. Because most major international companies are covered by these laws, they hold the promise of sharply curtailing the supply side of international bribery.

To make sure that the promise of the Convention is achieved, the OECD's Working Group on Bribery has been conducting a rigorous follow-up monitoring program since 1999. The first phase reviewed the laws enacted by the parties. The second phase assessed government enforcement programs and has included country visits to almost all of the parties. The monitoring program is described in more detail in Chapter One. It deserves high marks for professional thoroughness and for its courage in criticising even the most powerful governments.

In an independent civil society effort to assess government actions, Transparency International publishes an annual progress report on government enforcement. The 2008 report indicates there has been significant enforcement in 16 countries. This compares with 14 countries in 2007, 12 in 2006 and 8 in 2005. There have been substantial increases in the number of prosecutions in important exporting countries, including France, Germany and the US. In TI's assessment, the trend is positive, but there is still little or no enforcement by over half of the parties to the Convention. These include the UK, Japan and Canada, three of the largest exporters.

Because the Convention depends on a collective commitment to stop foreign bribery, its success will not be assured until all the major exporters meet their engagements. The present "half way there" situation is unstable. There is a danger of backsliding by governments now enforcing the Convention. These governments will come under increasing pressure from national companies to let them do what their competitors are doing, and these arguments will be difficult to resist during a period of declining export markets.

The progress of the Convention is also threatened by the UK government's termination in December 2006 of the investigation of bribery allegations involving a huge BAE order in Saudi Arabia. The UK asserted that national security interests overrode the obligation to prohibit foreign bribery. Even though the OECD strongly criticized the UK action, the House of Lords, in July 2008, upheld the termination, overturning a prior court ruling invalidating it. The threat posed by the BAE case is that other governments could also assert the right to override the Convention because of national security concerns. Unlimited, unilateral assertions of national security exceptions could undermine the Convention.

The Convention does not provide for a national security exception. However, there is room for debate concerning whether governments have an implicit right to assert such an exception. Many other treaties have resolved this issue by providing explicit national security exceptions, but establishing conditions limiting the use of them. Unless OECD adopts reasonable limitations on the use of national security exceptions, other governments may well be tempted to follow the UK's example and unilaterally assert them.

OECD's follow-up monitoring program has carefully documented the present deficiencies in enforcement. However, notwithstanding the efforts of the Working Group and the Secretary General, OECD is struggling to persuade reluctant governments to meet their commitments. This is difficult to do in OECD's consensus-based culture. The best hope for generating enough pressure to move forward is to secure the active cooperation of other interested stakeholders on the following steps:

- The business community faces intolerable problems if the Convention is unable to create a corruption-free level playing field for international trade and investment. Business leaders must use their influence to ensure that the Convention succeeds by persuading their governments to exercise sufficient peer pressure to ensure that:
  - Lagging governments enforce the prohibition against foreign bribery;
  - Reasonable limitations on the use of national security exceptions are adopted.
- Governments enforcing the Convention should exercise the required peer pressure through bilateral contacts and through fora such as the OECD Ministerial meetings and G8 meetings.
- Business organizations and NGOs should work actively with OECD and with governments to ensure that the current review of OECD instruments will result in:
  - Continuation of a rigorous monitoring program on a permanent basis;
  - New programs to (a) strengthen coverage of foreign subsidiaries and bribery of political parties, (b) eliminate the exclusion of facilitation payments and (c) determine how best to address private sector bribery.

UN Convention

After two years of negotiations in Vienna, the UN Convention Against Corruption (UNCAC) was adopted in 2003. It was signed by 140 governments and has been ratified by more than 120. UNCAC has a more comprehensive scope than any other anti-corruption convention. It includes a broad range of preventive measures designed to: strengthen governments' capacity to fight corruption; add extensive criminalization and law enforcement provisions covering domestic as well as foreign bribery, extortion and embezzlement by government officials; fight corruption in the private sector; provide arrangements for international cooperation, including mutual legal assistance facilitating investigation and prosecution across borders; introduce innovative provisions for asset recovery; and provide technical assistance and information exchange. UNCAC's worldwide membership and its broad scope provide a truly global framework for combating corruption

Based on surveys conducted by the UN Office on Drugs and Crime (UNODC), which serves as the Secretariat for UNCAC, government implementation of UNCAC's ambitious array of articles is quite uneven, both with respect to the countries that have taken action and the articles that have been implemented. This highlights the importance of follow-up monitoring. UNCAC's broad scope and large number of parties make monitoring even more essential than for other conventions, but also more difficult to agree upon. The conference in Vienna in 2002-2003, which adopted the Convention, was unable to reach agreement on monitoring and deferred the issue to the Conference of States Parties (CoSP) to be held after UNCAC went into effect.

Two such conferences have taken place. While there is agreement in principle on the need for a monitoring mechanism (or, in UN terminology, an "implementation review mechanism"), there is still no agreement on how this mechanism should be organized and its terms of reference. The principal obstacle is resistance by many developing countries belonging to the G77 group. These countries are concerned that monitoring would unfairly criticize countries that have difficulty implementing UNCAC. While there is greater support from industrialized countries, some have raised concerns about the cost of monitoring and about duplication of UNCAC monitoring and monitoring with other anti-corruption conventions. Overcoming the obstacles to agreement on a monitoring process remains a difficult challenge. Another Conference of States Parties will be held in Qatar at the end of 2009.

An effective monitoring mechanism is the key to enabling UNCAC to function as the global framework or combating corruption. Active cooperation by other stakeholders will be needed to enable the Convention to move to the next level.

- Business leaders must make clear to their governments that UNCAC deserves strong support and that the stalemate over monitoring must be overcome. The interests of the international business community are clear, because in a global economy UNCAC's global framework for combating corruption must be made to work. Moreover, most multinationals recognize that their future growth depends on their ability to expand in developing countries without compromising the integrity standards demanded in their home countries.
- International donors - including the World Bank, UNDP, OECD-DAC, the regional development banks and bilateral donors – must provide increased capacity-building assistance to developing countries to enable them to implement UNCAC. This is the single most important step needed to overcome G77 concerns about agreeing to a monitoring mechanism.
- The organizations monitoring other anti-corruption organizations-including OECD, GRECO, OAS and the African Union – must work with UNODC to agree upon cooperative arrangements to alleviate concerns about duplicative monitoring. Because all monitoring organizations have serious resource constraints, cooperation is in everyone's interest.

- Civil society and other private sector organizations – including ICC, TI the World Economic Forum and the Global Compact – can play an important role in promoting the foregoing initiatives.

International business initiatives

During the past several decades, there have been extensive efforts to curb corruption by business. The ICC Rules of Conduct have been made more rigorous. Transparency International has published its own Business Principles for Countering Bribery. The World Economic Forum has launched its Partnering Against Corruption Initiative (PACI). All three documents go beyond the provisions of the OECD and UN Conventions to clarify grey areas, such as gifts and entertainment and payments to agents and other intermediaries. The standards spelled out in all three documents are very similar. (They are also converging in their treatment of facilitation payments, where there had been differences between organizations.) The UN's Global Compact has been extended to include a commitment not to bribe and has recommended all three documents to its member companies as models for their use.

Many more companies have adopted anti-corruption policies. A decade ago, such policies were used primarily by US companies, but the OECD Convention has resulted in their adoption by companies from other OECD countries as well. There is also increasing recognition that adopting corporate policies is not enough and that rigorous implementation programs are necessary to ensure that all parts of an enterprise comply.

Anti-corruption programs tailored to the issues of particular industry sectors have been organized in several important industries - including aerospace and defence, private banking, construction, mining and other extractive industries. TI's Integrity Pacts, project-specific arrangements in which the project's sponsor and all bidders agree on procedures to prevent corruption, have been increasingly used.

The foregoing steps have been extremely valuable in developing the techniques needed to curb corruption. However, their impact on reducing it is still difficult to assess. The techniques have been utilized more extensively by large multinationals than by small- and medium-sized companies, and the extent to which they are employed differs substantially between countries, with higher use in countries where there is substantial enforcement of the OECD Convention. (For example, German businesses received a clear message to end foreign bribery from the prosecution and huge fines imposed on Siemens; the termination of the BAE case sends a different message to UK companies.)

The wider adoption of corporate anti-corruption programs may also be deterred by the increasing role in international trade of China, India, Russia and other countries not bound by the OECD Convention. While these countries are parties to the UN Convention, that Convention may not significantly impact the practices of their businesses until it becomes clear that governments will actively enforce its prohibitions against bribery.

To raise business initiatives to a level where there will be discernible reductions in bribery will require increased efforts, as well as greater cooperation, among corporations and with other stakeholders:

- Leaders of companies with high integrity standards have a strong incentive to promote improved compliance by their competitors.
- Industry sector anti-corruption initiatives provide an ideal forum for industry leaders to encourage adoption of improved standards for all competitors. Participation by independent organizations in the development of these standards would be helpful.
- Collection of data concerning how many companies have implemented anti-corruption programs would provide an important measure of progress. Differences in their use between companies in different industries and in different countries would indicate where additional work is needed.
- International organizations and governments engaged in major procurement projects should require all bidders to have rigorous anti-corruption programs in place as a condition for bidding.
- Business leaders should work with their governments to encourage cooperative action by the leading exporting countries to overcome extortion by public officials in countries where extortion is widespread.
- Corporate governance reforms will receive renewed attention as a result of the financial crisis. Business leaders should support stronger transparency and accountability requirements, including greater disclosure of anti-corruption programs and their implementation in annual reports, external verification of compliance with these programs and stronger whistleblower protection.
- Increased attention is needed to prevent bribery of public officials by intermediaries, such as sales agents, consultants, bankers, lawyers and Customs agents. Codes of conduct specifically applicable to different groups of intermediaries should be developed. In many countries, low pay of Customs officials is a cause of extortion. Cooperative projects should be conducted with participation by exporters, Customs agents and government officials to raise pay levels for Customs personnel, including provisions for increased fees in return for the elimination of illicit payments.

Cooperation by other stakeholders

International development agencies

International development agencies – including the World Bank, UNDP, regional MDBs and bilateral donors – have played an increasing role in preventing corruption in their own programs and in the countries in which they work. These efforts should be strengthened, and the leading development agencies, as well as OECD-DAC, should actively work in cooperation with other stakeholders along the lines indicated above.

Civil society and private sector organizations

ICC, Transparency International and other organizations have actively promoted anti-corruption initiatives, including the OECD Convention and UNCAC. Their continued involvement is essential, since they have substantial credibility with the public and the media; they can maintain a steady focus on anti-corruption when government interests flag; they can do independent research and analysis and pioneer innovative approaches; and they can take critical positions that are too controversial for governments and international organizations to advance.

The media

Public concern about widespread corruption has been the single most powerful driver for reform. The media have been a key here, by publicizing evidence of corruption in their investigative reporting.

Conclusion

Clearly, greater cooperation among all stakeholders is essential to move the anti-corruption agenda to the next level. To promote this cooperation, intensive dialogue across organizational lines is necessary. As soon as this dialogue has sufficiently advanced, a leadership meeting of the leading stakeholders should be held, with a focus on developing a consensus on attainable objectives over the next five years.

Even though serious obstacles must be overcome – both to achieve effective implementation of anti-corruption conventions and to have a broader adoption of corporate integrity programs – there must be no turning back. The damage inflicted by corruption on the global economy, on democratic institutions and on international development is well understood. Moving anti-corruption efforts to a higher level will make it possible to reduce and, in time, hopefully eliminate this scourge of international commerce.

Fritz Heimann is the author of Chapters 1 and 3 in this handbook.

Mark Pieth is a Professor of Criminal Law at Basel University in Switzerland and Chairman of the OECD Working Group on Bribery in International Business Transactions.

Appendices

Commission on anti-corruption Combating Extortion and Bribery : ICC Rules of Conduct and Recommendations

Prepared by the ICC Commission on anti-corruption

General introduction

The International Chamber of Commerce (ICC) has always been at the forefront of the drive for integrity in business life, because only a corruption free system makes it possible for all participants to compete on a level playing field.

The signing of the United Nations Convention on Corruption in December 2003 at Mérida, Mexico, marks a new era in the fight against extortion and bribery. This comprehensive international instrument paves the way for the establishment of a global prohibition of all forms of corruption. ICC, as the world business organization, welcomes this further evolution in the combat against corruption.

ICC has emphasized the critical role of compliance by enterprises with selfimposed rules based on their own values, while recognizing the basic responsibility of national governments and international organizations in the fight against corruption. Adhering to strict rules defined within the enterprise will help businesses fulfill their legal obligations in a more natural and effective way. The adoption and implementation of their own integrity programmes is therefore strongly recommended.

Already in 1977, in the aftermath of the international bribery scandals of the 1970s, ICC produced its first Report on Extortion and Bribery in International Business Transactions. This included the first version of the Rules of Conduct to Combat Extortion and Bribery recommended by ICC for voluntary application by enterprises. These Rules of Conduct strongly expressed the objective of ending both bribery and extortion. ICC also recommended that the United Nations adopt an international convention to prohibit corruption. UN efforts to reach such an agreement fell through in the 1980s.

It took another round of corruption scandals in the 1990s to revive international interest in matters of integrity. Again ICC was at the forefront and issued its second Report in 1996. The Organisation for Economic Cooperation and Development (OECD) became the key forum for anti-corruption reforms. In particular, the adoption in 1997 of the Convention on Combating Bribery of Foreign Public Officials represented a major milestone. This was recognized in a revised version of the ICC Report which was issued in 1999.

ICC has continued to work actively with the OECD and with other international organizations,. including the United Nations, the Council of Europe and the European Union, to promote awareness of the need for integrity and to further the combat against all forms of corruption in business transactions. ICC has emphasized that as much energy should be devoted to fight extortion or solicitation as to bribery. ICC has also insisted on the need to confront private-to-private corruption (corruption between private entities), as this form of bribery also distorts competition and can no longer be ignored in light of increasing moves to privatization as well as the blurring of lines between the private sector and the public sector.

The ICC Commission on anti-corruption has published "Fighting Corruption, A Corporate Practices Handbook", which provides detailed practical guidance for compliance with ICC Rules of Conduct and the OECD Convention. It is a handbook for all who wish to put into place an efficient and well-run integrity programme. The manual was first published in 1999 and substantially revised and expanded in 2003.

Because of the accelerating pace of anti-corruption developments, as well as ICC's work on corporate responsibility and corporate governance, the ICC Commission on anti-corruption decided to revisit and rethink ICC Rules of Conduct and to refine its stance on a number of integrity matters. Work on anti-corruption is never finished. Sustained efforts will still be necessary in the future. A better awareness is needed among public officials, in board rooms and at the working level. ICC is committed to contribute to this awareness.

Guy Sebban
ICC Secretary General Chair

François Vincke
ICC Commission on Anti-Corruption

Outline

The 2008 edition of ICC Rules of Conduct and Recommendations to Combat Extortion and Bribery consists of three parts:

- Part I contains substantive rules and implementation procedures for voluntary application by enterprises;
- Part II sets forth follow up activities by the ICC Commission on anti-corruption for the promotion of the Rules of Conduct;
- Part III covers the work of the ICC Commission on anti-corruption with international organizations and national governments to strengthen the legal and administrative framework to combat bribery and extortion.

Part I: Rules of Conduct to Combat Extortion and Bribery

Introduction

These Rules of Conduct are intended as a method of self-regulation by business against the background of applicable national laws. Their voluntary acceptance by business enterprises will promote high standards of integrity in business transactions, whether between enterprises and public bodies or between enterprises themselves. These Rules will play an important role in assisting enterprises to comply with their legal obligations and with the numerous anti-corruption initiatives at international level. They will also provide an appropriate basis for resisting attempts at extortion.

These Rules of Conduct are of a general nature constituting what is considered good commercial practice but are without direct legal effect. All enterprises should conform to the relevant laws and regulations of the countries in which they are established and in which they operate, and should observe both the letter and the spirit of these Rules. While the highest priority should continue to be directed to ending large scale extortion and bribery involving politicians and senior officials, the 2008 revision of the Rules also provides for action against facilitation payments to lower level officials.

For the purposes of these Rules, the term "enterprise" refers to any person or entity engaged in business and other economic activities, whether or not organized for profit, including any entity controlled by a state or a territorial subdivision thereof; it includes a parent and its controlled subsidiaries.

The success of ICC Rules will depend on the "tone at the top": a clear message from the chief executive that bribery and extortion are prohibited and that an effective compliance programme will be implemented.

To provide further guidance on the implementation of these Rules, the ICC Commission on anti-corruption has published "Fighting Corruption: A Corporate Practices Handbook". Each of the articles below includes a short cross reference to the relevant chapters of this handbook.

Article 1: Prohibition of Bribery and Extortion

Enterprises should prohibit bribery and extortion at all times and in any form, whether direct or indirect, including through agents and other intermediaries:

a) Bribery is the offering, promising, giving or accepting of any undue pecuniary or other advantage to or by:

- A public official, at national, local or international level;
- A political party, party official or candidate; and
- A director, officer, employee or agent of a private enterprise

in order to obtain or retain a business or other improper advantage, e.g., in connection with regulatory permits, taxation, customs, judicial and legislative proceedings.

b) Extortion or solicitation is the demanding of a bribe, whether or not coupled with a threat if the demand is refused. "Bribery" as used in these Rules shall include extortion.

c) Enterprises should not (i) kick back any portion of a contract payment to government officials or to employees of the other contracting party, or (ii) utilize intermediaries suchas agents,subcontractors,consultants or other third parties, to channel payments to government officials, or to employees of the other contracting party, their relatives, friends or business associates.

Defining bribery is the central theme of Chapter 3 of the handbook. The prohibition of private-to-private bribery is covered in Chapter 11.

Article 2: Agents and Other Intermediaries

Enterprises should make their anti-corruption policy known to all agents and other intermediaries and make it clear that they expect all activities carried out on their behalf to be compliant with their policy. More particularly, enterprises should take measures within their power to ensure:

a) That any payment made to any agent represents no more than an appropriate remuneration for legitimate services rendered by such agent;

b) That no part of any such payment is passed on by the agent as a bribe or otherwise in contravention of these Rules of Conduct;

c) That agents agree explicitly not to pay bribes. Enterprises should include in their contracts provisions to terminate agreements with agents if a bribe is paid, except for agreements with agents performing routine administrative or clerical tasks;

d) That they maintain a record of the names, terms of employment and payments to all agents who are retained by them in connection with transactions with public bodies, state or private enterprises. This record should be available for inspection by auditors and by appropriate, duly authorized governmental authorities under conditions of confidentiality.

The foregoing provisions should be applied to all agents or other intermediaries used by the enterprise to obtain orders and permits, including sales representatives, customs agents, lawyers and consultants.

Chapter 4 of the handbook looks specifically at issues raised by the use of agents and other intermediaries.

Article 3: Joint Ventures and Outsourcing Agreements

Enterprises should take measures within their power to ensure that anti-bribery provisions consistent with these Rules of Conduct are accepted by joint-venture partners as applicable to the joint venture and by parties to outsourcing agreements.

Chapter 3 touches upon the role of joint ventures.

Article 4: Political and Charitable Contributions and Sponsorships

a) Enterprises should only make contributions to political parties, party officials and candidates in accordance with applicable laws, and all requirements for public disclosure should be fully complied with. The amount and timing of political contributions should be reviewed to ensure that they are not used as a subterfuge for bribery.

b) Enterprises should take measures within their power to ensure that their charitable contributions and sponsorships are not used as a subterfuge for bribery. Charitable contributions and sponsorships should be transparent and in accordance with applicable law.

c) Enterprises should establish reasonable controls and procedures to ensure that improper political and charitable contributions are not made.Special care should be exercised in reviewing contributions to organizations in which prominent political figures, or their relatives, friends and business associates are involved.

Political contributions are further discussed in Chapter 10 of the handbook.

Article 5: Gifts, Hospitality and Expenses

Enterprises should establish procedures covering the offer or receipt of gifts, hospitality or expenses in order to ensure that such arrangements (a) are limited to reasonable and bona fide expenditures, and (b) do not improperly affect, or might be deemed to improperly affect, the outcome of a procurement or other business transaction.

Gifts, hospitality and expenses are one of the four critical issues analyzed in Chapter 3.

Article 6: Facilitation Payments

a) Enterprises should not make facilitation payments. In the event that an enterprise determines, after appropriate managerial review, that facilitation payments cannot be eliminated entirely, it should establish controls and procedures to ensure that their use is limited to small payments to low level officials for routine actions to which the enterprise is entitled.
b) The need for the continued use of facilitation payments should be reviewed periodically with the objective of eliminating them as soon as possible.

The critical issue of facilitation payments is also explored in Chapter 3 of the handbook.

Article 7: Corporate Policies

In order to prevent bribery and extortion, enterprises should implement comprehensive policies or codes reflecting these Rules of Conduct as well as their particular circumstances and specific business environment. These policies or codes should:

a) Provide guidance and training in identifying and avoiding bribery or extortion in the daily business dealings of the enterprise;
b) Offer confidential channels to raise concerns, seek advice or report violations without having to fear retaliation;
c) Include disciplinary procedures to sanction misconduct; and
d) Apply to all controlled subsidiaries, foreign and domestic.

Chapter 3 of the handbook examines the responsibilities of enterprises in providing the means to fight extortion and bribery. The issue of parent company responsibility for controlled subsidiaries is addressed also in Chapter 3 .

Article 8: Financial Recording and Auditing

a) All financial transactions must be properly and fairly recorded in appropriate books of account available for inspection by boards of directors, if applicable, or a corresponding body, as well as auditors.

b) There must be no "off the books" or secret accounts, nor may any documents be issued which do not properly and fairly record the transactions to which they relate.

c) Enterprises should take all necessary measures to establish independent systems of auditing, whether through internal or external auditors, in order to bring to light any transactions which contravene these Rules of Conduct. Appropriate corrective action must then be taken.

d) Enterprises should comply with all provisions of national tax laws and regulations, including those prohibiting the deduction of any form of bribe payment from taxable income.

Chapter 6 of the handbook offers further guidance on financial recording and auditing issues.

Article 9: Responsibilities

The board of directors or other body with ultimate responsibility for the enterprise, should:

a) Take reasonable steps to ensure compliance with these Rules of Conduct, including

   - Making resources available and supporting management in implementing the corporate policies reflecting them;
   - Establishing and maintaining proper systems of control and reporting procedures, including independent auditing;

b) Sanction violations and take appropriate corrective action; and

c) Make appropriate public disclosure of the enforcement of its anti-corruption policies or codes.

The audit committee of the board or other body with similar responsibility should conduct regular independent reviews of compliance with these Rules of Conduct and recommend corrective measures or policies as necessary. This can be done as part of a broader system of corporate compliance reviews.

Chapter 5 of the handbook deals specifically with the responsibilities of enterprises in the fight against corruption.

Part II: ICC Followup and Promotion of the Rules

To promote the widest possible use the Rules set forth in Part I, to propose initiatives to combat corruption and to stimulate cooperation between governments and world business, ICC has established a Commission on anti-corruption. This Commission is composed of business representatives from a wide range of business sectors and national backgrounds.

Among its primary tasks, the Commission shall:

1. Provide guidance on the implementation of the Rules of Conduct by promoting and updating the ICC handbook "Fighting Corruption: a Corporate Practices Manual";
2. Prepare ICC statements and develop views on major developments in the fight against extortion and bribery;
3. Report to the Secretary General and ICC's governing bodies on any major development in the fight against corruption that may have an impact on world business;
4. Maintain contacts with international organizations dealing with extortion and bribery, including civil society organizations, and, as appropriate, support their international initiatives;
5. Assist ICC national committees in promoting the use of the Rules of Conduct;
6. Organize or encourage the organization of conferences, seminars and other events to raise awareness and stimulate interest in, and discussion of, the Rules of Conduct among the business community;
7. Propose possible changes or improvements to ICC Rules of Conduct and Recommendations to Combat Extortion and Bribery to the ICC Executive Board, in light of new developments in the fight against extortion and bribery.

Part III: ICC Cooperation with International Organizations and National Governments

Introduction

The success of ICC Rules of Conduct in combating corruption through corporate selfregulation will be enhanced by actions by international organizations and by national governments to strengthen the legal and administrative framework for combating corruption. The political will of governments to enforce anti-corruption laws is of paramount importance. The need for complementary and mutually supportive action by the business community and by governments and international organizations was recognized in 1977 when the ICC issued its first Report on Extortion and Bribery, including the initial version of ICC Rules of the Conduct, and again when the Rules were revised and updated in 1996 and 1999.

In the period since the last revision of ICC Rules, the need to combat corruption has been widely recognized around the world, and considerable progress has been made in strengthening the legal framework for combating corruption. From the standpoint of international business the key step has been the adoption of the OECD Convention prohibiting bribery of foreign public officials, which ICC actively supported. In addition, several regional anti-corruption conventions have been adopted, and the UN Convention against Corruption has been signed by over one hundred countries. National governments are beginning to take action to implement the commitments embodied in these international conventions, although the response has been uneven.

The Global Compact in 2004 added working against corruption as one of its ten principles. The World Bank, the IMF and other international financial institutions have also launched important anti-corruption initiatives.

The ICC Commission on anti-corruption has played an active role in the development of the new framework for combating corruption. However, considerable further work is required to ensure that this framework is effectively implemented. The Commission expects to be active in the following areas:

International Conventions

OECD Convention

- Provide ICC support for OECD monitoring of national enforcement programmes.
    - ❖ Promote private sector participation in country reviews.
    - ❖ Endorse continuation of monitoring beyond the 2007 limit of current funding commitments.

- Encourage OECD and member governments to take steps to assist companies to resist extortion by foreign public officials.
- Urge action on "unresolved issues" identified in 1997:
  - ❖ Extend prohibition of foreign bribery to cover private sector bribery. This has been a major initiative of the ICC Commission, and has involved the study of private commercial bribery laws in collaboration with the Max Planck Institute in Freiburg. The next step should be the formation of a joint OECD/ICC study group to develop recommendations for action.
  - ❖ Clarify coverage of foreign subsidiaries; parent companies should require controlled subsidiaries to adopt anti-bribery policies.
  - ❖ Prohibit bribery of foreign political parties, party officials and candidates.

United Nations Convention Against Corruption (UNCAC)

- Encourage governments to ratify UNCAC promptly. UNCAC should secure balanced support from industrialized countries, as well as developing countries.
- Support establishment of an effective followup monitoring programme to ensure that parties implement and enforce UNCAC.
- Urge international donor agencies, such as UNDP and the World Bank, to help governments that need technical assistance to implement UNCAC.

Coordination of Conventions

The adoption of anti-corruption conventions by the OECD, the Organization of American States (OAS), the Council of Europe, the African Union and the UN gives a strong positive signal of the commitment by the international community to address the problem of corruption. However, from an international business standpoint, the proliferation of anti-corruption instruments raises concerns about inconsistent rules, overlapping enforcement and the lack of common definitions. The Commission will urge the organizations responsible for the various conventions to coordinate their work in order to promote a coherent approach along the following lines:

- The OECD Convention should remain the principal instrument focusing on the supply side of international corruption.
- Regional conventions – the instruments adopted by OAS, Council of Europe, African Union – should give priority to issues on which progress can be made by cooperation among their participating parties - such as technical assistance, preventive measures, criminalization and law enforcement, including combating extortion by public officials.

- UNCAC should give priority to issues requiring worldwide cooperation, particularly strengthening mutual legal assistance procedures for investigating and prosecuting foreign bribery cases and improving arrangements for repatriating the proceeds of corruption. UNCAC should also serve as the principal source for anti-corruption rules in areas which are not covered by regional conventions.
- Monitoring programs at OECD and at regional and UNCAC levels should be coordinated to avoid duplication, to share information and to utilize limited resources to best advantage.

International Organizations and Initiatives

World Bank and other International Financial Institutions

- The Commission will encourage the World Bank, IMF and other international financial institutions to strengthen procedures to prevent bribery on projects they finance, including requirements that contractors adopt antibribery compliance programmes.
- The Commission will encourage the World Bank, IMF and other international financial institutions to require governments to adopt transparent procurement rules and to ratify and implement UNCAC.

World Trade Organization (WTO)

- Because corruption causes serious distortions in international trade, the Commission will continue to urge WTO to address traderelated aspects of corruption. WTO action to promote the use of transparent procurement rules would reduce opportunities for corruption and help contribute to the strengthening of a rules based and non discriminatory global trading system.

Global Compact

- The Commission will cooperate with the Global Compact Office at the international and national level to encourage companies participating in the Global Compact to adopt corporate compliance programmes consistent with ICC Rules of Conduct to Combat Extortion and Bribery.

National Governments

The Commission will work with ICC national committees to encourage national governments to take the following measures to fight extortion and bribery:

- **Capacity Building**. Governments should provide adequate resources - including funding, staffing and training - for the organizations combating corruption. These resources should be aimed at raising public awareness of the economic and social consequences of corruption.
- **Strengthen Enforcement.** Even though laws prohibiting extortion and bribery have been on the books in virtually all countries, enforcement is weak or nonexistent in many countries. The Commission will urge governments to strengthen enforcement of antibribery laws, including laws prohibiting extortion by public officials and laws prohibiting commercial bribery. Governments should also establish reporting channels for complaints about corruption and provide protection for bona fide whistle blowers. Because it is difficult for local prosecutors to undertake foreign bribery cases, governments should assign responsibility for such cases to a national office.
- **Economic Regulations.** Governments should, as far as possible, minimize the use of systems requiring issuance of individual permits, authorizations, etc., because such systems offer scope for extortion and bribery. Where such systems cannot be eliminated, governments should take appropriate measures to prevent their abuse.
- **Public Procurement**. Governments should commit themselves to improve transparency in public procurement, including public bidding, and publication of the criteria upon which awards are based. Adoption of antibribery compliance programmes should be a condition for bidding on major government contracts. In particular, in the case of projects financed by an international financial institution, observance of these principles should be reflected in contractual arrangements between the parties.
- **Political Contributions.**Undisclosed political contributions can be a source of abuse. Governments should, subject to the specifics of their national political system, regulate the conditions under which political contributions can be made and how such contributions are to be reported by donors and recipients.
- **Accounting and Auditing.** Governments should require auditing by independent public auditors of the accounts of all economically significant enterprises. Governments should also support the adoption of strong and consistent international standards for accounting and auditing.
- **Export Credit Agencies.** Export credit agencies should include in their conditions that financing and guarantees are not provided for contracts secured through bribery and that sanctions shall be applied in the event of violations.
- **Official Development Assistance (ODA).** Development assistance programmes should require strict adherence to anti-corruption rules by government officials and contractors.

ICC Guidelines on Whistleblowing

Prepared by the ICC Commission on anti-corruption

A. Introduction

1. No abatement of corruption and economic fraud

Fraud remains one of the most problematic issues for business worldwide, no matter the company's country of operation, industry sector or size. An extensive survey, conducted in 2007 with 5428 companies in 40 countries, concluded that over 43 % of the respondents sustained one or more significant economic crimes during the two previous years. Despite the attention of regulators and companies' investment in controls, the actual level of economic crime and the associated financial and non-financial damages have not significantly decreased.

Economic fraud destroys shareholders' value, threatens enterprises' development, endangers employment opportunities and undermines good corporate governance. Enterprises should therefore consider putting into place efficient and appropriate internal tools to combat economic fraud and to fight corruption. Research indicates that companies that use effective guidelines and compliance programs are much less vulnerable to economic crime[1].

Potential fraudsters need to see that, due to internal risk management tools, there is a greater likelihood of detection and that those in breach of a company's ethical, regulatory and legal guidelines will be consistently subject to sanctions that fit the offences[2]. Fraud can be detected by internal audit, external audit, risk management, corporate security but also, and to a large extent, by whistleblowing.

A company's workforce represents a valuable source of information that can be utilized to identify a potential problem, and to deal with it, before it causes significant damage to the company's reputation or its stakeholders[3].

---

[1] PricewaterhouseCoopers, Investigations and Forensic Services, "Economic crime: people, culture and controls", 4th biennial Global Economic Crime Survey, 2007, p. 22.

[2] Ibidem, p. 4.

[3] Institute of Chartered Accountants in England and Wales, "Guidance for audit committees", March 2004.

2. Whistleblowing, an efficient fraud detection tool

Recent international professional research shows that whistleblowing, in addition to other instruments, such as people management and internal and external controls, provides the major source for detection of fraudulent behavior in enterprises. A study performed by an international accounting firm[4] reveals that not less than 25 % of the occurrences of fraud discovered in the enterprises surveyed came to light thanks to a whistleblowing system put into place by these companies.

There is however still some reluctance in parts of the business world to resort to internal fraud reporting by the company's employees, as it appears from another professional survey covering 13 European countries[5] that only 33 % of the respondents state that their company has a hotline. Cultural differences, legal requirements and psychological obstacles still make the introduction of whistle-blowing problematic in certain jurisdictions.

3. The ICC Rules of Conduct and Recommendations

Convinced that self regulation provides effective protection of corporate interests, ICC has developed over the years rules aiming at fighting corruption and other forms of economic fraud. In particular, ICC has encouraged companies to put into place efficient preventive policies which can shield them from the grave consequences economic fraud can entail.

The *2005 ICC Rules of Conduct on Combating Extortion and Bribery* recommend that anti-corruption policies and codes adopted by enterprises should "offer confidential channels to raise concerns, seek advice or report violations without fear of retaliation[6]." This ICC Recommendation is extensively commented in Chapter 7 of the ICC Corporate Practices Handbook "Fighting Corruption", written by Michael N. Davies, Q.C.

ICC France has taken the initiative to issue guidelines on the important question of putting into place whistleblowing mechanisms in enterprises.

4. Purpose of the ICC Guidelines on Whistleblowing

The purpose of these Guidelines is to help companies establish and implement internal whistleblowing programs, by setting forth practical indications, that can serve as a useful point of reference, while meeting, as much as possible, the objections formulated in certain countries about some aspects of a whistleblowing system.

[4] **KPMG Forensic, "Profile of a Fraudster", Survey, 2007, p. 26.**

[5] **Ernst & Young, "A Survey into Fraud Risk Mitigation in 13 European Countries".**

[6] **ICC Commission on Anti-Corruption, "Combating Extortion and Bribery: ICC Rules of Conduct and Recommendations, 2005 edition, article 7**

These Guidelines are based on the broad experience and practice of ICC member companies across a wide range of sectors and jurisdictions. They are also inspired by a large number of international and national legal provisions.

5. National and international sources of law on whistleblowing

Legal provisions covering whistleblowing, either internal or external, are listed below, as they serve as valuable indications for the organizing of reporting within companies:

a) International conventions

The InterAmerican Convention against Corruption (article III, section 8) of 29 March 1996, requires Parties to consider adopting systems for protecting public servants and private citizens who, in good faith, report acts of corruption, including protection of their identities.

The United Nations Convention against Corruption of 9 December 2003 (article 33) requires each State Party to consider incorporating into its domestic legal system *appropriate measures to provide protec tion against any unjustified treatment for any person who reports in good faith and on reasonable grounds to the competent authorities any facts concerning offences established in accordance in accordance with [the] Convention.*

The European Council Criminal Law Convention of 27 January 1999 (article 22) requires each Party to adopt *such measures as may be necessary to provide effective and appropriate protection for those who report the criminal offences established in accordance with* [the relevant provisions of the Convention].

The European Council Civil Law Convention of 4 November 1999 (article 9) requires that each Party provides *in its internal law for appropriate protection against any unjustified sanction for employees who have rea sonable grounds to suspect corruption and who report in good faith their suspicion to responsible persons or authorities.*

The African Union Convention on Preventing and Combating Corruption of 11 July 2003 (article 5) requires State Parties to adopt *measures that ensure citizens report instances of corruption without fear of consequent retaliation.*

b) Selected national legislation

1. United Kingdom: Public Interest Disclosure Act 1998 (PIDA) grants whistleblower protection to individuals who make certain disclosures in good faith and in the public interest and allows these individuals to bring action in respect of victimization.

2. United States: SarbanesOxley Act of 2002 (section 806) grants whistleblower protection for employees of publicly traded companies against retaliation in fraud cases.

   The New York Stock Exchange (NYSE) Listing Manual (Section 303A.10)[7] provides that listed companies must adopt a code of ethics for directors, officers and employees. In the commentary, it is stressed that each code of ethics must contain compliance standards and procedures that will facilitate the effective operation of the code and inter alia whistleblowing procedures and whistleblower protection.
3. France: Act nr. 20071598 of 13 November 2007 (article 9) amends the Labour Code and prohibits any discrimination against a person, who has reported or brought a witness report to an employer or to the authorities about corruption. Any discriminato ry act is to be declared null and void.

c) Recommendations by international public organizations

The OECD Guidelines for Multinational Enterprises of 2000 (chapter II, item 9) recommend that enterprises "refrain from discriminatory or disciplinary action against employees who make bona fide reports to management or, to the competent authorities, on practices that contravene the law, the Guidelines or the enterprise's policies[8]."

B. ICC Guidelines on Whistleblowing

1) Enterprises are encouraged to establish, within their organization and as an integral part of their integrity programme, a whistleblowing system, commensu rate with their size and resources.

2) Such whistleblowing system should aim to:

(i) Receive and entertain, in full confidentiality, all reasonable requests for advice and guidance on business conduct matters and ethical concerns raised by the employees of the enterprise and of its subsidiaries or affiliates (the group), but also, to any extent possible, by any of the group's agents, suppliers and customers; and to;

[7] **See also Section 4350 of the NASDAQ Listing Manual.**

[8] **The Commentary on this provision reads as follows:** *Following from effective self-regulatory practices, as a matter of course, enterprises are expected to promote employee awareness of company policies. Safeguards to protect bona fide "whistleblowing" activities are also recommended, including protection of employees who, in the absence of timely remedial action or in the face of reasonable risk of negative employment action, report practices that contravene the law to the competent authorities. While of particular relevance to anti-bribery and environmental initiatives, such protection is also relevant to other recommendations in the Guidelines.*

(ii) Receive and handle, Extortion and Bribery Rules of Conduct and Recommendations, which could seriously harm the enterprise or the group, if no remedial action is taken.

3) Enterprises should appoint high level personnel of undisputable repute and extensive work experience to be in charge of the management and administration of their whistleblowing units or ombudsservice. This personnel should be given a large autonomy within the enterprise and report to the highest echelon possible within the group.

As part of these arrangements, an enterprise may designate a firm, external to the group, specialized in receiving and handling whistleblowing reports. Such firm should be independent, of undisputable repute and should offer appropriate guarantees of professionalism and secrecy.

4) It is up to each individual enterprise to define the kind of communication channels it wants to use for whistleblowing purposes: oral or written communication, telephone based communication (toll free call help lines or hotlines) or computer based communication (Intranet) or any other tool which it considers adequate.

Enterprises should endeavor to use in these communication channels as many of the languages spoken in the different countries of operation as reasonably possible.

5) A whistleblowing system, being part and parcel of the enterprises voluntary ' integrity programmes, will only be successful if it is not overregulated from the outside.

Enterprises, however, should be aware that, in certain jurisdictions and cultural environments and because of inter alia data protection and labour law concerns, legal restrictions have been imposed on whistleblowing procedures which they will have to comply with.

6) Each individual enterprise may decide, taking into account the applicable law of every country, in which a whistleblowing system will be put into place:

i) Whether reporting under the whistleblowing system will be made compulsory or voluntary, and

ii) Whether reporting can be done on an anonymous as well as on a disclosed basis.

In deciding to opt for an anonymous whistleblowing system, a company may take into account its cultural environment, as well as issues relating to the protection of privacy and the risk of unfair reporting.

If an enterprise considers that reporting is made on a voluntary basis, its employees may opt to report a serious occurrence, as defined under § 2 above, under any other internal or external procedure, which is available.

7) All whistleblowers' reports should be diligently acknowledged, recorded and screened.

A whistleblower, whose report is not considered bona fide, should forthwith be told so and such report should be disregarded.

If there is abuse of the process, disciplinary action can be envisaged.

All bona fide reports should be investigated by the enterprise's whistleblowing unit and forwarded, under strict confidentiality rules, to the appropriate person(s) or department(s) in the enterprise or group.

As soon as reasonably possible, the main results of the due diligence examination should be appropriately communicated as feedback to the whistleblower.

The person whose behavior has been reported, should also be informed of the main object of the ongoing procedure, thereby allowing this person to present objections.

8) All employees should be in a position to report serious occurrences, as defined above, without fear of retaliation or of discriminatory or disciplinary action. Therefore, the whistleblower's employment, remuneration and career opportunities should be protected by the enterprise during a reasonable period of time.

Enterprises should maintain, to the fullest extent possible and at all times, the confidentiality of the data revealed through whistleblowing, and the identity of the whistleblower, subject to overriding legal requirements, and should protect such data with the most appropriate means.

OECD Convention on Combating Bribery of Foreign Public Officials in International Business Transactions

On 21 November 1997, OECD Member countries and five non-member countries, Argentina, Brazil, Bulgaria, Chile and the Slovak Republic, adopted a Convention on Combating Bribery of Foreign Public Officials in International Business Transactions. Signature of the Convention took place in Paris on 17 December 1997.

PREAMBLE

The Parties

Considering that bribery is a widespread phenomenon in international business transactions, including trade and investment, which raises serious moral and political concerns, undermines good governance and economic development, and distorts international competitive conditions;

Considering that all countries share a responsibility to combat bribery in international business transactions;

Having regard to the Revised Recommendation on Combating Bribery in International Business Transactions, adopted by the Council of the Organisation for Economic Cooperation and Development (OECD) on 23 May 1997, C(97)123/FINAL, which, inter alia, called for effective measures to deter, prevent and combat the bribery of foreign public officials in connection with international business transactions, in particular the prompt criminalisation of such bribery in an effective and co-ordinated manner and in conformity with the agreed common elements set out in that Recommendation and with the jurisdictional and other basic legal principles of each country;

Welcoming other recent developments which further advance international understanding and co-operation in combating bribery of public officials, including actions of the United Nations, the World Bank, the International Monetary Fund, the World Trade Organisation, the Organisation of American States, the Council of Europe and the European Union;

Welcoming the efforts of companies, business organisations and trade unions as well as other non-governmental organisations to combat bribery;

Recognising the role of governments in the prevention of solicitation of bribes from individuals and enterprises in international business transactions;
Recognising that achieving progress in this field requires not only efforts on a national level but also multilateral co-operation, monitoring and follow-up;

Recognising that achieving equivalence among the measures to be taken by the Parties is an essential object and purpose of the Convention, which requires that the Convention be ratified without derogations affecting this equivalence;

Have agreed as follows:

- **Article 1 – The Offence of Bribery of Foreign Public Officials**

1. Each Party shall take such measures as may be necessary to establish that it is a criminal offence under its law for any person intentionally to offer, promise or give any undue pecuniary or other advantage, whether directly or through intermediaries, to a foreign public official, for that official or for a third party, in order that the official act or refrain from acting in relation to the performance of official duties, in order to obtain or retain business or other improper advantage in the conduct of international business.

2. Each Party shall take any measures necessary to establish that complicity in, including incitement, aiding and abetting, or authorisation of an act of bribery of a foreign public official, shall be a criminal offence. Attempt and conspiracy to bribe a foreign public official shall be criminal offences to the same extent as attempt and conspiracy to bribe a public official of that Party.

3. The offences set out in paragraphs 1 and 2 above are hereinafter referred to as "bribery of a foreign public official".

4. For the purpose of this Convention:
   a) "foreign public official" means any person holding a legislative, administrative or judicial office of a foreign country, whether appointed or elected; any person exercising a public function for a foreign country, including for a public agency or public enterprise; and any official or agent of a public international organisation;
   b) "foreign country" includes all levels and subdivisions of government, from national to local;
   c) "act or refrain from acting in relation to the performance of official duties" includes any use of the public official's position, whether or not within the official's authorised competence.

- **Article 2 – Responsibility of Legal Persons**

Each Party shall take such measures as may be necessary, in accordance with its legal principles, to establish the liability of legal persons for the bribery of a foreign public official.

- **Article 3 – Sanctions**

1. The bribery of a foreign public official shall be punishable by effective, proportionate and dissuasive criminal penalties. The range of penalties shall be comparable to that applicable to the bribery of the Party's own public officials and shall, in the case of natural persons, include deprivation of liberty sufficient to enable effective mutual legal assistance and extradition.

2. In the event that, under the legal system of a Party, criminal responsibility is not applicable to legal persons, that Party shall ensure that legal persons shall be subject to effective, proportionate and dissuasive non-criminal sanctions, includ ing monetary sanctions, for bribery of foreign public officials.

3. Each Party shall take such measures as may be necessary to provide that the bribe and the proceeds of the bribery of a foreign public official, or property the value of which corresponds to that of such proceeds, are subject to seizure and confiscation or that monetary sanctions of comparable effect are applicable.

4. Each Party shall consider the imposition of additional civil or administrative sanctions upon a person subject to sanctions for the bribery of a foreign public official.

- **Article 4 – Jurisdiction**

1. Each Party shall take such measures as may be necessary to establish its jurisdiction over the bribery of a foreign public official when the offence is com mitted in whole or in part in its territory.

2. Each Party which has jurisdiction to prosecute its nationals for offences committed abroad shall take such measures as may be necessary to establish its jurisdiction to do so in respect of the bribery of a foreign public official, according to the same principles.

3. When more than one Party has jurisdiction over an alleged offence described in this Convention, the Parties involved shall, at the request of one of them, consult with a view to determining the most appropriate jurisdiction for prosecution.

4. Each Party shall review whether its current basis for jurisdiction is effective in the fight against the bribery of foreign public officials and, if it is not, shall take remedial steps.

- **Article 5 – Enforcement**

Investigation and prosecution of the bribery of a foreign public official shall be subject to the applicable rules and principles of each Party. They shall not be influenced by considerations of national economic interest, the potential effect upon relations with another State or the identity of the natural or legal persons involved.

- **Article 6 – Statute of Limitations**

Any statute of limitations applicable to the offence of bribery of a foreign public official shall allow an adequate period of time for the investigation and prosecution of this offence.

- **Article 7 – Money Laundering**

Each Party which has made bribery of its own public official a predicate offence for the purpose of the application of its money laundering legislation shall do so on the same terms for the bribery of a foreign public official, without regard to the place where the bribery occurred.

- **Article 8 – Accounting**

1. In order to combat bribery of foreign public officials effectively, each Party shall take such measures as may be necessary, within the framework of its laws and regulations regarding the maintenance of books and records, financial statement disclosures, and accounting and auditing standards, to prohibit the establishment of off-the-books accounts, the making of off-the-books or inadequately identified transactions, the recording of non-existent expenditures, the entry of liabilities with incorrect identification of their object, as well as the use of false documents, by companies subject to those laws and regulations, for the purpose of bribing foreign public officials or of hiding such bribery.
2. Each Party shall provide effective, proportionate and dissuasive civil, administrative or criminal penalties for such omissions and falsifications in respect of the books, records, accounts and financial statements of such companies.

- **Article 9 – Mutual Legal Assistance**

1. Each Party shall, to the fullest extent possible under its laws and relevant treaties and arrangements, provide prompt and effective legal assistance to another Party for the purpose of criminal investigations and proceedings brought by a Party concerning offences within the scope of this Convention and for non-criminal proceedings within the scope of this Convention brought by a Party against a legal person. The requested Party shall inform the requesting Party, without delay, of any additional information or documents needed to support the request for assistance and, where requested, of the status and outcome of the request for assistance.

2. Where a Party makes mutual legal assistance conditional upon the existence of dual criminality, dual criminality shall be deemed to exist if the offence for which the assistance is sought is within the scope of this Convention.
3. A Party shall not decline to render mutual legal assistance for criminal matters within the scope of this Convention on the ground of bank secrecy.

- **Article 10 – Extradition**

1. Bribery of a foreign public official shall be deemed to be included as an extraditable offence under the laws of the Parties and the extradition treaties between them.

2. If a Party which makes extradition conditional on the existence of an extradition treaty receives a request for extradition from another Party with which it has no extradition treaty, it may consider this Convention to be the legal basis for extradition in respect of the offence of bribery of a foreign public official.

3. Each Party shall take any measures necessary to assure either that it can extradite its nationals or that it can prosecute its nationals for the offence of bribery of a foreign public official. A Party which declines a request to extradite a person for bribery of a foreign public official solely on the ground that the person is its national shall submit the case to its competent authorities for the purpose of prosecution.

4. Extradition for bribery of a foreign public official is subject to the conditions set out in the domestic law and applicable treaties and arrangements of each Party. Where a Party makes extradition conditional upon the existence of dual criminality, that condition shall be deemed to be fulfilled if the offence for which extradition is sought is within the scope of Article 1 of this Convention.

- **Article 11 – Responsible Authorities**

For the purposes of Article 4, paragraph 3, on consultation, Article 9, on mutual legal assistance and Article 10, on extradition, each Party shall notify to the Secretary-General of the OECD an authority or authorities responsible for making and receiving requests, which shall serve as channel of communication for these matters for that Party, without prejudice to other arrangements between Parties.

- **Article 12 – Monitoring and Follow-up**

The Parties shall co-operate in carrying out a programme of systematic follow-up to monitor and promote the full implementation of this Convention. Unless otherwise decided by consensus of the Parties, this shall be done in the framework of the OECD Working Group on Bribery in International Business Transactions and according to its terms of reference, or within the framework and terms of reference of any successor to its functions, and Parties shall bear the costs of the programme in accordance with the rules applicable to that body.

- **Article 13 – Signature and Accession**

1. Until its entry into force, this Convention shall be open for signature by OECD members and by non-members which have been invited to become full participants in its Working Group on Bribery in International Business Transactions.

2. Subsequent to its entry into force, this Convention shall be open to accession by any non-signatory which is a member of the OECD or has become a full participant in the Working Group on Bribery in International Business Transactions or any successor to its functions. For each such non-signatory, the Convention shall enter into force on the sixtieth day following the date of deposit of its instrument of accession.

- **Article 14 – Ratification and Depositary**

This Convention is subject to acceptance, approval or ratification by the Signatories, in accordance with their respective laws.
Instruments of acceptance, approval, ratification or accession shall be deposited with the Secretary-General of the OECD, who shall serve as Depositary of this Convention.

- **Article 15 – Entry into Force**

1. This Convention shall enter into force on the sixtieth day following the date upon which five of the ten countries which have the ten largest export shares (see annex), and which represent by themselves at least sixty per cent of the combined total exports of those ten countries, have deposited their instruments of acceptance, approval, or ratification. For each signatory depositing its instrument after such entry into force, the Convention shall enter into force on the sixtieth day after deposit of its instrument.

2. If, after 31 December 1998, the Convention has not entered into force under paragraph 1 above, any signatory which has deposited its instrument of acceptance, approval or ratification may declare in writing to the Depositary its readiness to accept entry into force of this Convention under this paragraph 2. The Convention shall enter into force for such a signatory on the sixtieth day following the date upon which such declarations have been deposited by at least two signatories. For each signatory depositing its declaration after such entry into force, the Convention shall enter into force on the sixtieth day following the date of deposit.

- **Article 16 – Amendment**

Any Party may propose the amendment of this Convention. A proposed amendment shall be submitted to the Depositary, which shall communicate it to the other Parties at least sixty days before convening a meeting of the Parties to consider the proposed amendment. An amendment adopted by consensus of the Parties, or by such other means as the Parties may determine by consensus, shall enter into force sixty days after the deposit of an instrument of ratification, acceptance or approval by all of the Parties, or in such other circumstances as may be specified by the Parties at the time of adoption of the amendment.

- **Article 17 – Withdrawal**

A Party may withdraw from this Convention by submitting written notification to the Depositary. Such withdrawal shall be effective one year after the date of the receipt of the notification. After withdrawal, co-operation shall continue between the Parties and the Party which has withdrawn on all requests for assistance or extradition made before the effective date of withdrawal which remain pending.

Official Commentaries to the OECD Convention on Combating Bribery of Officials in International Business Transactions

Adopted by the OECD Negotiating Conference on 21 November 1997

General

1. This Convention deals with what, in the law of some countries, is called "active corruption" or "active bribery", meaning the offence committed by the person who promises or gives the bribe, as contrasted with "passive bribery", the offence committed by the official who receives the bribe. The Convention does not utilise the term "active bribery" simply to avoid it being misread by the non-technical reader as implying that the briber has taken the initiative and the recipient is a passive victim. In fact, in a number of situations, the recipient will have induced or pressured the briber and will have been, in that sense, the more active.

2. This Convention seeks to assure a functional equivalence among the measures taken by the Parties to sanction bribery of foreign public officials, without requiring uniformity or changes in fundamental principles of a Party's legal system.

- **Article 1 – The Offence of Bribery of Foreign Public Officials**

Re. paragraph 1:

3. Article 1 establishes a standard to be met by Parties, but does not require them to utilise its precise terms in defining the offence under their domestic laws. A Party may use various approaches to fulfill its obligations, provided that conviction of a person for the offence does not require proof of elements beyond those which would be required to be proved if the offence were defined as in this paragraph. For example, a statute prohibiting the bribery of agents generally which does not specifically address bribery of a foreign public official, and a statute specifically limited to this case, could both comply with this Article. Similarly, a statute which defined the offence in terms of payments "to induce a breach of the official's duty" could meet the standard provided that it was understood that every public official had a duty to exercise judgement or discretion impartially and this was an "autonomous" definition not requiring proof of the law of the particular official's country.

4. It is an offence within the meaning of paragraph 1 to bribe to obtain or retain business or other improper advantage whether or not the company concerned was the best qualified bidder or was otherwise a company which could properly have been awarded the business.

5. "Other improper advantage" refers to something to which the company concerned was not clearly entitled, for example, an operating permit for a factory which fails to meet the statutory requirements.

6. The conduct described in paragraph 1 is an offence whether the offer or promise is made or the pecuniary or other advantage is given on that person's own behalf or on behalf of any other natural person or legal entity.

7. It is also an offence irrespective of, inter alia, the value of the advantage, its results, perceptions of local custom, the tolerance of such payments by local authorities, or the alleged necessity of the payment in order to obtain or retai n business or other improper advantage.

8. It is not an offence, however, if the advantage was permitted or required by the written law or regulation of the foreign public official's country, including case law.

9. Small "facilitation" payments do not constitute payments made "to obtain or retain business or other improper advantage" within the meaning of paragraph 1 and, accordingly, are also not an offence. Such payments, which, in some countries, are made to induce public officials to perform their functions, such as issuing licenses or permits, are generally illegal in the foreign country con-cerned. Other countries can and should address this corrosive phenomenon by such means as support for programmes of good governance. However, criminalisation by other countries does not seem a practical or effective complementary action.

10. Under the legal system of some countries, an advantage promised or given to any person, in anticipation of his or her becoming a foreign public official, fall s within the scope of the offences described in Article 1, paragraph 1 or 2. Under the legal system of many countries, it is considered technically distinct from the offences covered by the present Convention. However, there is a commonly shared concern and intent to address this phenomenon through further work.

Re. paragraph 2:

11. The offences set out in paragraph 2 are understood in terms of their normal con tent in national legal systems. Accordingly, if authorisation, incitement, or one of the other listed acts, which does not lead to further action, is not itself punishable under a Party's legal system, then the Party would not be required to make it punishable with respect to bribery of a foreign public official.

Re. paragraph 4:

12. "Public function" includes any activity in the public interest, delegated by a foreign country, such as the performance of a task delegated by it in connection with public procurement.

13. A "public agency" is an entity constituted under public law to carry out specific tasks in the public interest.

14. A "public enterprise" is any enterprise, regardless of its legal form, over which a government, or governments, may, directly or indirectly, exercise a dominant influence. This is deemed to be the case, inter alia, when the government or governments hold the majority of the enterprise's subscribed capital, control the majority of votes attaching to shares issued by the enterprise or ca n appoint a majority of the members of the enterprise's administrative or managerial body or supervisory board.

15. An official of a public enterprise shall be deemed to perform a public function unless the enterprise operates on a normal commercial basis in the relevant market, i.e., on a basis which is substantially equivalent to that of a private enterprise, without preferential subsidies or other privileges.

16. In special circumstances, public authority may in fact be held by persons (e , political party officials in single party states) not formally designated as public officials. Such persons, through their de facto performance of a public function, may, under the legal principles of some countries, be considered to be for eign public officials.

17. "Public international organisation" includes any international organisation formed by states, governments, or other public international organisations, whatever the form of organisation and scope of competence, including, for example, a regional economic integration organisation such as the European Communities.

18. "Foreign country" is not limited to states, but includes any organised foreign area or entity, such as an autonomous territory or a separate customs territory.

19. One case of bribery which has been contemplated under the definition in pragraph 4.c is where an executive of a company gives a bribe to a senior official of a government, in order that this official use his office — though acting outside his competence — to make another official award a contract to that company.

- **Article 2 – Responsibility of Legal Persons**

20. In the event that, under the legal system of a Party, criminal responsibility is not applicable to legal persons, that Party shall not be required to establish such criminal responsibility.

- **Article 3 – Sanctions**

Re. paragraph 3:

21. The "proceeds" of bribery are the profits or other benefits derived by the briber from the transaction or other improper advantage obtained or retained through bribery.
22. The term "confiscation" includes forfeiture where applicable and means the permanent deprivation of property by order of a court or other competent authority. This paragraph is without prejudice to rights of victims.
23. Paragraph 3 does not preclude setting appropriate limits to monetary sanctions.

Re paragraph 4:

24. Among the civil or administrative sanctions, other than non-criminal fines, which might be imposed upon legal persons for an act of bribery of a foreign public official are: exclusion from entitlement to public benefits or aid; temporary or permanent disqualification from participation in public procurement or from the practice of other commercial activities; placing under judicial supervision; and a judicial winding-up order.

- **Article 4 – Jurisdiction**

Re paragraph 1:

25. The territorial basis for jurisdiction should be interpreted broadly so that an extensive physical connection to the bribery act is not required.

Re paragraph 2:

26. Nationality jurisdiction is to be established according to the general principles and conditions in the legal system of each Party. These principles deal with such matters as dual criminality. However, the requirement of dual criminality should be deemed to be met if the act is unlawful where it occurred, even if under a different criminal statute. For countries which apply nationality jurisdiction only to certain types of offences, the reference to "principles" includes the principles upon which such selection is based.

- **Article 5 – Enforcement**

27. Article 5 recognises the fundamental nature of national regimes of prosecutorial discretion. It recognises as well that, in order to protect the independence of prosecution, such discretion is to be exercised on the basis of professional motives and is not to be subject to improper influence by concerns of a political nature. Article 5 is complemented by paragraph 6 of the Annex to the 1997 OECD Revised Recommendation on Combating Bribery in International Business Transactions, C(97)123/FINAL (hereinafter, "1997 OECD Recommendation"), which recommends, inter alia, that complaints of bribery of foreign public officials should be seriously investigated by competent authorities and that adequate resources should be provided by national governments to permit effective prosecution of such bribery. Parties will have accepted this Recommendation, including its monitoring and follow-up arrangements.

- **Article 6 – Statut of Limitations**

Any statute of limitations applicable to the offence of bribery of a foreign public officialshall allow an adequate period of time for the investigation and prosecution of this offence.

- **Article 7 – Money Laundering**

28. In Article 7, "bribery of its own public official" is intended broadly, so that bribery of a foreign public official is to be made a predicate offence for money laundering legislation on the same terms, when a Party has made either active or passive bribery of its own public official such an offence. When a Party has made only passive bribery of its own public officials a predicate offence for money laundering purposes, this article requires that the laundering of the bribe payment be subject to money laundering legislation.

- **Article 8 – Accounting**

29. Article 8 is related to section V of the 1997 OECD Recommendation, which all Parties will have accepted and which is subject to follow-up in the OECD Working Group on Bribery in International Business Transactions. This paragraph contains a series of recommendations concerning accounting requirements, inde pendent external audit and internal company controls the implementation of which will be important to the overall effectiveness of the fight against bribery in international business. However, one immediate consequence of the implementation of this Convention by the Parties will be that companies which are required to issue financial statements disclosing their material contingent liabilities will need to take into account the full potential liabilities under this Convention, in particular its Articles 3 and 8, as well as other losses which might flow from conviction of the company or its agents for bribery. This also has implications for the execution of professional responsibilities of auditors regarding indications of bribery of foreign public officials. In addition, the accounting offences referred to in Article 8 will generally occur in the company's home country, when the bribery offence itself may have been committed in another country, and this can fill gaps in the effective reach of the Convention.

- **Article 9 – Mutual Legal Assistance**

30. Parties will have also accepted, through paragraph 8 of the Agreed Common Elements annexed to the 1997 OECD Recommendation, to explore and under take means to improve the efficiency of mutual legal assistance.

Re paragraph 1:

31. Within the framework of paragraph 1 of Article 9, Parties should, upon request, facilitate or encourage the presence or availability of persons, including persons in custody, who consent to assist in investigations or participate in proceedings. Parties should take measures to be able, in appropriate cases, to transfer

temporarily such a person in custody to a Party requesting it and to credit time in custody in the requesting Party to the transferred person's sentence in the requested Party. The Parties wishing to use this mechanism should also take measures to be able, as a requesting Party, to keep a transferred person in custody and return this person without necessity of extradition proceedings.

Re paragraph 2:

32. Paragraph 2 addresses the issue of identity of norms in the concept of dual criminality. Parties with statutes as diverse as a statute prohibiting the bribery of agents generally and a statute directed specifically at bribery of foreign public officials should be able to co-operate fully regarding cases whose facts fall within the scope of the offences described in this Convention.

- **Article 10 – Extradition**

Re paragraph 2:

33. A Party may consider this Convention to be a legal basis for extradition if, for one or more categories of cases falling within this Convention, it requires an extradition treaty. For example, a country may consider it a basis for extradition of its nationals if it requires an extradition treaty for that category but does not require one for extradition of non-nationals.

- **Article 11 – Responsible Authorities**

For the purposes of Article 4, paragraph 3, on consultation, Article 9, on mutual legal assistance and Article 10, on extradition, each Party shall notify to the Secretary-Generalof the OECD an authority or authorities responsible for making and receiving requests,which shall serve as channel of communication for these matters for that Party, withoutprejudice to other arrangements between Parties.

- **Article 12 – Monitoring and Follow-up**

34. The current terms of reference of the OECD Working Group on Bribery which are relevant to monitoring and follow-up are set out in Section VIII of the 1997 OECD Recommendation. They provide for: i) receipt of notifications and other information submitted to it by the [participating]countries;

    i) receipt of notification and otger information submitted to it by the [participating] countries.

    ii) regular reviews of steps taken by [participating] countries to implement the Recommendation and to make proposals, as appropriate, to assist [participating] countries in its implementation; these reviews will be based on the following complementary systems:

        - a system of self evaluation, where [participating] countries' responses on the basis of a questionnaire will provide a basis for assessing the implementation of the Recommendation;

- a system of mutual evaluation, where each [participating] country will be examined in turn by the Working Group on Bribery, on the basis of a report which will provide an objective assessment of the progress of the [participating] country in implementing the Recommendation.

iii) examination of specific issues relating to bribery in international business transactions; v) provision of regular information to the public on its work and activities and on implementation of the Recommendation.

35. The costs of monitoring and follow-up will, for OECD Members, be handled through the normal OECD budget process. For non-members of the OECD, the current rules create an equivalent system of cost sharing, which is described in the Resolution of the Council Concerning Fees for Regular Observer Countries and Non-Member Full Participants in OECD Subsidiary Bodies, C(96)223/FINAL.
36. The follow-up of any aspect of the Convention which is not also follow-up of the 1997 OECD Recommendation or any other instrument accepted by all the participants in the OECD Working Group on Bribery will be carried out by the Parties to the Convention and, as appropriate, the participants party to another, corresponding instrument.

- **Article 13 – Signature and Accession:**

37. The Convention will be open to non-members which become full participants in the OECD Working Group on Bribery in International Business Transactions. Full participation by non-members in this Working Group is encouraged and arranged under simple procedures. Accordingly, the requirement of full participation in the Working Group, which follows from the relationship of the Convention to other aspects of the fight against bribery in international business, should not be seen as an obstacle by countries wishing to participate in that fight. The Council of the OECD has appealed to non-members to adhere to the 1997 OECD Recommendation and to participate in any institutional follow up or implementation mechanism, i.e., in the Working Group. The current procedures regarding full participation by non-members in the Working Group may be found in the Resolution of the Council concerning the Participation of Non-Member Economies in the Work of Subsidiary Bodies of the Organisation, C(96)64/REV1/FINAL. In addition to accepting the Revised Recommendation of the Council on Combating Bribery, a full participant also accepts the Recommendation on the Tax Deductibility of Bribes of Foreign Public Officials, adopted on 11 April 1996, C(96)27/FINAL.

United Nations Convention against Corruption

Preamble

The States Parties to this Convention,

Concerned about the seriousness of problems and threats posed by corruption to the stability and security of societies, undermining the institutions and values of democracy, ethical values and justice and jeopardizing sustainable development and the rule of law,

Concerned also about the links between corruption and other forms of crime, in particular organized crime and economic crime, including money-laundering,

Concerned further about cases of corruption that involve vast quantities of assets, which may constitute a substantial proportion of the resources of States, and that threaten the political stability and sustainable development of those States,

Convinced that corruption is no longer a local matter but a transnational phenomenon that affects all societies and economies, making international cooperation to prevent and control it essential,

Convinced also that a comprehensive and multidisciplinary approach is required to prevent and combat corruption effectively,

Convinced further that the availability of technical assistance can play an important role in enhancing the ability of States, including by strengthening capacity and by institution-building, to prevent and combat corruption effectively,

Convinced that the illicit acquisition of personal wealth can be particularly damaging to democratic institutions, national economies and the rule of law,

Determined to prevent, detect and deter in a more effective manner international transfers of illicitly acquired assets and to strengthen international cooperation in asset recovery,

Acknowledging the fundamental principles of due process of law in criminal proceedings and in civil or administrative proceedings to adjudicate property rights,

Bearing in mind that the prevention and eradication of corruption is a responsibility of all States and that they must cooperate with one another, with the support and involvement of individuals and groups outside the public sector, such as civil society, non-governmental organizations and community-based organizations, if their efforts in this area are to be effective,

Bearing also in mind the principles of proper management of public affairs and public property, fairness, responsibility and equality before the law and the need to safeguard integrity and to foster a culture of rejection of corruption,

Commending the work of the Commission on Crime Prevention and Criminal Justice and the United Nations Office on Drugs and Crime in preventing and combating corruption,

Recalling the work carried out by other international and regional organizations in this field, including the activities of the African Union, the Council of Europe, the Customs Cooperation Council (also known as the World Customs Organization), the European Union, the League of Arab States, the Organisation for Economic Cooperation and Development and the Organization of American States,

Taking note with appreciation of multilateral instruments to prevent and combat corruption, including, inter alia, the Inter-American Convention against Corruption, adopted by the Organization of American States on 29 March 1996,[1] the Convention on the Fight against Corruption involving Officials of the European Communities or Officials of Member States of the European Union, adopted by the Council of the European Union on 26 May 1997,[2] the Convention on Combating Bribery of Foreign Public Officials in International Business Transactions, adopted by the Organisation for Economic Cooperation and Development on 21 November 1997,[3] the Criminal Law Convention on Corruption, adopted by the Committee of Ministers of the Council of Europe on 27 January 1999,[4] the Civil Law Convention on Corruption, adopted by the Committee of Ministers of the Council of Europe on 4 November 1999,[5] and the African Union Convention on Preventing and Combating Corruption, adopted by the Heads of State and Government of the African Union on 12 July 2003,

Welcoming the entry into force on 29 September 2003 of the United Nations Convention against Transnational Organized Crime,[6]

Have agreed as follows:

1 See E/1996/99.
2 *Official Journal of the European Communities*, C 195, 25 June 1997.
3 See *Corruption and Integrity Improvement Initiatives in Developing Countries* (United Nations publication, Sales No. E.98.III.B.18).
4 Council of Europe, *European Treaty Series*, No. 173.
5 Ibid., No. 174.
6 General Assembly resolution 55/25, annex I.

Chapter I

General provisions

Article 1
Statement of purpose

The purposes of this Convention are:

(a) To promote and strengthen measures to prevent and combat corruption more efficiently and effectively;

(b) To promote, facilitate and support international cooperation and technical assistance in the prevention of and fight against corruption, including in asset recovery;

(c) To promote integrity, accountability and proper management of public affairs and public property.

Article 2
Use of terms

For the purposes of this Convention:

(a) "Public official" shall mean: (i) any person holding a legislative, executive, administrative or judicial office of a State Party, whether appointed or elected, whether permanent or temporary, whether paid or unpaid, irrespective of that person's seniority; (ii) any other person who performs a public function, including for a public agency or public enterprise, or provides a public service, as defined in the domestic law of the State Party and as applied in the pertinent area of law of that State Party; (iii) any other person defined as a "public official" in the domestic law of a State Party. However, for the purpose of some specific measures contained in chapter II of this Convention, "public official" may mean any person who performs a public function or provides a public service as defined in the domestic law of the State Party and as applied in the pertinent area of law of that State Party;

(b) "Foreign public official" shall mean any person holding a legislative, executive, administrative or judicial office of a foreign country, whether appointed or elected; and any person exercising a public function for a foreign country, including for a public agency or public enterprise;

(c) "Official of a public international organization" shall mean an international civil servant or any person who is authorized by such an organization to act on behalf of that organization;

(d) "Property" shall mean assets of every kind, whether corporeal or incorporeal, movable or immovable, tangible or intangible, and legal documents or instruments evidencing title to or interest in such assets;

(e) "Proceeds of crime" shall mean any property derived from or obtained, directly or indirectly, through the commission of an offence;

(f) "Freezing" or "seizure" shall mean temporarily prohibiting the transfer, conversion, disposition or movement of property or temporarily assuming custody or control of property on the basis of an order issued by a court or other competent authority;

(g) "Confiscation", which includes forfeiture where applicable, shall mean the permanent deprivation of property by order of a court or other competent authority;

(h) "Predicate offence" shall mean any offence as a result of which proceeds have been generated that may become the subject of an offence as defined in article 23 of this Convention;

(i) "Controlled delivery" shall mean the technique of allowing illicit or suspect consignments to pass out of, through or into the territory of one or more States, with the knowledge and under the supervision of their competent authorities, with a view to the investigation of an offence and the identification of persons involved in the commission of the offence.

Article 3
Scope of application

1. This Convention shall apply, in accordance with its terms, to the prevention, investigation and prosecution of corruption and to the freezing, seizure, confiscation and return of the proceeds of offences established in accordance with this Convention.

2. For the purposes of implementing this Convention, it shall not be necessary, except as otherwise stated herein, for the offences set forth in it to result in damage or harm to state property.

Article 4
Protection of sovereignty

1. States Parties shall carry out their obligations under this Convention in a manner consistent with the principles of sovereign equality and territorial integrity of States and that of non-intervention in the domestic affairs of other States.

2. Nothing in this Convention shall entitle a State Party to undertake in the territory of another State the exercise of jurisdiction and performance of functions that are reserved exclusively for the authorities of that other State by its domestic law.

Chapter II
Preventive measures

Article 5
Preventive anti-corruption policies and practices

1. Each State Party shall, in accordance with the fundamental principles of its legal system, develop and implement or maintain effective, coordinated anti-corruption policies that promote the participation of society and reflect the principles of the rule of law, proper management of public affairs and public property, integrity, transparency and accountability.

2. Each State Party shall endeavour to establish and promote effective practices aimed at the prevention of corruption.

3. Each State Party shall endeavour to periodically evaluate relevant legal instruments and administrative measures with a view to determining their adequacy to prevent and fight corruption.

4. States Parties shall, as appropriate and in accordance with the fundamental principles of their legal system, collaborate with each other and with relevant international and regional organizations in promoting and developing the measures referred to in this article. That collaboration may include participation in international programmes and projects aimed at the prevention of corruption.

Article 6
Preventive anti-corruption body or bodies

1. Each State Party shall, in accordance with the fundamental principles of its legal system, ensure the existence of a body or bodies, as appropriate, that prevent corruption by such means as:

(a) Implementing the policies referred to in article 5 of this Convention and, where appropriate, overseeing and coordinating the implementation of those policies;

(b) Increasing and disseminating knowledge about the prevention of corruption.

2. Each State Party shall grant the body or bodies referred to in paragraph 1 of this article the necessary independence, in accordance with the fundamental principles of its legal system, to enable the body or bodies to carry out its or their functions effectively and free from any undue influence. The necessary material resources and specialized staff, as well as the training that such staff may require to carry out their functions, should be provided.

3. Each State Party shall inform the Secretary-General of the United Nations of the name and address of the authority or authorities that may assist other States Parties in developing and implementing specific measures for the prevention of corruption.

Article 7
Public sector

1. Each State Party shall, where appropriate and in accordance with the fundamental principles of its legal system, endeavour to adopt, maintain and strengthen systems for the recruitment, hiring, retention, promotion and retirement of civil servants and, where appropriate, other non-elected public officials:

(a) That are based on principles of efficiency, transparency and objective criteria such as merit, equity and aptitude;

(b) That include adequate procedures for the selection and training of individuals for public positions considered especially vulnerable to corruption and the rotation, where appropriate, of such individuals to other positions;

(c) That promote adequate remuneration and equitable pay scales, taking into account the level of economic development of the State Party;

(d) That promote education and training programmes to enable them to meet the requirements for the correct, honourable and proper performance of public functions and that provide them with specialized and appropriate training to enhance their awareness of the risks of corruption inherent in the performance of their functions. Such programmes may make reference to codes or standards of conduct in applicable areas.

2. Each State Party shall also consider adopting appropriate legislative and administrative measures, consistent with the objectives of this Convention and in accordance with the fundamental principles of its domestic law, to prescribe criteria concerning candidature for and election to public office.

3. Each State Party shall also consider taking appropriate legislative and administrative measures, consistent with the objectives of this Convention and in accordance with the fundamental principles of its domestic law, to enhance transparency in the funding of candidatures for elected public office and, where applicable, the funding of political parties.

4. Each State Party shall, in accordance with the fundamental principles of its domestic law, endeavour to adopt, maintain and strengthen systems that promote transparency and prevent conflicts of interest.

Article 8
Codes of conduct for public officials

1. In order to fight corruption, each State Party shall promote, inter alia, integrity, honesty and responsibility among its public officials, in accordance with the fundamental principles of its legal system.

2. In particular, each State Party shall endeavour to apply, within its own institutional and legal systems, codes or standards of conduct for the correct, honourable and proper performance of public functions.

3. For the purposes of implementing the provisions of this article, each State Party shall, where appropriate and in accordance with the fundamental principles of its legal system, take note of the relevant initiatives of regional, interregional and multilateral organizations, such as the International Code of Conduct for Public Officials contained in the annex to General Assembly resolution 51/59 of 12 December 1996.

4. Each State Party shall also consider, in accordance with the fundamental principles of its domestic law, establishing measures and systems to facilitate the reporting by public officials of acts of corruption to appropriate authorities, when such acts come to their notice in the performance of their functions.

5. Each State Party shall endeavour, where appropriate and in accordance with the fundamental principles of its domestic law, to establish measures and systems requiring public officials to make declarations to appropriate authorities regarding, inter alia, their outside activities, employment, investments, assets and substantial gifts or benefits from which a conflict of interest may result with respect to their functions as public officials.

6. Each State Party shall consider taking, in accordance with the fundamental principles of its domestic law, disciplinary or other measures against public officials who violate the codes or standards established in accordance with this article.

Article 9
Public procurement and management of public finances

1. Each State Party shall, in accordance with the fundamental principles of its legal system, take the necessary steps to establish appropriate systems of procurement, based on transparency, competition and objective criteria in decision-making, that are effective, inter alia, in preventing corruption. Such systems, which may take into account appropriate threshold values in their application, shall address, inter alia:

(a) The public distribution of information relating to procurement procedures and contracts, including information on invitations to tender and relevant or pertinent information on the award of contracts, allowing potential tenderers sufficient time to prepare and submit their tenders;

(b) The establishment, in advance, of conditions for participation, including selection and award criteria and tendering rules, and their publication;

(c) The use of objective and predetermined criteria for public procurement decisions, in order to facilitate the subsequent verification of the correct application of the rules or procedures;

(d) An effective system of domestic review, including an effective system of appeal, to ensure legal recourse and remedies in the event that the rules or procedures established pursuant to this paragraph are not followed;

(e) Where appropriate, measures to regulate matters regarding personnel responsible for procurement, such as declaration of interest in particular public procurements, screening procedures and training requirements.

2. Each State Party shall, in accordance with the fundamental principles of its legal system, take appropriate measures to promote transparency and accountability in the management of public finances. Such measures shall encompass, inter alia:

(a) Procedures for the adoption of the national budget;

(b) Timely reporting on revenue and expenditure;

(c) A system of accounting and auditing standards and related oversight;

(d) Effective and efficient systems of risk management and internal control;

(e) Where appropriate, corrective action in the case of failure to comply with the requirements established in this paragraph.

3. Each State Party shall take such civil and administrative measures as may be necessary, in accordance with the fundamental principles of its domestic law, to preserve the integrity of accounting books, records, financial statements or other documents related to public expenditure and revenue and to prevent the falsification of such documents.

Article 10
Public reporting

Taking into account the need to combat corruption, each State Party shall, in accordance with the fundamental principles of its domestic law, take such measures as may be necessary to enhance transparency in its public administration, including with regard to its organization, functioning and decision-making processes, where appropriate. Such measures may include, inter alia:

(a) Adopting procedures or regulations allowing members of the general public to obtain, where appropriate, information on the organization, functioning and decision-making processes of its public administration and, with due regard for the protection of privacy and personal data, on decisions and legal acts that concern members of the public;

(b) Simplifying administrative procedures, where appropriate, in order to facilitate public access to the competent decision-making authorities; and

(c) Publishing information, which may include periodic reports on the risks of corruption in its public administration.

Article 11
Measures relating to the judiciary and prosecution services

1. Bearing in mind the independence of the judiciary and its crucial role in combating corruption, each State Party shall, in accordance with the fundamental principles of its legal system and without prejudice to judicial independence, take measures to strengthen integrity and to prevent opportunities for corruption among members of the judiciary. Such measures may include rules with respect to the conduct of members of the judiciary.

2. Measures to the same effect as those taken pursuant to paragraph 1 of this article may be introduced and applied within the prosecution service in those States Parties where it does not form part of the judiciary but enjoys independence similar to that of the judicial service.

Article 12
Private sector

1. Each State Party shall take measures, in accordance with the fundamental principles of its domestic law, to prevent corruption involving the private sector, enhance accounting and auditing standards in the private sector and, where appropriate, provide effective, proportionate and dissuasive civil, administrative or criminal penalties for failure to comply with such measures.

2. Measures to achieve these ends may include, inter alia:

(a) Promoting cooperation between law enforcement agencies and relevant private entities;

(b) Promoting the development of standards and procedures designed to safeguard the integrity of relevant private entities, including codes of conduct for the correct, honourable and proper performance of the activities of business and all relevant professions and the prevention of conflicts of interest, and for the promotion of the use of good commercial practices among businesses and in the contractual relations of businesses with the State;

(c) Promoting transparency among private entities, including, where appropriate, measures regarding the identity of legal and natural persons involved in the establishment and management of corporate entities;

(d) Preventing the misuse of procedures regulating private entities, including procedures regarding subsidies and licences granted by public authorities for commercial activities;

(e) Preventing conflicts of interest by imposing restrictions, as appropriate and for a reasonable period of time, on the professional activities of former public officials or on the employment of public officials by the private sector after their resignation or retirement, where such activities or employment relate directly to the functions held or supervised by those public officials during their tenure;

(f) Ensuring that private enterprises, taking into account their structure and size, have sufficient internal auditing controls to assist in preventing and detecting acts of corruption and that the accounts and required financial statements of such private enterprises are subject to appropriate auditing and certification procedures.

3. In order to prevent corruption, each State Party shall take such measures as may be necessary, in accordance with its domestic laws and regulations regarding the maintenance of books and records, financial statement disclosures and accounting and auditing standards, to prohibit the following acts carried out for the purpose of committing any of the offences established in accordance with this Convention:

(a) The establishment of off-the-book accounts;

(b) The making of off-the-book or inafequately identified transactions;

(c) The recording of non-existent expenditure;

(d) The entry of liabilities with incorrect identification of their objects;

(e) The use of false document;and

(f) The intentional destruction of bookkeeping documents earlier than foreseen by the law.

4. Each State Party shall disallow the tax deductibility of expenses that constitute bribes, the latter being one of the constituent elements of the offences established in accordance with articles 15 and 16 of this Convention and, where appropriate, other expenses incurred in furtherance of corrupt conduct.

Article 13
Participation of society

1. Each State Party shall take appropriate measures, within its means and in accordance with fundamental principles of its domestic law, to promote the active participation of individuals and groups outside the public sector, such as civil society, non-governmental organizations and community-based organizations, in the prevention of and the fight against corruption and to raise public awareness regarding the existence, causes and gravity of and the threat posed by corruption. This participation should be strengthened by such measures as:

(a) Enhancing the transparency of and promoting the contribution of the public to decision-making processes;

(b) Ensuring that the public has effective access to information;

(c) Undertaking public information activities that contribute to non-tolerance of corruption, as well as public education programmes, including school and university curricula;

(d) Respecting, promoting and protecting the freedom to seek, receive, publish and disseminate information concerning corruption. That freedom may be subject to certain restrictions, but these shall only be such as are provided for by law and are necessary:

(i) For respect of the rights or reputations of others; (ii) For the protection of national security or *ordre public* or of public health or morals.

2. Each State Party shall take appropriate measures to ensure that the relevant anti-corruption bodies referred to in this Convention are known to the public and shall provide access to such bodies, where appropriate, for the reporting, including anonymously, of any incidents that may be considered to constitute an offence established in accordance with this Convention.

Article 14
Measures to prevent money-laundering

1. Each State Party shall:

(a) Institute a comprehensive domestic regulatory and supervisory regime for banks and non-bank financial institutions, including natural or legal persons that provide formal or informal services for the transmission of money or value and, where appropriate, other bodies particularly susceptible to money-laundering, within its competence, in order to deter and detect all forms of money-laundering, which regime shall emphasize requirements for customer and, where appropriate, beneficial owner identification, record-keeping and the reporting of suspicious transactions;

(b) Without prejudice to article 46 of this Convention, ensure that administrative, regulatory, law enforcement and other authorities dedicated to combating money-laundering (including, where appropriate under domestic law, judicial authorities) have the ability to cooperate and exchange information at the national and international levels within the conditions prescribed by its domestic law and, to that end, shall consider the establishment of a financial intelligence unit to serve as a national centre for the collection, analysis and dissemination of information regarding potential money-laundering.

2. States Parties shall consider implementing feasible measures to detect and monitor the movement of cash and appropriate negotiable instruments across their borders, subject to safeguards to ensure proper use of information and without impeding in any way the movement of legitimate capital. Such measures may include a requirement that individuals and businesses report the cross-border transfer of substantial quantities of cash and appropriate negotiable instruments.

3. States Parties shall consider implementing appropriate and feasible measures to require financial institutions, including money remitters:

(a) To include on forms for the electronic transfer of funds and related messages accurate and meaningful information on the originator;

(b) To maintain such information throughout the payment chain; and

(c) To apply enhanced scrutiny to transfers of funds that do not contain complete information on the originator.

4. In establishing a domestic regulatory and supervisory regime under the terms of this article, and without prejudice to any other article of this Convention, States Parties are called upon to use as a guideline the relevant initiatives of regional, interregional and multilateral organizations against money-laundering.

5. States Parties shall endeavour to develop and promote global, regional, subregional and bilateral cooperation among judicial, law enforcement and financial regulatory authorities in order to combat money- laundering.

Chapter III
Criminalization and law enforcement

Article 15
Bribery of national public officials

Each State Party shall adopt such legislative and other measures as may be necessary to establish as criminal offences, when committed intentionally:

(a) The promise, offering or giving, to a public official, directly or indirectly, of an undue advantage, for the official himself or herself or another person or entity, in order that the official act or refrain from acting in the exercise of his or her official duties;

(b) The solicitation or acceptance by a public official, directly or indirectly, of an undue advantage, for the official himself or herself or another person or entity, in order that the official act or refrain from acting in the exercise of his or her official duties.

Article 16
Bribery of foreign public officials and officials of public international organizations

1. Each State Party shall adopt such legislative and other measures as may be necessary to establish as a criminal offence, when committed intentionally, the promise, offering or giving to a foreign public official or an official of a public international organization, directly or indirectly, of an undue advantage, for the official himself or herself or another person or entity, in order that the official act or refrain from acting in the exercise of his or her official duties, in order to obtain or retain business or other undue advantage in relation to the conduct of international business.

2. Each State Party shall consider adopting such legislative and other measures as may be necessary to establish as a criminal offence, when committed intentionally, the solicitation or acceptance by a foreign public official or an official of a public international organization, directly or indirectly, of an undue advantage, for the official himself or herself or another person or entity, in order that the official act or refrain from acting in the exercise of his or her official duties.

Article 17
Embezzlement, misappropriation or other diversion of property by a public official

Each State Party shall adopt such legislative and other measures as may be necessary to establish as criminal offences, when committed intentionally, the embezzlement, misappropriation or other diversion by a public official for his or her benefit or for the benefit of another person or entity, of any property, public or private funds or securities or any other thing of value entrusted to the public official by virtue of his or her position.

Article 18
Trading in influence

Each State Party shall consider adopting such legislative and other measures as may be necessary to establish as criminal offences, when committed intentionally:

(a) The promise, offering or giving to a public official or any other person, directly or indirectly, of an undue advantage in order that the public official or the person abuse his or her real or supposed influence with a view to obtaining from an administration or public authority of the State Party an undue advantage for the original instigator of the act or for any other person;

(b) The solicitation or acceptance by a public official or any other person, directly or indirectly, of an undue advantage for himself or herself or for another person in order that the public official or the person abuse his or her real or supposed influence with a view to obtaining from an administration or public authority of the State Party an undue advantage.

Article 19
Abuse of functions

Each State Party shall consider adopting such legislative and other measures as may be necessary to establish as a criminal offence, when committed intentionally, the abuse of functions or position, that is, the performance of or failure to perform an act, in violation of laws, by a public official in the discharge of his or her functions, for the purpose of obtaining an undue advantage for himself or herself or for another person or entity.

Article 20
Illicit enrichment

Subject to its constitution and the fundamental principles of its legal system, each State Party shall consider adopting such legislative and other measures as may be necessary to establish as a criminal offence, when committed intentionally, illicit enrichment, that is, a significant increase in the assets of a public official that he or she cannot reasonably explain in relation to his or her lawful income.

Article 21
Bribery in the private sector

Each State Party shall consider adopting such legislative and other measures as may be necessary to establish as criminal offences, when committed intentionally in the course of economic, financial or commercial activities:

(a) The promise, offering or giving, directly or indirectly, of an undue advantage to any person who directs or works, in any capacity, for a private sector entity, for the person himself or herself or for another person, in order that he or she, in breach of his or her duties, act or refrain from acting;

(b) The solicitation or acceptance, directly or indirectly, of an undue advantage by any person who directs or works, in any capacity, for a private sector entity, for the person himself or herself or for another person, in order that he or she, in breach of his or her duties, act or refrain from acting.

Article 22
Embezzlement of property in the private sector

Each State Party shall consider adopting such legislative and other measures as may be necessary to establish as a criminal offence, when committed intentionally in the course of economic, financial or commercial activities, embezzlement by a person who directs or works, in any capacity, in a private sector entity of any property, private funds or securities or any other thing of value entrusted to him or her by virtue of his or her position.

Article 23
Laundering of proceeds of crime

1. Each State Party shall adopt, in accordance with fundamental principles of its domestic law, such legislative and other measures as may be necessary to establish as criminal offences, when committed intentionally:

(a) (i) The conversion or transfer of property, knowing that such property is the proceeds of crime, for the purpose of concealing or disguising the illicit origin of the property or of helping any person who is involved in the commission of the predicate offence to evade the legal consequences of his or her action;

(ii) The concealment or disguise of the true nature, source, location, dispo sition, movement or ownership of or rights with respect to property, know ing that such property is the proceeds of crime;

(b) Subject to the basic concepts of its legal system:

(i) The acquisition, possession or use of property, knowing, at the time of receipt, that such property is the proceeds of crime;

(ii) Participation in, association with or conspiracy to commit, attempts to commit and aiding, abetting, facilitating and counselling the commission of any of the offences established in accordance with this article.

2. For purposes of implementing or applying paragraph 1 of this article:

(a) Each State Party shall seek to apply paragraph 1 of this article to the widest range of predicate offences;

(b) Each State Party shall include as predicate offences at a minimum a comprehensive range of criminal offences established in accordance with this Convention;

(c) For the purposes of subparagraph (b) above, predicate offences shall include offences committed both within and outside the jurisdiction of the State Party in question. However, offences committed outside the jurisdiction of a State Party shall constitute predicate offences only when the relevant conduct is a criminal offence under the domestic law of the State where it is committed and would be a criminal offence under the domestic law of the State Party implementing or applying this article had it been committed there;

(d) Each State Party shall furnish copies of its laws that give effect to this article and of any subsequent changes to such laws or a description thereof to the Secretary-General of the United Nations;

(e) If required by fundamental principles of the domestic law of a State Party, it may be provided that the offences set forth in paragraph 1 of this article do not apply to the persons who committed the predicate offence.

Article 24
Concealment

Without prejudice to the provisions of article 23 of this Convention, each State Party shall consider adopting such legislative and other measures as may be necessary to establish as a criminal offence, when committed intentionally after the commission of any of the offences established in accordance with this Convention without having participated in such offences, the concealment or continued retention of property when the person involved knows that such property is the result of any of the offences established in accordance with this Convention.

Article 25
Obstruction of justice

Each State Party shall adopt such legislative and other measures as may be necessary to establish as criminal offences, when committed intentionally:

(a) The use of physical force, threats or intimidation or the promise, offering or giving of an undue advantage to induce false testimony or to interfere in the giving of testimony or the production of evidence in a proceeding in relation to the commission of offences established in accordance with this Convention;

(b) The use of physical force, threats or intimidation to interfere with the exercise of official duties by a justice or law enforcement official in relation to the commission of offences established in accordance with this Convention. Nothing in this subparagraph shall prejudice the right of States Parties to have legislation that protects other categories of public official.

Article 26
Liability of legal persons

1. Each State Party shall adopt such measures as may be necessary, consistent with its legal principles, to establish the liability of legal persons for participation in the offences established in accordance with this Convention.

2. Subject to the legal principles of the State Party, the liability of legal persons may be criminal, civil or administrative.

3. Such liability shall be without prejudice to the criminal liability of the natural persons who have committed the offences.

4. Each State Party shall, in particular, ensure that legal persons held liable in accordance with this article are subject to effective, proportionate and dissuasive criminal or non-criminal sanctions, including monetary sanctions.

Article 27
Participation and attempt

1. Each State Party shall adopt such legislative and other measures as may be necessary to establish as a criminal offence, in accordance with its domestic law, participation in any capacity such as an accomplice, assistant or instigator in an offence established in accordance with this Convention.

2. Each State Party may adopt such legislative and other measures as may be necessary to establish as a criminal offence, in accordance with its domestic law, any attempt to commit an offence established in accordance with this Convention.

3. Each State Party may adopt such legislative and other measures as may be necessary to establish as a criminal offence, in accordance with its domestic law, the preparation for an offence established in accordance with this Convention.

Article 28
Knowledge, intent and purpose as elements of an offence

Knowledge, intent or purpose required as an element of an offence established in accordance with this Convention may be inferred from objective factual circumstances.

Article 29
Statute of limitations

Each State Party shall, where appropriate, establish under its domestic law a long statute of limitations period in which to commence proceedings for any offence established in accordance with this Convention and establish a longer statute of limitations period or provide for the suspension of the statute of limitations where the alleged offender has evaded the administration of justice.

Article 30
Prosecution, adjudication and sanctions

1. Each State Party shall make the commission of an offence established in accordance with this Convention liable to sanctions that take into account the gravity of that offence.

2. Each State Party shall take such measures as may be necessary to establish or maintain, in accordance with its legal system and constitutional principles, an appropriate balance between any immunities or jurisdictional privileges accorded to its public officials for the performance of their functions and the possibility, when necessary, of effectively investigating, prosecuting and adjudicating offences established in accordance with this Convention.

3. Each State Party shall endeavour to ensure that any discretionary legal powers under its domestic law relating to the prosecution of persons for offences established in accordance with this Convention are exercised to maximize the effectiveness of law enforcement measures in respect of those offences and with due regard to the need to deter the commission of such offences.

4. In the case of offences established in accordance with this Convention, each State Party shall take appropriate measures, in accordance with its domestic

law and with due regard to the rights of the defence, to seek to ensure that conditions imposed in connection with decisions on release pending trial or appeal take into consideration the need to ensure the presence of the defendant at subsequent criminal proceedings.

5. Each State Party shall take into account the gravity of the offences concerned when considering the eventuality of early release or parole of persons convicted of such offences.

6. Each State Party, to the extent consistent with the fundamental principles of its legal system, shall consider establishing procedures through which a public official accused of an offence established in accordance with this Convention may, where appropriate, be removed, suspended or reassigned by the appropriate authority, bearing in mind respect for the principle of the presumption of innocence.

7. Where warranted by the gravity of the offence, each State Party, to the extent consistent with the fundamental principles of its legal system, shall consider establishing procedures for the disqualification, by court order or any other appropriate means, for a period of time determined by its domestic law, of persons convicted of offences established in accordance with this Convention from:

(a) Holding public office; and

(b) Holding office in an enterprise owned in whole or in part by the State.

8. Paragraph 1 of this article shall be without prejudice to the exercise of disciplinary powers by the competent authorities against civil servants.

9. Nothing contained in this Convention shall affect the principle that the description of the offences established in accordance with this Convention and of the applicable legal defences or other legal principles controlling the lawfulness of conduct is reserved to the domestic law of a State Party and that such offences shall be prosecuted and punished in accordance with that law.

10. States Parties shall endeavour to promote the reintegration into society of persons convicted of offences established in accordance with this Convention.

Article 31
Freezing, seizure and confiscation

1. Each State Party shall take, to the greatest extent possible within its domestic legal system, such measures as may be necessary to enable confiscation of:

(a) Proceeds of crime derived from offences established in accordance with this Convention or property the value of which corresponds to that of such proceeds;

(b) Property, equipment or other instrumentalities used in or destined for use in offences established in accordance with this Convention.

2. Each State Party shall take such measures as may be necessary to enable the identification, tracing, freezing or seizure of any item referred to in paragraph 1 of this article for the purpose of eventual confiscation.

3. Each State Party shall adopt, in accordance with its domestic law, such legislative and other measures as may be necessary to regulate the administration by

the competent authorities of frozen, seized or confiscated property covered in paragraphs 1 and 2 of this article.

4. If such proceeds of crime have been transformed or converted, in part or in full, into other property, such property shall be liable to the measures referred to in this article instead of the proceeds.

5. If such proceeds of crime have been intermingled with property acquired from legitimate sources, such property shall, without prejudice to any powers relating to freezing or seizure, be liable to confiscation up to the assessed value of the intermingled proceeds.

6. Income or other benefits derived from such proceeds of crime, from property into which such proceeds of crime have been transformed or converted or from property with which such proceeds of crime have been intermingled shall also be liable to the measures referred to in this article, in the same manner and to the same extent as proceeds of crime.

7. For the purpose of this article and article 55 of this Convention, each State Party shall empower its courts or other competent authorities to order that bank, financial or commercial records be made available or seized. A State Party shall not decline to act under the provisions of this paragraph on the ground of bank secrecy.

8. States Parties may consider the possibility of requiring that an offender demonstrate the lawful origin of such alleged proceeds of crime or other property liable to confiscation, to the extent that such a requirement is consistent with the fundamental principles of their domestic law and with the nature of judicial and other proceedings.

9. The provisions of this article shall not be so construed as to prejudice the rights of bona fide third parties.

10. Nothing contained in this article shall affect the principle that the measures to which it refers shall be defined and implemented in accordance with and subject to the provisions of the domestic law of a State Party.

Article 32
Protection of witnesses, experts and victims

1. Each State Party shall take appropriate measures in accordance with its domestic legal system and within its means to provide effective protection from potential retaliation or intimidation for witnesses and experts who give testimony concerning offences established in accordance with this Convention and, as appropriate, for their relatives and other persons close to them.

2. The measures envisaged in paragraph 1 of this article may include, inter alia, without prejudice to the rights of the defendant, including the right to due process:

(a) Establishing procedures for the physical protection of such persons, such as, to the extent necessary and feasible, relocating them and permitting, where appropriate, non-disclosure or limitations on the disclosure of information concerning the identity and whereabouts of such persons;

(b) Providing evidentiary rules to permit witnesses and experts to give testimony in a manner that ensures the safety of such persons, such as permitting testimony to be given through the use of communications technology such as video or other adequate means.

3. States Parties shall consider entering into agreements or arrangements with other States for the relocation of persons referred to in paragraph 1 of this article.

4. The provisions of this article shall also apply to victims insofar as they are witnesses.

5. Each State Party shall, subject to its domestic law, enable the views and concerns of victims to be presented and considered at appropriate stages of criminal proceedings against offenders in a manner not prejudicial to the rights of the defence.

Article 33
Protection of reporting persons

Each State Party shall consider incorporating into its domestic legal system appropriate measures to provide protection against any unjustified treatment for any person who reports in good faith and on reasonable grounds to the competent authorities any facts concerning offences established in accordance with this Convention.

Article 34
Consequences of acts of corruption

With due regard to the rights of third parties acquired in good faith, each State Party shall take measures, in accordance with the fundamental principles of its domestic law, to address consequences of corruption. In this context, States Parties may consider corruption a relevant factor in legal proceedings to annul or rescind a contract, withdraw a concession or other similar instrument or take any other remedial action.

Article 35
Compensation for damage

Each State Party shall take such measures as may be necessary, in accordance with principles of its domestic law, to ensure that entities or persons who have suffered damage as a result of an act of corruption have the right to initiate legal proceedings against those responsible for that damage in order to obtain compensation.

Article 36
Specialized authorities

Each State Party shall, in accordance with the fundamental principles of its legal system, ensure the existence of a body or bodies or persons specialized in combating corruption through law enforcement. Such body or bodies or persons shall be granted the necessary independence, in accordance with the fundamental principles of the legal system of the State Party, to be able to carry out their functions effectively and without any undue influence. Such persons or staff of such body or bodies should have the appropriate training and resources to carry out their tasks.

Article 37
Cooperation with law enforcement authorities

1. Each State Party shall take appropriate measures to encourage persons who participate or who have participated in the commission of an offence established in accordance with this Convention to supply information useful to competent authorities for investigative and evidentiary purposes and to provide factual, specific help to competent authorities that may contribute to depriving offenders of the proceeds of crime and to recovering such proceeds.

2. Each State Party shall consider providing for the possibility, in appropriate cases, of mitigating punishment of an accused person who provides substantial cooperation in the investigation or prosecution of an offence established in accordance with this Convention.

3. Each State Party shall consider providing for the possibility, in accordance with fundamental principles of its domestic law, of granting immunity from prosecution to a person who provides substantial cooperation in the investigation or prosecution of an offence established in accordance with this Convention.

4. Protection of such persons shall be, mutatis mutandis, as provided for in article 32 of this Convention.

5. Where a person referred to in paragraph 1 of this article located in one State Party can provide substantial cooperation to the competent authorities of another State Party, the States Parties concerned may consider entering into agreements or arrangements, in accordance with their domestic law, concerning the potential provision by the other State Party of the treatment set forth in paragraphs 2 and 3 of this article.

Article 38
Cooperation between national authorities

Each State Party shall take such measures as may be necessary to encourage, in accordance with its domestic law, cooperation between, on the one hand, its public authorities, as well as its public officials, and, on the other hand, its authorities responsible for investigating and prosecuting criminal offences. Such cooperation may include:

(a) Informing the latter authorities, on their own initiative, where there are reasonable grounds to believe that any of the offences established in accordance with articles 15, 21 and 23 of this Convention has been committed; or

(b) Providing, upon request, to the latter authorities all necessary information.

Article 39
Cooperation between national authorities and the private sector

1. Each State Party shall take such measures as may be necessary to encourage, in accordance with its domestic law, cooperation between national investigating and prosecuting authorities and entities of the private sector, in particular financial institutions, relating to matters involving the commission of offences established in accordance with this Convention.

2. Each State Party shall consider encouraging its nationals and other persons with a habitual residence in its territory to report to the national investigating and prosecuting authorities the commission of an offence established in accordance with this Convention.

Article 40
Bank secrecy

Each State Party shall ensure that, in the case of domestic criminal investigations of offences established in accordance with this Convention, there are appropriate mechanisms available within its domestic legal system to overcome obstacles that may arise out of the application of bank secrecy laws.

Article 41
Criminal record

Each State Party may adopt such legislative or other measures as may be necessary to take into consideration, under such terms as and for the purpose that it deems appropriate, any previous conviction in another State of an alleged offender for the purpose of using such information in criminal proceedings relating to an offence established in accordance with this Convention.

Article 42
Jurisdiction

1. Each State Party shall adopt such measures as may be necessary to establish its jurisdiction over the offences established in accordance with this Convention when:

(a) The offence is committed in the territory of that State Party; or

(b) The offence is committed on board a vessel that is flying the flag of that State Party or an aircraft that is registered under the laws of that State Party at the time that the offence is committed.

2. Subject to article 4 of this Convention, a State Party may also establish its jurisdiction over any such offence when:

(a) The offence is committed against a national of that State Party; or

(b) The offence is committed by a national of that State Party or a stateless person who has his or her habitual residence in its territory; or

(c) The offence is one of those established in accordance with article 23, paragraph 1 (b) (ii), of this Convention and is committed outside its territory with a view to the commission of an offence established in accordance with article 23, paragraph 1 (a) (i) or (ii) or (b) (i), of this Convention within its territory; or

(d) The offence is committed against the State Party.

3. For the purposes of article 44 of this Convention, each State Party shall take such measures as may be necessary to establish its jurisdiction over the offences established in accordance with this Convention when the alleged offender is present in its territory and it does not extradite such person solely on the ground that he or she is one of its nationals.

4. Each State Party may also take such measures as may be necessary to establish its jurisdiction over the offences established in accordance with this Convention when the alleged offender is present in its territory and it does not extradite him or her.

5. If a State Party exercising its jurisdiction under paragraph 1 or 2 of this article has been notified, or has otherwise learned, that any other States Parties are conducting an investigation, prosecution or judicial proceeding in respect of the

same conduct, the competent authorities of those States Parties shall, as appropriate, consult one another with a view to coordinating their actions.

6. Without prejudice to norms of general international law, this Convention shall not exclude the exercise of any criminal jurisdiction established by a State Party in accordance with its domestic law.

Chapter IV International cooperation

Article 43
International cooperation

1. States Parties shall cooperate in criminal matters in accordance with articles 44 to 50 of this Convention. Where appropriate and consistent with their domestic legal system, States Parties shall consider assisting each other in investigations of and proceedings in civil and administrative matters relating to corruption.

2. In matters of international cooperation, whenever dual criminality is considered a requirement, it shall be deemed fulfilled irrespective of whether the laws of the requested State Party place the offence within the same category of offence or denominate the offence by the same terminology as the requesting State Party, if the conduct underlying the offence for which assistance is sought is a criminal offence under the laws of both States Parties.

Article 44
Extradition

1. This article shall apply to the offences established in accordance with this Convention where the person who is the subject of the request for extradition is present in the territory of the requested State Party, provided that the offence for which extradition is sought is punishable under the domestic law of both the requesting State Party and the requested State Party.

2. Notwithstanding the provisions of paragraph 1 of this article, a State Party whose law so permits may grant the extradition of a person for any of the offences covered by this Convention that are not punishable under its own domestic law.

3. If the request for extradition includes several separate offences, at least one of which is extraditable under this article and some of which are not extraditable by reason of their period of imprisonment but are related to offences established in accordance with this Convention, the requested State Party may apply this article also in respect of those offences.

4. Each of the offences to which this article applies shall be deemed to be included as an extraditable offence in any extradition treaty existing between States Parties. States Parties undertake to include such offences as extraditable offences in every extradition treaty to be concluded between them. A State Party whose

law so permits, in case it uses this Convention as the basis for extradition, shall not consider any of the offences established in accordance with this Convention to be a political offence.

5. If a State Party that makes extradition conditional on the existence of a treaty receives a request for extradition from another State Party with which it has no extradition treaty, it may consider this Convention the legal basis for extradition in respect of any offence to which this article applies.

6. A State Party that makes extradition conditional on the existence of a treaty shall:

(a) At the time of deposit of its instrument of ratification, acceptance or approval of or accession to this Convention, inform the Secretary-General of the United Nations whether it will take this Convention as the legal basis for cooperation on extradition with other States Parties to this Convention; and

(b) If it does not take this Convention as the legal basis for cooperation on extradition, seek, where appropriate, to conclude treaties on extradition with other States Parties to this Convention in order to implement this article.

7. States Parties that do not make extradition conditional on the existence of a treaty shall recognize offences to which this article applies as extraditable offences between themselves.

8. Extradition shall be subject to the conditions provided for by the domestic law of the requested State Party or by applicable extradition treaties, including, inter alia, conditions in relation to the minimum penalty requirement for extradition and the grounds upon which the requested State Party may refuse extradition.

9. States Parties shall, subject to their domestic law, endeavour to expedite extradition procedures and to simplify evidentiary requirements relating thereto in respect of any offence to which this article applies.

10. Subject to the provisions of its domestic law and its extradition treaties, the requested State Party may, upon being satisfied that the circumstances so warrant and are urgent and at the request of the requesting State Party, take a person whose extradition is sought and who is present in its territory into custody or take other appropriate measures to ensure his or her presence at extradition proceedings.

11. A State Party in whose territory an alleged offender is found, if it does not extradite such person in respect of an offence to which this article applies solely on the ground that he or she is one of its nationals, shall, at the request of the State Party seeking extradition, be obliged to submit the case without undue delay to its competent authorities for the purpose of prosecution. Those authorities shall take their decision and conduct their proceedings in the same manner as in the case of any other offence of a grave nature under the domestic law of that State Party. The States Parties concerned shall cooperate with each other, in particular on procedural and evidentiary aspects, to ensure the efficiency of such prosecution.

12. Whenever a State Party is permitted under its domestic law to extradite or otherwise surrender one of its nationals only upon the condition that the person will be returned to that State Party to serve the sentence imposed as a result of the trial or proceedings for which the extradition or surrender of the person was sought and that State Party and the State Party seeking the extradition of the person agree with this option and other terms that they may deem appropriate, such conditional extradition or surrender shall be sufficient to discharge the obligation set forth in paragraph 11 of this article.

13. If extradition, sought for purposes of enforcing a sentence, is refused because the person sought is a national of the requested State Party, the requested State Party shall, if its domestic law so permits and in conformity with the requirements of such law, upon application of the requesting State Party, consider the enforcement of the sentence imposed under the domestic law of the requesting State Party or the remainder thereof.

14. Any person regarding whom proceedings are being carried out in connection with any of the offences to which this article applies shall be guaranteed fair treatment at all stages of the proceedings, including enjoyment of all the rights and guarantees provided by the domestic law of the State Party in the territory of which that person is present.

15. Nothing in this Convention shall be interpreted as imposing an obligation to extradite if the requested State Party has substantial grounds for believing that the request has been made for the purpose of prosecuting or punishing a person on account of that person's sex, race, religion, nationality, ethnic origin or political opinions or that compliance with the request would cause prejudice to that person's position for any one of these reasons.

16. States Parties may not refuse a request for extradition on the sole ground that the offence is also considered to involve fiscal matters.

17. Before refusing extradition, the requested State Party shall, where appropriate, consult with the requesting State Party to provide it with ample opportunity to present its opinions and to provide information relevant to its allegation.

18. States Parties shall seek to conclude bilateral and multilateral agreements or arrangements to carry out or to enhance the effectiveness of extradition.

Article 45
Transfer of sentenced persons

States Parties may consider entering into bilateral or multilateral agreements or arrangements on the transfer to their territory of persons sentenced to imprisonment or other forms of deprivation of liberty for offences established in accordance with this Convention in order that they may complete their sentences there.

Article 46
Mutual legal assistance

1. States Parties shall afford one another the widest measure of mutual legal assistance in investigations, prosecutions and judicial proceedings in relation to the offences covered by this Convention.

2. Mutual legal assistance shall be afforded to the fullest extent possible under relevant laws, treaties, agreements and arrangements of the requested State Party with respect to investigations, prosecutions and judicial proceedings in relation to the offences for which a legal person may be held liable in accordance with article 26 of this Convention in the requesting State Party.

3. Mutual legal assistance to be afforded in accordance with this article may be requested for any of the following purposes:

(a) Taking evidence or statements from persons;

(b) Effecting service of judicial documents;

(c) Executing searches and seizures, and freezing;

(d) Examining objects and sites;

(e) Providing information, evidentiary items and expert evaluations;

(f) Providing originals or certified copies of relevant documents and records, including government, bank, financial, corporate or business records;

(g) Identifying or tracing proceeds of crime, property, instrumentalities or other things for evidentiary purposes;

(h) Facilitating the voluntary appearance of persons in the requesting State Party;

(i) Any other type of assistance that is not contrary to the domestic law of the requested State Party;

(j) Identifying, freezing and tracing proceeds of crime in accordance with the provisions of chapter V of this Convention;

(k) The recovery of assets, in accordance with the provisions of chapter V of this Convention.

4. Without prejudice to domestic law, the competent authorities of a State Party may, without prior request, transmit information relating to criminal matters to a competent authority in another State Party where they believe that such information could assist the authority in undertaking or successfully concluding inquiries and criminal proceedings or could result in a request formulated by the latter State Party pursuant to this Convention.

5. The transmission of information pursuant to paragraph 4 of this article shall be without prejudice to inquiries and criminal proceedings in the State of the competent authorities providing the information. The competent authorities receiving the information shall comply with a request that said information remain confidential, even temporarily, or with restrictions on its use. However, this shall not prevent the receiving State Party from disclosing in its proceedings information that is exculpatory to an accused person. In such a case, the receiving State Party shall notify the transmitting State Party prior to the disclosure and, if so requested, consult with the transmitting State Party. If, in an exceptional case, advance notice is not possible, the receiving State Party shall inform the transmitting State Party of the disclosure without delay.

6. The provisions of this article shall not affect the obligations under any other treaty, bilateral or multilateral, that governs or will govern, in whole or in part, mutual legal assistance.

7. Paragraphs 9 to 29 of this article shall apply to requests made pursuant to this article if the States Parties in question are not bound by a treaty of mutual legal assistance. If those States Parties are bound by such a treaty, the corresponding provisions of that treaty shall apply unless the States Parties agree to apply paragraphs 9 to 29 of this article in lieu thereof. States Parties are strongly encouraged to apply those paragraphs if they facilitate cooperation.

8. States Parties shall not decline to render mutual legal assistance pursuant to this article on the ground of bank secrecy.

9. (a) A requested State Party, in responding to a request for assistance pursuant to this article in the absence of dual criminality, shall take into account the purposes of this Convention, as set forth in article 1;

(b) States Parties may decline to render assistance pursuant to this article on the ground of absence of dual criminality. However, a requested State Party shall, where consistent with the basic concepts of its legal system, render assistance that does not involve coercive action. Such assistance may be refused when requests involve matters of a *de minimis* nature or matters for which the cooperation or assistance sought is available under other provisions of this Convention;

(c) Each State Party may consider adopting such measures as may be necessary to enable it to provide a wider scope of assistance pursuant to this article in the absence of dual criminality.

10. A person who is being detained or is serving a sentence in the territory of one State Party whose presence in another State Party is requested for purposes of identification, testimony or otherwise providing assistance in obtaining evidence for investigations, prosecutions or judicial proceedings in relation to offences covered by this Convention may be transferred if the following conditions are met:

(a) The person freely gives his or her informed consent;

(b) The competent authorities of both States Parties agree, subject to such conditions as those States Parties may deem appropriate.

11. For the purposes of paragraph 10 of this article:

(a) The State Party to which the person is transferred shall have the authority and obligation to keep the person transferred in custody, unless otherwise requested or authorized by the State Party from which the person was transferred;

(b) The State Party to which the person is transferred shall without delay implement its obligation to return the person to the custody of the State Party from which the person was transferred as agreed beforehand, or as otherwise agreed, by the competent authorities of both States Parties;

(c) The State Party to which the person is transferred shall not require the State Party from which the person was transferred to initiate extradition proceedings for the return of the person;

(d) The person transferred shall receive credit for service of the sentence being served in the State from which he or she was transferred for time spent in the custody of the State Party to which he or she was transferred.

12. Unless the State Party from which a person is to be transferred in accordance with paragraphs 10 and 11 of this article so agrees, that person, whatever his or her nationality, shall not be prosecuted, detained, punished or subjected to any other restriction of his or her personal liberty in the territory of the State to which that person is transferred in respect of acts, omissions or convictions prior to his or her departure from the territory of the State from which he or she was transferred.

13. Each State Party shall designate a central authority that shall have the responsibility and power to receive requests for mutual legal assistance and either to execute them or to transmit them to the competent authorities for execution. Where a State Party has a special region or territory with a separate system of mutual legal assistance, it may designate a distinct central authority that shall have the same function for that region or territory. Central authorities shall ensure the speedy and proper execution or transmission of the requests received. Where the central authority transmits the request to a competent authority for execution, it shall encourage the speedy and proper execution of the request by the competent authority. The Secretary-General of the United Nations shall be notified of the central authority designated for this purpose at the time each State Party deposits its instrument of ratification, acceptance or approval of or accession to this Convention. Requests for mutual legal assistance and any communication related thereto shall be transmitted to the central authorities designated by the States Parties. This requirement shall be without prejudice to the right of a State Party to require that such requests and communications be addressed to it through diplomatic channels and, in urgent circumstances, where the States Parties agree, through the International Criminal Police Organization, if possible.

14. Requests shall be made in writing or, where possible, by any means capable of producing a written record, in a language acceptable to the requested State Party, under conditions allowing that State Party to establish authenticity. The Secretary-General of the United Nations shall be notified of the language or languages acceptable to each State Party at the time it deposits its instrument of ratification, acceptance or approval of or accession to this Convention. In urgent circumstances and where agreed by the States Parties, requests may be made orally but shall be confirmed in writing forthwith.

15. A request for mutual legal assistance shall contain:

(a) The identity of the authority making the request;

(b) The subject matter and nature of the investigation, prosecution or judicial proceeding to which the request relates and the name and functions of the authority conducting the investigation, prosecution or judicial proceeding;

(c) A summary of the relevant facts, except in relation to requests for the purpose of service of judicial documents;

(d) A description of the assistance sought and details of any particular procedure that the requesting State Party wishes to be followed;

(e) Where possible, the identity, location and nationality of any person concerned; and

(f) The purpose for which the evidence, information or action is sought.

16. The requested State Party may request additional information when it appears necessary for the execution of the request in accordance with its domestic law or when it can facilitate such execution.

17. A request shall be executed in accordance with the domestic law of the requested State Party and, to the extent not contrary to the domestic law of the requested State Party and where possible, in accordance with the procedures specified in the request.

18. Wherever possible and consistent with fundamental principles of domestic law, when an individual is in the territory of a State Party and has to be heard as a witness or expert by the judicial authorities of another State Party, the first State Party may, at the request of the other, permit the hearing to take place by video conference if it is not possible or desirable for the individual in question to appear in person in the territory of the requesting State Party. States Parties may agree that the hearing shall be conducted by a judicial authority of the requesting State Party and attended by a judicial authority of the requested State Party.

19. The requesting State Party shall not transmit or use information or evidence furnished by the requested State Party for investigations, prosecutions or judicial proceedings other than those stated in the request without the prior consent of the requested State Party. Nothing in this paragraph shall prevent the requesting State Party from disclosing in its proceedings information or evidence that is exculpatory to an accused person. In the latter case, the requesting State Party shall notify the requested State Party prior to the disclosure and, if so requested,

shall notify the requested State Party prior to the disclosure and, if so requested, consult with the requested State Party. If, in an exceptional case, advance notice is not possible, the requesting State Party shall inform the requested State Party of the disclosure without delay.

20. The requesting State Party may require that the requested State Party keep confidential the fact and substance of the request, except to the extent necessary to execute the request. If the requested State Party cannot comply with the requirement of confidentiality, it shall promptly inform the requesting State Party.

21. Mutual legal assistance may be refused:

(a) If the request is not made in conformity with the provisions of this article;

(b) If the requested State Party considers that execution of the request is likely to prejudice its sovereignty, security, *ordre public* or other essential interests;

(c) If the authorities of the requested State Party would be prohibited by its domestic law from carrying out the action requested with regard to any similar offence, had it been subject to investigation, prosecution or judicial proceedings under their own jurisdiction;

(d) If it would be contrary to the legal system of the requested State Party relating to mutual legal assistance for the request to be granted.

22. States Parties may not refuse a request for mutual legal assistance on the sole ground that the offence is also considered to involve fiscal matters.

23. Reasons shall be given for any refusal of mutual legal assistance.

24. The requested State Party shall execute the request for mutual legal assistance as soon as possible and shall take as full account as possible of any deadlines suggested by the requesting State Party and for which reasons are given, preferably in the request. The requesting State Party may make reasonable requests for information on the status and progress of measures taken by the requested State Party to satisfy its request. The requested State Party shall respond to reasonable requests by the requesting State Party on the status, and progress in its handling, of the request. The requesting State Party shall promptly inform the requested State Party when the assistance sought is no longer required.

25. Mutual legal assistance may be postponed by the requested State Party on the ground that it interferes with an ongoing investigation, prosecution or judicial proceeding.

26. Before refusing a request pursuant to paragraph 21 of this article or postponing its execution pursuant to paragraph 25 of this article, the requested State Party shall consult with the requesting State Party to consider whether assistance may be granted subject to such terms and conditions as it deems necessary. If the requesting State Party accepts assistance subject to those conditions, it shall comply with the conditions.

27. Without prejudice to the application of paragraph 12 of this article, a witness, expert or other person who, at the request of the requesting State Party, consents to give evidence in a proceeding or to assist in an investigation, prosecution or judicial proceeding in the territory of the requesting State Party shall not be prosecuted, detained, punished or subjected to any other restriction of his or her personal liberty in that territory in respect of acts, omissions or convictions prior to his or her departure from the territory of the requested State Party. Such safe conduct shall cease when the witness, expert or other person having had, for a period of fifteen consecutive days or for any period agreed upon by the States Parties from the date on which he or she has been officially informed that his or her presence is no longer required by the judicial authorities, an opportunity of leaving, has nevertheless remained voluntarily in the territory of the requesting State Party or, having left it, has returned of his or her own free will.

28. The ordinary costs of executing a request shall be borne by the requested State Party, unless otherwise agreed by the States Parties concerned. If expenses of a substantial or extraordinary nature are or will be required to fulfill the request, the States Parties shall consult to determine the terms and conditions under which the request will be executed, as well as the manner in which the costs shall be borne.

29. The requested State Party:

(a) Shall provide to the requesting State Party copies of government records, documents or information in its possession that under its domestic law are available to the general public;

(b) May, at its discretion, provide to the requesting State Party in whole, in part or subject to such conditions as it deems appropriate, copies of any government records, documents or information in its possession that under its domestic law are not available to the general public.

30. States Parties shall consider, as may be necessary, the possibility of concluding bilateral or multilateral agreements or arrangements that would serve the purposes of, give practical effect to or enhance the provisions of this article.

Article 47
Transfer of criminal proceedings

States Parties shall consider the possibility of transferring to one another proceedings for the prosecution of an offence established in accordance with this Convention in cases where such transfer is considered to be in the interests of the proper administration of justice, in particular in cases where several jurisdictions are involved, with a view to concentrating the prosecution.

Article 48
Law enforcement cooperation

1. States Parties shall cooperate closely with one another, consistent with their respective domestic legal and administrative systems, to enhance the effectiveness of law enforcement action to combat the offences covered by this Convention. States Parties shall, in particular, take effective measures:

(a) To enhance and, where necessary, to establish channels of communication between their competent authorities, agencies and services in order to facilitate the secure and rapid exchange of information concerning all aspects of the offences covered by this Convention, including, if the States Parties concerned deem it appropriate, links with other criminal activities;

(b) To cooperate with other States Parties in conducting inquiries with respect to offences covered by this Convention concerning:

(i) The identity, whereabouts and activities of persons suspected of i nvolvement in such offences or the location of other persons concerned;

(ii) The movement of proceeds of crime or property derived from the commission of such offences;

(iii) The movement of property, equipment or other instrumentalities used or intended for use in the commission of such offences;

(c) To provide, where appropriate, necessary items or quantities of substances for analytical or investigative purposes;

(d) To exchange, where appropriate, information with other States Parties concerning specific means and methods used to commit offences covered by this Convention, including the use of false identities, forged, altered or false documents and other means of concealing activities;

(e) To facilitate effective coordination between their competent authorities, agencies and services and to promote the exchange of personnel and other experts, including, subject to bilateral agreements or arrangements between the States Parties concerned, the posting of liaison officers;

(f) To exchange information and coordinate administrative and other measures taken as appropriate for the purpose of early identification of the offences covered by this Convention.

2. With a view to giving effect to this Convention, States Parties shall consider entering into bilateral or multilateral agreements or arrangements on direct cooperation between their law enforcement agencies and, where such agreements or arrangements already exist, amending them. In the absence of such agreements or arrangements between the States Parties concerned, the States Parties may consider this Convention to be the basis for mutual law enforcement cooperation in respect of the offences covered by this Convention. Whenever appropriate, States Parties shall make full use of agreements or arrangements, including international or regional organizations, to enhance the cooperation between their law enforcement agencies.

3. States Parties shall endeavour to cooperate within their means to respond to offences covered by this Convention committed through the use of modern technology.

Article 49
Joint investigations

States Parties shall consider concluding bilateral or multilateral agreements or arrangements whereby, in relation to matters that are the subject of investigations, prosecutions or judicial proceedings in one or more States, the competent authorities concerned may establish joint investigative bodies. In the absence of such agreements or arrangements, joint investigations may be undertaken by agreement on a case-by-case basis. The States Parties involved shall ensure that the sovereignty of the State Party in whose territory such investigation is to take place is fully respected.

Article 50
Special investigative techniques

1. In order to combat corruption effectively, each State Party shall, to the extent permitted by the basic principles of its domestic legal system and in accordance with the conditions prescribed by its domestic law, take such measures as may be necessary, within its means, to allow for the appropriate use by its competent authorities of controlled delivery and, where it deems appropriate, other special investigative techniques, such as electronic or other forms of surveillance and undercover operations, within its territory, and to allow for the admissibility in court of evidence derived therefrom.

2. For the purpose of investigating the offences covered by this Convention, States Parties are encouraged to conclude, when necessary, appropriate bilateral or multilateral agreements or arrangements for using such special investigative techniques in the context of cooperation at the international level. Such agreements or arrangements shall be concluded and implemented in full compliance with the principle of sovereign equality of States and shall be carried out strictly in accordance with the terms of those agreements or arrangements.

3. In the absence of an agreement or arrangement as set forth in paragraph 2 of this article, decisions to use such special investigative techniques at the international level shall be made on a case-by-case basis and may, when necessary, take into consideration financial arrangements and understandings with respect to the exercise of jurisdiction by the States Parties concerned.

4. Decisions to use controlled delivery at the international level may, with the consent of the States Parties concerned, include methods such as intercepting and allowing the goods or funds to continue intact or be removed or replaced in whole or in part.

Chapter V
Asset recovery

Article 51
General provision

The return of assets pursuant to this chapter is a fundamental principle of this Convention, and States Parties shall afford one another the widest measure of cooperation and assistance in this regard.

Article 52
Prevention and detection of transfers of proceeds of crime

1. Without prejudice to article 14 of this Convention, each State Party shall take such measures as may be necessary, in accordance with its domestic law, to require financial institutions within its jurisdiction to verify the identity of customers, to take reasonable steps to determine the identity of beneficial owners of funds deposited into high-value accounts and to conduct enhanced scrutiny of accounts sought or maintained by or on behalf of individuals who are, or have been, entrusted with prominent public functions and their family members and close associates. Such enhanced scrutiny shall be reasonably designed to detect suspicious transactions for the purpose of reporting to competent authorities and should not be so construed as to discourage or prohibit financial institutions from doing business with any legitimate customer.

2. In order to facilitate implementation of the measures provided for in paragraph 1 of this article, each State Party, in accordance with its domestic law and inspired by relevant initiatives of regional, interregional and multilateral organizations against money-laundering, shall:

(a) Issue advisories regarding the types of natural or legal person to whose accounts financial institutions within its jurisdiction will be expected to apply enhanced scrutiny, the types of accounts and transactions to which to pay particular attention and appropriate account-opening, maintenance and record-keeping measures to take concerning such accounts; and

(b) Where appropriate, notify financial institutions within its jurisdiction, at the request of another State Party or on its own initiative, of the identity of particular natural or legal persons to whose accounts such institutions will be expected to apply enhanced scrutiny, in addition to those whom the financial institutions may otherwise identify.

3. In the context of paragraph 2 (a) of this article, each State Party shall implement measures to ensure that its financial institutions maintain adequate records, over an appropriate period of time, of accounts and transactions involving the persons mentioned in paragraph 1 of this article, which should, as a minimum, contain information relating to the identity of the customer as well as, as far as possible, of the beneficial owner.

4. With the aim of preventing and detecting transfers of proceeds of offences established in accordance with this Convention, each State Party shall implement appropriate and effective measures to prevent, with the help of its regulatory and oversight bodies, the establishment of banks that have no physical presence and that are not affiliated with a regulated financial group. Moreover, States Parties may consider requiring their financial institutions to refuse to enter into or continue a correspondent banking relationship with such institutions and to guard against establishing relations with foreign financial institutions that permit their accounts to be used by banks that have no physical presence and that are not affiliated with a regulated financial group.

5. Each State Party shall consider establishing, in accordance with its domestic law, effective financial disclosure systems for appropriate public officials and shall provide for appropriate sanctions for non-compliance. Each State Party shall also consider taking such measures as may be necessary to permit its competent authorities to share that information with the competent authorities in other States Parties when necessary to investigate, claim and recover proceeds of offences established in accordance with this Convention.

6. Each State Party shall consider taking such measures as may be necessary, in accordance with its domestic law, to require appropriate public officials having an interest in or signature or other authority over a financial account in a foreign country to report that relationship to appropriate authorities and to maintain appropriate records related to such accounts. Such measures shall also provide for appropriate sanctions for non-compliance.

Article 53
Measures for direct recovery of property

Each State Party shall, in accordance with its domestic law:

(a) Take such measures as may be necessary to permit another State Party to initiate civil action in its courts to establish title to or ownership of property acquired through the commission of an offence established in accordance with this Convention;

(b) Take such measures as may be necessary to permit its courts to order those who have committed offences established in accordance with this Convention to pay compensation or damages to another State Party that has been harmed by such offences; and

(c) Take such measures as may be necessary to permit its courts or competent authorities, when having to decide on confiscation, to recognize another State Party's claim as a legitimate owner of property acquired through the commission of an offence established in accordance with this Convention.

Article 54
Mechanisms for recovery of property through international cooperation in confiscation

1. Each State Party, in order to provide mutual legal assistance pursuant to article 55 of this Convention with respect to property acquired through or involved in the commission of an offence established in accordance with this Convention, shall, in accordance with its domestic law:

(a) Take such measures as may be necessary to permit its competent authorities to give effect to an order of confiscation issued by a court of another State Party;

(b) Take such measures as may be necessary to permit its competent authorities, where they have jurisdiction, to order the confiscation of such property of foreign origin by adjudication of an offence of money-laundering or such other offence as may be within its jurisdiction or by other procedures authorized under its domestic law; and

(c) Consider taking such measures as may be necessary to allow confiscation of such property without a criminal conviction in cases in which the offender cannot be prosecuted by reason of death, flight or absence or in other appropriate cases.

2. Each State Party, in order to provide mutual legal assistance upon a request made pursuant to paragraph 2 of article 55 of this Convention, shall, in accordance with its domestic law:

(a) Take such measures as may be necessary to permit its competent authorities to freeze or seize property upon a freezing or seizure order issued by a court or competent authority of a requesting State Party that provides a reasonable basis for the requested State Party to believe that there are sufficient grounds for taking such actions and that the property would eventually be subject to an order of confiscation for purposes of paragraph 1 (a) of this article;

(b) Take such measures as may be necessary to permit its competent authorities to freeze or seize property upon a request that provides a reasonable basis for the requested State Party to believe that there are sufficient grounds for taking such actions and that the property would eventually be subject to an order of confiscation for purposes of paragraph 1 (a) of this article; and

(c) Consider taking additional measures to permit its competent authorities to preserve property for confiscation, such as on the basis of a foreign arrest or criminal charge related to the acquisition of such property.

Article 55
International cooperation for purposes of confiscation

1. A State Party that has received a request from another State Party having jurisdiction over an offence established in accordance with this Convention for confiscation of proceeds of crime, property, equipment or other instrumentalities referred to in article 31, paragraph 1, of this Convention situated in its territory shall, to the greatest extent possible within its domestic legal system:

(a) Submit the request to its competent authorities for the purpose of obtaining an order of confiscation and, if such an order is granted, give effect to it; or

b) Submit to its competent authorities, with a view to giving effect to it to the extent requested, an order of confiscation issued by a court in the territory of the requesting State Party in accordance with articles 31, paragraph 1, and 54, paragraph 1 (a), of this Convention insofar as it relates to proceeds of crime, property, equipment or other instrumentalities referred to in article 31, paragraph 1, situated in the territory of the requested State Party.

2. Following a request made by another State Party having jurisdiction over an offence established in accordance with this Convention, the requested State Party shall take measures to identify, trace and freeze or seize proceeds of crime, property, equipment or other instrumentalities referred to in article 31, paragraph 1, of this Convention for the purpose of eventual confiscation to be ordered either by the requesting State Party or, pursuant to a request under paragraph 1 of this article, by the requested State Party.

3. The provisions of article 46 of this Convention are applicable, mutatis mutandis, to this article. In addition to the information specified in article 46, paragraph 15, requests made pursuant to this article shall contain:

(a) In the case of a request pertaining to paragraph 1 (a) of this article, a description of the property to be confiscated, including, to the extent possible, the location and, where relevant, the estimated value of the property and a statement of the facts relied upon by the requesting State Party sufficient to enable the requested State Party to seek the order under its domestic law;

(b) In the case of a request pertaining to paragraph 1 (b) of this article, a legally admissible copy of an order of confiscation upon which the request is based issued by the requesting State Party, a statement of the facts and information as to the extent to which execution of the order is requested, a statement specifying the measures taken by the requesting State Party to provide adequate notification to bona fide third parties and to ensure due process and a statement that the confiscation order is final;

(c) In the case of a request pertaining to paragraph 2 of this article, a statement of the facts relied upon by the requesting State Party and a description of the actions requested and, where available, a legally admissible copy of an order on which the request is based.

4. The decisions or actions provided for in paragraphs 1 and 2 of this article shall be taken by the requested State Party in accordance with and subject to the provisions of its domestic law and its procedural rules or any bilateral or multilateral agreement or arrangement to which it may be bound in relation to the requesting State Party.

5. Each State Party shall furnish copies of its laws and regulations that give effect to this article and of any subsequent changes to such laws and regulations or a description thereof to the Secretary-General of the United Nations.

6. If a State Party elects to make the taking of the measures referred to in paragraphs 1 and 2 of this article conditional on the existence of a relevant treaty, that State Party shall consider this Convention the necessary and sufficient treaty basis.

7. Cooperation under this article may also be refused or provisional measures lifted if the requested State Party does not receive sufficient and timely evidence or if the property is of a *de minimis* value.

8. Before lifting any provisional measure taken pursuant to this article, the requested State Party shall, wherever possible, give the requesting State Party an opportunity to present its reasons in favour of continuing the measure.

9. The provisions of this article shall not be construed as prejudicing the rights of bona fide third parties.

Article 56
Special cooperation

Without prejudice to its domestic law, each State Party shall endeavour to take measures to permit it to forward, without prejudice to its own investigations, prosecutions or judicial proceedings, information on proceeds of offences established in accordance with this Convention to another State Party without prior request, when it considers that the disclosure of such information might assist the receiving State Party in initiating or carrying out investigations, prosecutions or judicial proceedings or might lead to a request by that State Party under this chapter of the Convention.

Article 57
Return and disposal of assets

1. Property confiscated by a State Party pursuant to article 31 or 55 of this Convention shall be disposed of, including by return to its prior legitimate owners, pursuant to paragraph 3 of this article, by that State Party in accordance with the provisions of this Convention and its domestic law.

2. Each State Party shall adopt such legislative and other measures, in accordance with the fundamental principles of its domestic law, as may be necessary to enable its competent authorities to return confiscated property, when acting on the request made by another State Party, in accordance with this Convention, taking into account the rights of bona fide third parties.

3. In accordance with articles 46 and 55 of this Convention and paragraphs 1 and 2 of this article, the requested State Party shall:

(a) In the case of embezzlement of public funds or of laundering of embezzled public funds as referred to in articles 17 and 23 of this Convention, when confiscation was executed in accordance with article 55 and on the basis of a final judgement in the requesting State Party, a requirement that can be waived by the requested State Party, return the confiscated property to the requesting State Party;

(b) In the case of proceeds of any other offence covered by this Convention, when the confiscation was executed in accordance with article 55 of this Convention and on the basis of a final judgement in the requesting State Party, a requirement that can be waived by the requested State Party, return the confiscated property to the requesting State Party, when the requesting State Party reasonably establishes its prior ownership of such confiscated property to the requested State Party or when the requested State Party recognizes damage to the requesting State Party as a basis for returning the confiscated property;

(c) In all other cases, give priority consideration to returning confiscated property to the requesting State Party, returning such property to its prior legitimate owners or compensating the victims of the crime.

4. Where appropriate, unless States Parties decide otherwise, the requested State Party may deduct reasonable expenses incurred in investigations, prosecutions or judicial proceedings leading to the return or disposition of confiscated property pursuant to this article.

5. Where appropriate, States Parties may also give special consideration to concluding agreements or mutually acceptable arrangements, on a case-by-case basis, for the final disposal of confiscated property.

Article 58
Financial intelligence unit

States Parties shall cooperate with one another for the purpose of preventing and combating the transfer of proceeds of offences established in accordance with this Convention and of promoting ways and means of recovering such proceeds and, to that end, shall consider establishing a financial intelligence unit to be responsible for receiving, analysing and disseminating to the competent authorities reports of suspicious financial transactions.

Article 59
Bilateral and multilateral agreements and arrangements

States Parties shall consider concluding bilateral or multilateral agreements or arrangements to enhance the effectiveness of international cooperation undertaken pursuant to this chapter of the Convention.

Chapter VI
Technical assistance and information exchange

Article 60
Training and technical assistance

1. Each State Party shall, to the extent necessary, initiate, develop or improve specific training programmes for its personnel responsible for preventing and combating corruption. Such training programmes could deal, inter alia, with the following areas:

(a) Effective measures to prevent, detect, investigate, punish and control corruption, including the use of evidence-gathering and investigative methods;

(b) Building capacity in the development and planning of strategic anti-corruption policy;

(c) Training competent authorities in the preparation of requests for mutual legal assistance that meet the requirements of this Convention;

(d) Evaluation and strengthening of institutions, public service management and the management of public finances, including public procurement, and the private sector;

(e) Preventing and combating the transfer of proceeds of offences established in accordance with this Convention and recovering such proceeds;

(f) Detecting and freezing of the transfer of proceeds of offences established in accordance with this Convention;

(g) Surveillance of the movement of proceeds of offences established in accordance with this Convention and of the methods used to transfer, conceal or disguise such proceeds;

(h) Appropriate and efficient legal and administrative mechanisms and methods for facilitating the return of proceeds of offences established in accordance with this Convention;

(i) Methods used in protecting victims and witnesses who cooperate with judicial authorities; and

(j) Training in national and international regulations and in languages.

2. States Parties shall, according to their capacity, consider affording one another the widest measure of technical assistance, especially for the benefit of developing countries, in their respective plans and programmes to combat corruption, including material support and training in the areas referred to in paragraph 1 of this article, and training and assistance and the mutual exchange of relevant experience and specialized knowledge, which will facilitate international cooperation between States Parties in the areas of extradition and mutual legal assistance.

3. States Parties shall strengthen, to the extent necessary, efforts to maximize operational and training activities in international and regional organizations and in the framework of relevant bilateral and multilateral agreements or arrangements.

4. States Parties shall consider assisting one another, upon request, in conducting evaluations, studies and research relating to the types, causes, effects and costs of corruption in their respective countries, with a view to developing, with the participation of competent authorities and society, strategies and action plans to combat corruption.

5. In order to facilitate the recovery of proceeds of offences established in accordance with this Convention, States Parties may cooperate in providing each other with the names of experts who could assist in achieving that objective.

6. States Parties shall consider using subregional, regional and international conferences and seminars to promote cooperation and technical assistance and to stimulate discussion on problems of mutual concern, including the special problems and needs of developing countries and countries with economies in transition.

7. States Parties shall consider establishing voluntary mechanisms with a view to contributing financially to the efforts of developing countries and countries with economies in transition to apply this Convention through technical assistance programmes and projects.

8. Each State Party shall consider making voluntary contributions to the United Nations Office on Drugs and Crime for the purpose of fostering, through the Office, programmes and projects in developing countries with a view to implementing this Convention.

Article 61
Collection, exchange and analysis of information on corruption

1. Each State Party shall consider analysing, in consultation with experts, trends in corruption in its territory, as well as the circumstances in which corruption offences are committed.

2. States Parties shall consider developing and sharing with each other and through international and regional organizations statistics, analytical expertise concerning corruption and information with a view to developing, insofar as possible, common definitions, standards and methodologies, as well as information on best practices to prevent and combat corruption.

3. Each State Party shall consider monitoring its policies and actual measures to combat corruption and making assessments of their effectiveness and efficiency.

Article 62
Other measures: implementation of the Convention through economic development and technical assistance

1. States Parties shall take measures conducive to the optimal implementation of this Convention to the extent possible, through international cooperation, taking into account the negative effects of corruption on society in general, in particular on sustainable development.

2. States Parties shall make concrete efforts to the extent possible and in coordination with each other, as well as with international and regional organizations:

(a) To enhance their cooperation at various levels with developing countries, with a view to strengthening the capacity of the latter to prevent and combat corruption;

(b) To enhance financial and material assistance to support the efforts of developing countries to prevent and fight corruption effectively and to help them implement this Convention successfully;

(c) To provide technical assistance to developing countries and countries with economies in transition to assist them in meeting their needs for the implementation of this Convention. To that end, States Parties shall endeavour to make adequate and regular voluntary contributions to an account specifically designated for that purpose in a United Nations funding mechanism. States Parties may also give special consideration, in accordance with their domestic law and the provisions of this Convention, to contributing to that account a percentage of the money or of the corresponding value of proceeds of crime or property confiscated in accordance with the provisions of this Convention;

(d) To encourage and persuade other States and financial institutions as appropriate to join them in efforts in accordance with this article, in particular by providing more training programmes and modern equipment to developing countries in order to assist them in achieving the objectives of this Convention.

3. To the extent possible, these measures shall be without prejudice to existing foreign assistance commitments or to other financial cooperation arrangements at the bilateral, regional or international level.

4. States Parties may conclude bilateral or multilateral agreements or arrangements on material and logistical assistance, taking into consideration the financial arrangements necessary for the means of international cooperation provided for by this Convention to be effective and for the prevention, detection and control of corruption.

Chapter VII
Mechanisms for implementation

Article 63
Conference of the States Parties to the Convention

1. A Conference of the States Parties to the Convention is hereby established to improve the capacity of and cooperation between States Parties to achieve the objectives set forth in this Convention and to promote and review its implementation.

2. The Secretary-General of the United Nations shall convene the Conference of the States Parties not later than one year following the entry into force of this Convention. Thereafter, regular meetings of the Conference of the States Parties shall be held in accordance with the rules of procedure adopted by the Conference.

3. The Conference of the States Parties shall adopt rules of procedure and rules governing the functioning of the activities set forth in this article, including

rules concerning the admission and participation of observers, and the payment of expenses incurred in carrying out those activities.

4. The Conference of the States Parties shall agree upon activities, procedures and methods of work to achieve the objectives set forth in paragraph 1 of this article, including:

(a) Facilitating activities by States Parties under articles 60 and 62 and chapters II to V of this Convention, including by encouraging the mobilization of voluntary contributions;

(b) Facilitating the exchange of information among States Parties on patterns and trends in corruption and on successful practices for preventing and combating it and for the return of proceeds of crime, through, inter alia, the publication of relevant information as mentioned in this article;

(c) Cooperating with relevant international and regional organizations and mechanisms and non-governmental organizations;

(d) Making appropriate use of relevant information produced by other international and regional mechanisms for combating and preventing corruption in order to avoid unnecessary duplication of work;

(e) Reviewing periodically the implementation of this Convention by its States Parties;

(f) Making recommendations to improve this Convention and its implementation;

(g) Taking note of the technical assistance requirements of States Parties with regard to the implementation of this Convention and recommending any action it may deem necessary in that respect.

5. For the purpose of paragraph 4 of this article, the Conference of the States Parties shall acquire the necessary knowledge of the measures taken by States.

Parties in implementing this Convention and the difficulties encountered by them in doing so through information provided by them and through such supplemental review mechanisms as may be established by the Conference of the States Parties.

6. Each State Party shall provide the Conference of the States Parties with information on its programmes, plans and practices, as well as on legislative and administrative measures to implement this Convention, as required by the Conference of the States Parties. The Conference of the States Parties shall examine the most effective way of receiving and acting upon information, including, inter alia, information received from States Parties and from competent international organizations. Inputs received from relevant non-governmental organizations duly accredited in accordance with procedures to be decided upon by the Conference of the States Parties may also be considered.

7. Pursuant to paragraphs 4 to 6 of this article, the Conference of the States Parties shall establish, if it deems it necessary, any appropriate mechanism or body to assist in the effective implementation of the Convention.

Article 64
Secretariat

1. The Secretary-General of the United Nations shall provide the necessary secretariat services to the Conference of the States Parties to the Convention.

2. The secretariat shall:

(a) Assist the Conference of the States Parties in carrying out the activities set forth in article 63 of this Convention and make arrangements and provide the necessary services for the sessions of the Conference of the States Parties;

(b) Upon request, assist States Parties in providing information to the Conference of the States Parties as envisaged in article 63, paragraphs 5 and 6, of this Convention; and

(c) Ensure the necessary coordination with the secretariats of relevant international and regional organizations.

Chapter VIII
Final provisions

Article 65
Implementation of the Convention

1. Each State Party shall take the necessary measures, including legislative and administrative measures, in accordance with fundamental principles of its domestic law, to ensure the implementation of its obligations under this Convention.

2. Each State Party may adopt more strict or severe measures than those provided for by this Convention for preventing and combating corruption.

Article 66
Settlement of disputes

1. States Parties shall endeavour to settle disputes concerning the interpretation or application of this Convention through negotiation.

2. Any dispute between two or more States Parties concerning the interpretation or application of this Convention that cannot be settled through negotiation within a reasonable time shall, at the request of one of those States Parties, be submitted to arbitration. If, six months after the date of the request for arbitration, those States Parties are unable to agree on the organization of the arbitration, any one of those States Parties may refer the dispute to the International Court of Justice by request in accordance with the Statute of the Court.

3. Each State Party may, at the time of signature, ratification, acceptance or approval of or accession to this Convention, declare that it does not consider itself bound by paragraph 2 of this article. The other States Parties shall not be bound by paragraph 2 of this article with respect to any State Party that has made such a reservation.

4. Any State Party that has made a reservation in accordance with paragraph 3 of this article may at any time withdraw that reservation by notification to the Secretary-General of the United Nations.

Article 67
Signature, ratification, acceptance, approval and accession

1. This Convention shall be open to all States for signature from 9 to 11 December 2003 in Merida, Mexico, and thereafter at United Nations Headquarters in New York until 9 December 2005.

2. This Convention shall also be open for signature by regional economic integration organizations provided that at least one member State of such organization has signed this Convention in accordance with paragraph 1 of this article.

3. This Convention is subject to ratification, acceptance or approval. Instruments of ratification, acceptance or approval shall be deposited with the Secretary-General of the United Nations. A regional economic integration organization may deposit its instrument of ratification, acceptance or approval if at least one of its member States has done likewise. In that instrument of ratification, acceptance or approval, such organization shall declare the extent of its competence with respect to the matters governed by this Convention. Such organization shall also inform the depositary of any relevant modification in the extent of its competence.

4. This Convention is open for accession by any State or any regional economic integration organization of which at least one member State is a Party to this Convention. Instruments of accession shall be deposited with the Secretary-General of the United Nations. At the time of its accession, a regional economic integration organization shall declare the extent of its competence with respect to matters governed by this Convention. Such organization shall also inform the depositary of any relevant modification in the extent of its competence.

Article 68
Entry into force

1. This Convention shall enter into force on the ninetieth day after the date of deposit of the thirtieth instrument of ratification, acceptance, approval or accession. For the purpose of this paragraph, any instrument deposited by a regional economic integration organization shall not be counted as additional to those deposited by member States of such organization.

2. For each State or regional economic integration organization ratifying, accepting, approving or acceding to this Convention after the deposit of the thirtieth instrument of such action, this Convention shall enter into force on the thirtieth day after the date of deposit by such State or organization of the relevant instrument or on the date this Convention enters into force pursuant to paragraph 1 of this article, whichever is later.

Article 69
Amendment

1. After the expiry of five years from the entry into force of this Convention, a State Party may propose an amendment and transmit it to the Secretary-General of the United Nations, who shall thereupon communicate the proposed amendment to the States Parties and to the Conference of the States Parties to the Convention for the purpose of considering and deciding on the proposal. The Conference of the States Parties shall make every effort to achieve consensus on

each amendment. If all efforts at consensus have been exhausted and no agreement has been reached, the amendment shall, as a last resort, require for its adoption a two-thirds majority vote of the States Parties present and voting at the meeting of the Conference of the States Parties.

2. Regional economic integration organizations, in matters within their competence, shall exercise their right to vote under this article with a number of votes equal to the number of their member States that are Parties to this Convention. Such organizations shall not exercise their right to vote if their member States exercise theirs and vice versa.

3. An amendment adopted in accordance with paragraph 1 of this article is subject to ratification, acceptance or approval by States Parties.

4. An amendment adopted in accordance with paragraph 1 of this article shall enter into force in respect of a State Party ninety days after the date of the deposit with the Secretary-General of the United Nations of an instrument of ratification, acceptance or approval of such amendment.

5. When an amendment enters into force, it shall be binding on those States Parties which have expressed their consent to be bound by it. Other States Parties shall still be bound by the provisions of this Convention and any earlier amendments that they have ratified, accepted or approved.

Article 70
Denunciation

1. A State Party may denounce this Convention by written notification to the Secretary-General of the United Nations. Such denunciation shall become effective one year after the date of receipt of the notification by the Secretary-General.

2. A regional economic integration organization shall cease to be a Party to this Convention when all of its member States have denounced it.

Article 71
Depositary and languages

1. The Secretary-General of the United Nations is designated depositary of this Convention.

2. The original of this Convention, of which the Arabic, Chinese, English, French, Russian and Spanish texts are equally authentic, shall be deposited with the Secretary-General of the United Nations.

IN WITNESS WHEREOF, the undersigned plenipotentiaries, being duly authorized thereto by their respective Governments, have signed this Convention.

Council of Europe Criminal Law Convention on Corruption – Summary

Open for signature by the member States of the Council of Europe and the non-member States which have participated in its elaboration, in Strasbourg, on 27 January 1999.

Entry into force: 1 July 2002.

Summary of the treaty

The Criminal Law Convention on Corruption is an ambitious instrument aiming at the coordinated criminalisation of a large number of corrupt practices. It also provides for complementary criminal law measures and for improved international co-operation in the prosecution of corruption offences. The Convention is open to the accession of non-member States. Its implementation will be monitored by the "Group of States against Corruption GRECO", which started functioning on 1st May 1999.

The Convention is wide-ranging in scope, and complements existing legal instruments.

It covers the following forms of corrupt behaviour normally considered as specific types of corruption:

- active and passive bribery of domestic and foreign public officials;
- active and passive bribery of national and foreign parliamentarians and of mem bers of international parliamentary assemblies;
- active and passive bribery in the private sector;
- active and passive bribery of international civil servants;
- active and passive bribery of domestic, foreign and international judges and officials of international courts;
- active and passive trading in influence;
- money-laundering of proceeds from corruption offences;
- accounting offences (invoices, accounting documents, etc.) connected with corruption offences.

States are required to provide for effective and dissuasive sanctions and measures, including deprivation of liberty that can lead to extradition. Legal entities will also be liable for offences committed to benefit them, and will be subject to effective criminal or non-criminal sanctions, including monetary sanctions.

The Convention also incorporates provisions concerning aiding and abetting, immunity, criteria for determining the jurisdiction of States, liability of legal persons, the setting up of specialised anti-corruption bodies, protection of persons collaborating with investigating or prosecuting authorities, gathering of evidence and confiscation of proceeds.

It provides for enhanced international co-operation (mutual assistance, extradition and the provision of information) in the investigation and prosecution of corruption offences.

It will come into force when it has been ratified by 14 states. As soon as they ratify it, States which do not already belong to GRECO will automatically become members.

The countries having ratified the Council of Europe Criminal Law Convention on Corruption as of March 2003 are: Albania, Bosnia and Herzegovina, Bulgaria, Croatia, Cyprus, Czech Republic, Denmark, Estonia, Finland, Hungary, Latvia, Lithuania, Netherlands, Poland, Portugal, Romania, Slovakia, Slovenia, Macedonia and the State Union of Serbia and Montenegro.
Further information on this treaty, including the full text, can be found at http://conventions.coe.int.

About the authors

François Vincke

François Vincke was admitted to the Brussels Bar after a distinguished career of more than two decades serving as company lawyer, General Counsel and Secretary General of a multinational energy and chemicals corporation. He received his degrees from the *Facultés universitaires Notre-Dame de la Paix* in Namur, *cum laude*, from the *Katholieke Universiteit Leuven*, *magna cum laude* and from the *Europa-Instituut* of the University of Amsterdam. He was assistant professor at the *Universitaire Instelling Antwerpen*.He was for six years lay judge in the Commercial Court of Brussels.

François Vincke serves as Chairman of the Anti-corruption Commission of the International Chamber of Commerce in Paris since 1994. This commission has written the "Rules and Recommendations on Extortion and Bribery in International Business Transactions" of ICC, which were originally issued in 1977, rewritten in 1996, revised in 1999 and adapted in 2005.

He is the co-editor and co-author of the following books: "Fighting Corruption, a Corporate Practices Manual", ICC Publishing, Paris, 2003, "L'entreprise face à la mondialisation, opportunités et risques, strategies juridiques", Brussels and Paris, 2006 and "The Fight against corruption in Belgium. Good corporate Practice", Bruylant, Brussels, 2008. He is co-author of the books "Legal tracks, I, Essays on contemporary corporate and finance law", Brussels, 2003 and "Legal tracks, II, Essays on international and domestic contracts and torts", Brussels, 2005.

He authored numerous articles on corporate governance, corporate practices (mainly addressing self regulation and anti-corruption) and competition and is often asked to speak about these subjects in various fora.

Fritz Heimann

Fritz Heimann an American corporate lawyer, is the Vice Chair of ICC's Anti-Corruption Commission. He is the co-editor of "Fighting Corruption" and wrote four of its chapters. He is one of the founders of Transparency International and leads TI's work on international conventions. He was formerly Associate General Counsel of the General Electic Company.

Heimann is the co-author with Ben Heineman of *"The Long War Against Corruption"*,Foreign Affairs, May/June 2006, and *"Arrested Development: The Fight Against International Corporate Bribery"*, National Interest, November/December 2007.

Contributors

Carlos Natera

Carlos Natera is an international lawyer with experience in common law and civil law systems. During his LL.M. he majored in international business with emphasis in intellectual property, anti-corruption issues in global development, money laundering, corporate compliance and project and anti-terrorism financing. He has produced "The Role of the Israel Money Laundering Prohibition Authority to Combat Corruption" and "An Overview of Thailand's Anti-Corruption Legislation." He took special training for the Foreign Corrupt Practices Act and has written about fraud in manufacturing in Thailand.

David Lyman

David Lyman is a graduate of Duke University (B.S.E.E.) in North Carolina, USA in 1958, and Hastings College of the Law (J.D.) in San Francisco, California in 1965. He joined Tilleke & Gibbins, Thailand's oldest law firm, in 1967 following a career in the U.S. Navy Submarine Service, became a senior partner in 1984, and is currently the law firm's Chairman and Chief Values Officer (CVO).

François Georges

François Georges graduated from the French Ecole Supérieure de Commerce et d'Administration des Entreprises (equivalent to a MBA). More than thirty five years of experience, mainly with EDF, one of the world's leading energy companies (last position as Head of international corporate relations). Expertise in the field of international relations, sustainable development, corporate social responsibility and the fight against corruption. Since 2008, UN Global Compact senior advisor on the tenth principle (anti-corruption), Chairman of the French ICC commission on anti-corruption and member of its international commission. Also French foreign trade advisor and Senator of Junior Chamber international.

Frank Piantidosi

Mr. Piantidosi is the Chairman and Chief Executive Officer of Deloitte Financial Advisory Services LLP ("Deloitte FAS"), and he also serves as the global leader of the Forensic & Dispute Services ("F&DS") practices of the Deloitte Touche Tohmatsu member firms and their affiliates ("DTT Member Firms").

With over two decades dedicated to the development of the forensic investigations and dispute consulting discipline, Mr. Piantidosi's experience transcends borders. He led the engagement relating to the Volcker Commission's investigation of Swiss banks on behalf of Holocaust victims, which resulted in a $1.2 billion settlement and the return of hundreds of millions of dollars worth of assets to victims and their heirs.

Jermyn P. Brooks

Jermyn P. Brooks qualified as both a UK chartered accountant and as a German Wirtschaftsprüfer, spending his accounting career with PricewaterhouseCoopers, from which he retired as Global Managing Partner in the year 2000. Since that time Jermyn has developed initiatives within Transparency International, the anti-corruption NGO, focusing on the private sector and now leads this effort as Director of Private Sector Programmes, being a frequent writer and speaker on the relationship between good accountability and sound ethical standards in business.

John Raven

John Raven is a Consultant to the World Bank, based in Brussels, Belgium. He was formerly Director General of the International Express Carriers Conference and is Adviser to the ICC Commission on Customs and Trade Regulations.

Jean-Pierre Méan

Jean-Pierre Méan has been General Counsel and Chief Compliance Officer for SGS SA, the world leading verification, inspection and certification company from 1996 until 2008. In 2002 and 2003, he was Chief Compliance Officer for the European Bank for Development and Reconstruction in London before returning to his position at SGS. He is now a consultant on anticorruption and integrity and is representing Ethic Intelligence in Switzerland, an organisation certifying corporate anti-corruption systems.

Dr. Méan holds a doctor of laws degree from the University of Basle and an LL.M. from Harvard Law School and is admitted to the bar in Switzerland and Canada. He is Vice President of the Swiss Chapter of Transparency International and a member and of the Anticorruption Commission of the International Chamber of Commerce.

Mark Pieth

Mark Pieth is a Professor of Criminal Law at Basel University, Chairman of the OECD Working Group on Bribery in International Business Transactions, and Member of Swiss Federal Gaming Commission, Chairman of the Board of the Basel Institute on Governance. Formerly Member of the Independent Inquiry Committee into the Iraq Oil-for-Food Programme, the Financial Action Task Force on Money Laundering (FATF) and Head of Section of Economic and Organised Crime at Swiss Ministry of Justice & Police, member of Chemical Action Task Force on Precursor Chemicals, Chairman, UN Intergovernmental Expert Group Commission to determine the extent of illicit trafficking in drugs. Mark Pieth has published extensively in the fields of economic and organised crime, money laundering, corruption, sentencing and criminal procedure.

Maximilian Burger-Scheidlin

Maximilian Burger-Scheidlin is Executive Director of ICC Austria and a member of the ICC and BIAC Commisions on Anti-Corrution, Paris. He extensively consults companies on foreign trade contracts, cross cultural negotiation tactics and on the prevention of commercial crime (corruption, counterfeiting, import-export fraud, espionage etc.). He is a lecturer at the Donau-University, Austria and member if the ICC World Council.

Michael N. Davies Q.C

Michael Davies joined General Electric Canada as Associate General Counsel and, in 1987, was appointed Vice President, General Counsel and Secretary of the company. He retired in 2002. For almost ten years, he was Chair of the Bribery and Corruption Committee of the Canadian Council for International Business and in that capacity has been an active member of the ICC Commission on Anti-Corruption and of the Business and Industry Advisory (BIAC) Task Force on Corruption & Bribery to the OECD Working Group on Bribery in International Business Transactions. He was one of the founders of Transparency International and was, for many years, a director and Vice Chair of the Canadian Chapter of TI.

Phyllis A. Erikson

Phyllis A. Erikson, the retired Vice President, General Counsel and Secretary of L.M. Huber Corporation, chaired the working group that developed the Anti-Bribery Toolkit for small and medium-sized enterprises for the Transparency International USA website.

Sandy Merber

Sandy graduated from Rensselaer Polytechnic Institute in Troy, New York, in 1970 with a degree in Physics, and received his JD from Georgetown University in 1975. From 1975 to 1984, he was Staff Attorney, Assistant to the Director, and Deputy Assistant Director at the Federal Trade Commission Bureau of Competition. In 1985 he was appointed Assistant General Counsel of the US Department of the Treasury, where he was the principal legal advisor to the Assistant Secretary for Enforcement, and was responsible for legal support for the Customs Service; Bureau of Alcohol, Tobacco and Firearms; Secret Service; and Office of Foreign Assets Control. Sandy joined GE in 1989, and is a part of the International Law and Policy group.

Thomas Pletscher

Thomas Pletscher is a Member of the Executive Board of economiesuisse, Vice-Chair of the ICC Commission on Anti-Corruption and Chair of BIAC Task Force on Bribery and Corruption. As head of the legal and competition department at economie suisse, his main areas of personal responsibility include general legal issues, competition policy, corporate governance, financial market regulations, information society and security policy. He chairs the Swiss Experts group on Corporate Governance which issues the Swiss Code of Best Practice in Corporate Governance. In addition, he is a member of the Swiss Federal Competition Authority. He is also Secretary General of ICC Switzerland.

ICC at a Glance

ICC is the world business organization, a representative body that speaks with authority on behalf of enterprises from all sectors in every part of the world.

The fundamental mission of ICC is to promote trade and investment across frontiers and help business corporations meet the challenges and opportunities of globalization. Its conviction that trade is a powerful force for peace and prosperity dates from the organization's origins early in the last century. The small group of far-sighted business leaders who founded ICC called themselves "the merchants of peace".

Because its member companies and associations are themselves engaged in international business, ICC has unrivalled authority in making rules that govern the conduct of business across borders. Although these rules are voluntary, they are observed in countless thousands of transactions every day and have become part of the fabric of international trade.

ICC also provides essential services, foremost among them the ICC International Court of Arbitration, the world's leading arbitral institution. Another service is the World Chambers Federation, ICC's worldwide network of chambers of commerce, fostering interaction and exchange of chamber best practice.

Within a year of the creation of the United Nations, ICC was granted consultative status at the highest level with the UN and its specialized agencies.

Business leaders and experts drawn from the ICC membership establish the business stance on broad issues of trade and investment policy as well as on vital technical and sectoral subjects. These include financial services, information technologies, telecommunications, marketing ethics, the environment, trans-portation, competition law and intellectual property.

ICC was founded in 1919. Today it groups thousands of member companies and associations from over 130 countries. National committees work with their members to address the concerns of business in their countries and convey to their governments the business views formulated by ICC.

Some ICC Specialized Divisions

- ICC International Court of Arbitration (Paris)
- ICC International Centre for Expertise (Paris)
- ICC World Chambers Federation (Paris)
- ICC Institute of World Business Law (Paris)
- ICC Centre for Maritime Co-operation (London)
- ICC Commercial Crime Services (London)
- ICC Services (Paris):
    - **Publications**

ICC Publications Department is committed to offering the best resources on business and trade for the international community.

The content of ICC publications is derived from the work of ICC commissions, institutions and individual international experts. The specialized list covers a range of topics including international banking, international trade reference and terms (Incoterms), law and arbitration, counterfeiting and fraud, model commercial contracts and environmental issues.

Publications are available in both traditional paper and electronic formats from the ICC Business Bookstore.

- **Events**

ICC's programme of conferences and seminars is the essential channel for passing on the world business organization's expertise to a wider audience.

ICC Events, a Department of ICC Services, spotlights policy issues of direct concern to business such as banking techniques and practices, e-business, IT and telecoms, piracy and counterfeiting.

ICC Events also runs training courses on international arbitration and negotiating international contracts for business people, corporate counsel, lawyers and legal practitioners involved in international trade.

Source Products for Global Business

ICC's specialized list of publications covers a range of topics including international banking, international trade reference and terms (Incoterms), law and arbitration, counterfeiting and fraud, model commercial contracts and environmental issues.

ICC products are available from ICC national committees which exist in over 80 countries around the world. Contact details for a national committee in your country are available at **www.iccwbo.org**

You may also order ICC products online from the ICC Business Bookstore at **www.iccbooks.com**

ICC Services
Publications
38 Cours Albert 1er
75008 Paris
France
Tel. +33 1 49 53 29 23
Fax +33 1 49 53 29 02
e-mail pub@iccwbo.org